THE
MASKS
OF
LUCIFER

THE
MASKS
OF
LUCIFER

TECHNOLOGY AND THE OCCULT IN
TWENTIETH-CENTURY POPULAR LITERATURE

DAVID MORRIS

Many thanks Sandra
— is it it amazing what
you can get up to in
Adult Education

Dave

B.T.Batsford Ltd · London

For ANGELA, with love,
who said nothing
and
KATE, with fun,
who applauded the vicar's
indiscretion in the woodshed with
the verger
while Daphne ran
the tombola with a fixed
smile.

First published 1992

Typeset by J&L Composition Ltd, Filey, North Yorkshire
and printed in Great Britain by
Billings Ltd, Worcester

Published by B.T. Batsford Ltd
4 Fitzhardinge Street, London W1H 0AH

A CIP catalogue record for this book is available from the British Library

ISBN 0 7134 6706 1

CONTENTS

ACKNOWLEDGEMENTS

I would like to thank Michael Green and Maureen McNeil of the Centre for Contemporary Cultural Studies at Birmingham University for their constant help and stimulation during the course of my researches.

In particular I would like to thank my friend and colleague Lynn Miller for her unstinting help in proof reading and her constant advice in reshaping an unwieldy thesis into a presentable text. If thickets remain, the fault is mine.

My thanks are also due to Geoff Holt for the illustrations, some of which were prepared from much-damaged originals.

INTRODUCTION

This work began with clearly defined aims. They were to study the variety of theories that have been advanced to account for flying saucer phenomena and to investigate the extent to which the texts that proposed these theories could be said to constitute a popular culture. As the work progressed these limitations had to be abandoned. It rapidly became obvious that other, but related, themes would have to be considered – the Ancient Astronaut thesis of von Daniken, and Velikovsky's variant of catastrophism being two such examples.

A considerable number of texts was now included within this wider scope (see Bibliography 1), the majority of which shared basic cultural assumptions and rejections – for instance an anti-Darwinian theme runs throughout the genre. The texts also share a particularly assertive style which derives, to some extent, from the circumstance that while they are not works of fiction (and are quite distinct from Science Fiction[1], neither are they works of fact, and I have used the term 'suppositional' to describe their particular style of advocacy.

The study of texts dealing with flying saucers and related themes led into unexpected areas. In order to understand the belief system that flying saucer theories were based upon it was necessary to make an excursion into nineteenth-century occultism in general and the cosmogony developed by Madame Blavatsky in particular. Hence Chapter 1 will give a brief outline of that system and of the 'environment of ideas' that favoured its acceptance in the late nineteenth century.

Since the texts that deal with flying saucers and the Ancient Astronaut theory make necessary associations with contemporary technology while at the same time proposing derivatives from occult thinking of the previous century, I have used the term 'Techno-Occultism' to encompass the corpus of texts studied. The term is cumbersome, as are the subvariants used in later chapters to identify particular strands of Techno-Occultism, but at least they will be seen to be useful and self-explanatory.

A further excursion is made in the second chapter, which gives a detailed examination of Velikovsky's catastrophism and its reception in America in 1950. The problem here is that Velikovsky's work does not easily sit under the heading of Techno-Occultism. Nevertheless the brief but successful heyday of Velikovsky's theories provides a remarkably detailed example of how a theory that springs from the same world perception as Techno-Occultism can successfully feed upon the anxieties of the society that received them: it is too close to Techno-Occultism to be ignored.

Chapters 3, 4 and 5 each deal in some detail with a major variant of Techno-Occultism, examining the reasons for their success and discussing the contemporary social and political circumstances that helped to produce that success. The final chapter begins to address the complex problem of readership and the sustained popularity of the genre over a period of almost half a century.

One excursion that was not necessary, however, was that into other critical analyses within the field. Remarkably, at the time of writing, the type of text being studied had been totally neglected in all surveys of popular literature. In spite of the fact that the complete corpus of texts would run to well over two hundred titles and that several of that number had amassed sales figures of over a million, there was no reference to the works of Velikovsky or von Daniken in such different accounts of popular literature as John Sutherland's *Best Sellers* (1981) or Victor Neuburg's *The Batsford Companion to Popular Literature* (1982). This omission is due partly to the texts not fitting within the fact–fiction polarity, and there seems to be an implicit notion that the term 'bestseller' refers to a work of fiction. Also of significance is the distinction, that will be developed later, between a *popular* culture and a *popularized* culture. The texts under discussion tend more to the former concept, their success frequently taking the publishing world by surprise, remarkable sales figures often being achieved without any of the promotional 'hype' that often precedes the release of a bestseller onto the market.

Finally this work will, I hope, add to other, recent works in the field of contemporary cultural studies that stress the variety and complexity of popular cultures (and here the plural is important). For too long the academic study of popular culture (and here the singular is important) was bracketed within prescriptive pessimisms. The Frankfurt School with its assumption of a complete homology between collective consciousness and 'mass' culture provided one example; the analysis of Eliot and the Leavises that insisted upon the perennial nostalgia of the old order passing and the consequent decline of cultural products, provided another. The result was to deny both the complexity and the variety of contemporary popular cultures. The perception still remained that popularity poses problems. As J.A. Sutherland comments in his introduction to *Fiction and The Fiction Industry* (1978), we '. . . fear the plentifulness of our age and the ruthless energy of its industry'. Finally I dare to hope that at least one of the original aims when setting out upon this work will have been realized and that the study of Techno-Occultism goes some way towards revealing the refreshing ambiguity inherent in the term 'a popular culture'.

1

THEOSOPHY AND ROMANTIC OCCULTISM

IDENTIFICATION

The cover illustration of Robert Charroux's *Masters of the World* (1979) shows a huge, low sun, golden and red, setting over a burnished, empty, desert landscape. Silhouetted, small and characteristically angled, against the orb of the setting sun are three flying saucers, the artefacts of a fabulous technology. The cover text reads, 'In the dawn of Time they came from Space to become ... Masters of the World.' Here is the determining fusion of magical past and future, of myth and technology. Charroux, a best-selling author in the field, a narrow progenitor of Erich von Daniken's more celebrated essays on the Ancient Astronaut Theory, offers in *Masters of the World* a text that is quite typical of the genre, both in style and content.

In keeping with the keynote theme of a fabulous technology being the evidence and means of human salvation, Charroux writes (p. 15)

> We have abundant evidence that our planet was visited by extraterrestrial beings who were called gods, angels, initiators or demons.
>
> Twentieth century man can no longer believe in those gods and angels who organised social life, taught agriculture and the smelting of metals, brought wheat and initiatic potions and seduced pretty women. He can no longer believe in clouds and heavenly chariots inhabited by ethereal, immortal creatures.
>
> His experience, technological achievements and intelligence make him inclined to give rational explanations for those outdated images ... A self propelled object in the atmosphere is an aeroplane.

The situation could not seem clearer: the break with religious teaching is complete, the scriptural imagery is discarded, utterly redundant, and a more contemporary range of symbol and imagery, derived from technology, is to be presented. And yet the matter is not that simple, and there persists throughout Charroux's work glimpses of the Blavatskian cosmology that has formed the seminal core of what is termed Romantic Occultism, when he argues:

> Then came the Hebrews. That was the final blow. . . . New myths and religions were launched for the purpose of hypnotising the masses and turning them away from the original truths.   (Charroux 1979, p. 19)

and:

> It can therefore be said that all civilisations earlier than 3,000 BC were typically Venusian.   (Charroux 1979, p. 20)

and:

> The psychosis still continues in our time: text-books, books on mythology and encyclopaedias conceal the truth and present only the traditional mandatory version.   (Charroux 1979, p. 21)

or:

> . . . the Hebrews wanted to impose the One God and therefore had to Satanise the ancestral gods . . . How hard it is to make anyone believe that those vilified gods were innocent victims.
>   Startling as it may seem, the Hebrews are Aryans. (Charroux 1979, pp. 22–3)

Consideration of these statements, given within the opening pages of *Masters of the World*, convinces that here is a work that is not just concerned with simply replacing scriptural imagery and account with technological imagery and account, and that within these assertions a complete and alternative cosmology is being hinted at. Evidently Hebraic history plays an important role – one which is quite different from the tradition of Christian interpretation and one that is not yet played out, for the terms 'psychosis' and 'mandatory' are pointedly suggestive of humanity living under the weight of an enormous error, in the thrall of some far-reaching conspiracy. The nature of that conspiracy is clear – a transvaluation, with the 'true gods' being 'Satanized' and with the 'vilified' Satan becoming the innocent victim of Hebraic evil.

Here then is a remarkable situation. An author wishing to argue that the intervention of extra-terrestrials, borne in flying saucers – craft fashioned with advanced metallurgy and powered by advanced engines – played a decisive role in the evolution of humankind, would be expected to jettison religious account and to dismiss myth systems as being the creation of relatively primitive minds struggling to come to terms with the witness of a technology that was beyond their comprehension. But Charroux is going much further. What is being offered here is a cosmology that, with its emphasis on Satan-Lucifer as a god of good, plunges straight into the imagery of Romantic Occultism. Here is allusion in tone and tenet that leads back to that syncretic occult system erected by Madame Blavatsky, known as Theosophy, and maintained by Charroux with some insistence, for clearly the claim that ' . . . all civilisations earlier than 3,000 BC were typically Venusian' presents enormous difficulties for the techno-exegete writing in 1967, when the text was first published in France.

It must be remembered that these are not fictive texts as in science fiction, though by 1967 few science fiction authors would risk a civiliza-tion derived from Venus in historical times. Charroux's is a suppositional text and evidently he is prepared to pay the price for the incorporation of the whole of Blavatsky's cosmology, albeit in adumbration and with the translation of spirits into astronauts.

The *Masters of the World* is not an isolated work, as is shown by a perusal of Bibliography One, which consists of over a hundred titles whose texts are concerned either with flying saucer speculation or related themes such as: ancient astronauts being the creators of humanity; Atlantis as the seat of a palaeo-technological society; world cataclysm brought about by moral decline coupled with unbridled scientific advance. The titles that make up Bibliography One are mostly of paperback editions that have been issued by major publishing houses. Most have been previously available in hardback format. Many have undergone several re-editions; all of the Daniken texts for instance, but so too lesser-known works such as Richard Winer's *The Devil's Triangle*, which underwent no less than nineteen printing issues between September 1974 and March 1975. Further, many of the listed texts authenticate themselves *inter alia*. 'The most exciting challenge in cosmology since *Chariots of the Gods?*', queries the cover text of Sassoon and Dale's *The Manna Machine*. 'The most controversial view of the past since *Chariots of the Gods?*', echoes the cover text of Noorbergen's *Secrets of the Lost Races*.

A consensual theme that runs throughout these texts is that of a future social order being determined by a fabulous technology and yet also predicate to an ancien regime that derives from a magical palaeo-historical past. This theme, the fusion of technology and magic, of past and future, is figuratively rendered by the flying saucer, a symbol that is able to assume simultaneous and contradictory readings with remarkable facility.

Yet as a counterpoint to such a fusion the theme of Catastrophe offers continuity between mythic past and a technologically determined future threatened by immediate doom. The fabulous technological artefact – the flying saucer – is messenger of the future and signal for human salvation, while the counterpoint of Catastrophe provides a metaphor for modern hubris. Thus the texts of Techno-Occultism can mythologize hope and despair, expectation and fear, a most energetic complex of root themes.

Yet in all this talk of Catastrophe, of a magical past lost to recorded history but universally vouchsafed in legend, there is clearly more than a hint of occult belief. As will be demonstrated, Daniken and Drake, like Charroux, in pursuing the Ancient Astronaut thesis drew upon the work of Madame Blavatsky and her Theosophical system, as do Leslie and Adamski in developing their interpretation of flying saucer appearances. While Techno-Occultism makes a remarkable break from occult tradition with the espousal of a fabulous technology and the rendering of the esoteric as technical artefact, its thematic assertions remain based in the Romantic Occultism of the late nineteenth century in general, and in the work of Blavatsky in particular.

Clearly then a brief analysis of Blavatsky's work and of the Theosophical Society that she founded must constitute the first step towards a study of Techno-Occultism.

A Brief History of the Theosophical Society

Helena Petrovna Blavatsky (*née* von Hahn) was born in 1831 at Ekaterinoslav in the Ukraine. At the age of eighteen she married Nikifor Blavatsky, Vice-Governor of the province of Erivan. Helena left her husband soon after their marriage and returned to her grandfather's home, from whence she was shipped off to join her father. At the seaport of Poti she struck up an acquaintance with the captain of an English steamer and was taken off to Constantinople, from where she began a series of bizarre adventures whose extent and veracity will never be determined. In 1874, however, Madame Blavatsky was to be found in America, at the Vermont farm of Chittenden, the home of the famous spirit mediums, the Eddys. Here she met a fellow enthusiast for occult phenomena, Colonel Olcott, an American lawyer, who now gave some direction to her hitherto purposeless wanderings.

Olcott soon became aware that Blavatsky had occult mediumistic powers and this fascinated him; his reason for being at the Eddy farmstead was to write up reports of the 'phenomena' that had been produced there. The two of them struck up an alliance and founded a 'Miracle Club', essentially a spiritualist society. Soon Olcott began receiving letters by the spiritualist technique of apportage, letters claiming to be from a mysterious person signing himself Tuit Bey, of the 'Brotherhood of Luxor', a body of which Blavatsky, as a result of her earlier wanderings, claimed intimate knowledge. The colonel, excited by this precipitated letter, became ever more immersed in occult study, and together with Madame Blavatsky and William Quem Judge founded the Theosophical Society in 1875.[1]

Not satisfied with founding the T.S. (the society and its various sub-sections formed later, as too its leading members, were all usually referred to by their initials) Blavatsky began writing a massive book *Isis Unveiled*, which was published in 1877. The work was a huge and often bewildering compilation which appeared in two volumes, entitled *Science and Theology*, each of over 600 closely printed pages. Its preface proclaimed the work to have been the 'fruit of a somewhat intimate acquaintance with Eastern adepts and study of their science'. A rambling and confused work, it has been described by James Webb in his detailed survey of late nineteenth-century occultism, *The Flight From Reason*, as a product of a 'magpie-like accumulation of mysticism, tall stories and archaeology' (J. Webb 1971, p. 46).

What did nevertheless appear through the 'spiritual porridge' was that, whatever else may be said about Theosophy, it set itself firmly against both the whole spirit of contemporary materialist science and also the beleaguered orthodoxy of the Christian faith, assailed as it was by the recent advances of that science. Blavatsky proclaimed that 'defying the hand of Time, the vain inquiry of profane science, the insults of revealed religions', the Brotherhood would disclose its 'riddles to none but the legatees of those by whom they were entrusted with the MYSTERY' (Blavatsky 1877, vol. 1, p. 573). In its assault on both organized religion and progressive science, proclaiming the authority of mediumistic and adept knowledge, the T.S. was possibly unique.

Shortly after the publication of *Isis Unveiled* Blavatsky and Olcott set sail for India in 1878, travelling via London. In India the T.S. established itself at Adyar, near Madras, and flourished.

Blavatsky's Indian experiences, perhaps inevitably, led to a change of direction for Theosophy: no more is heard of the mysterious Brotherhood of Luxor and it is no longer Ancient Egypt that is the source of divine knowledge, but Tibet. This later Theosophy, with its Hindu and Buddhist elements, proclaimed that Theosophists were specially chosen to be the light-bearers of the newly evolving global society. Those who had chosen the T.S. to be such an instrument were known as 'The Masters' – men made perfect by a life of spiritual devotion in Tibet and who had as their task the direction of humanity's evolution. This, however, was a spiritual evolution, of which the evolutionary scheme proposed by Darwin was but a fragment, a mere materialist shadow of a greater spiritual manifold. Thus the creed that Blavatsky had accrued for the T.S. constituted a complete and unifying vision of the cosmos, in which humanity's evolutionary destiny was to play a central role in the evolution of the universe. Her scheme detailed not only past aeons and the development of fabulous civilizations, lost to historical record, but also drew precise perspectives for the coming millennia of life on this and other planets.

Of those Masters who were the guardians of occult knowledge and whose task it was to shape the course of spiritual evolution of humanity on earth, two in particular were taken by the T.S. under its special protection. These Masters were designated as Morya and Kut Humi, and Blavatsky claimed that she had been initiated by them in Tibet and that she was their Chela or pupil.

Beneath the valley in which the Masters lived, so the Theosophists were told, lay huge subterranean caverns containing an 'occult museum', under the charge of Kut Humi. It was in these hidden treasure caves and libraries that were kept the books that Blavatsky was able to read by the 'astral light'. One such work was the Book of Dzyan, said to be the oldest manuscript in the world, and from which she took the account of creation given in her later work *The Secret Doctrine*.

Blavatsky returned to Europe, reaching London in 1884, coincidentally arriving just as Sinnett's book *The Occult World* was being published. A.P. Sinnett, the editor of the influential Anglo-Indian newspaper, *The Pioneer*, became a notable convert to Theosophy. His works, *Esoteric Buddhism* and *The Occult World* served to introduce Theosophy to Europe and they were popular works at the time. *The Occult World*, which contained an account of his meeting with Blavatsky and of her remarkable powers, served to arouse considerable interest in occult matters in England, and it was in London that Blavatsky was to settle and write her last work, *The Secret Doctrine*. This, like *Isis Unveiled*, was in two massive volumes, entitled *Cosmogenesis* and *Anthropogenesis* respectively. *The Secret Doctrine* incorporated the new wisdom of spiritual evolution and of the occult destiny of humanity as well as overhauling and restating much of what had been given in *Isis Unveiled*.

For a time H.P.B. and her Theosophy became a 'cause célèbre' and converts, largely from the moneyed classes, flocked to be associated with the inspiring guru and her all-embracing spiritual wisdom. Theosophical lodges sprang up in most European countries, with yet more being set up in America, the land of the movement's birth. In London Theosophy became the talk of Society and it made many notable converts, some of them briefly like the young W.B. Yeats and the wife of Oscar Wilde, others for life, such as the secularist and birth control advocate, Annie Besant, 'Militant Annie', fresh from her triumph in leading the Match Girls' strike of 1888.

Following her 'capture', Mrs Besant's involvement in the affairs of the T.S. was immediate. She quickly became joint-editor with Blavatsky of *Lucifer*, the Society's official organ, and within a few months she was President of the Blavatsky Lodge. By the autumn of 1888, together with Herbert Burrows, one of the S.D.F. leaders and a slightly earlier convert to Theosophy, she had compiled *A Short Glossary of Theosophical Terms*.

The conversion of Annie Besant (A.B.) to the Theosophist cause was Madame Blavatsky's last coup; she died in May 1891. It was one, however, that was to change both the nature and the course of the movement which had, during her life, been almost completely dominated by the powerful personality of its enigmatic and, at times, preposterous founder.

But Helena Petrovna Blavatsky's thought, 'although far from clear, had a certain power which that of her successors lacked' (J. Webb 1971, p. 53) and, while the essential doctrines of the T.S. in no way changed after the death of its founder, nevertheless the movement, now under the joint leadership of Annie Besant and C.W. Leadbeater, changed its complexion. Annie Besant brought to the Society all her experience of mass meetings, pamphleteering and touring gained in her earlier association with Bradlaugh and the National Secular Society, from which she had broken as a result of her conversion to Theosophy. Together with William Quem Judge she went out into the North of England,

> barnstorming together, talking on Theosophical terms, particularly reincarnation, at well known places like Bradford, Manchester, Liverpool, Sheffield, Birmingham, with an average attendance of eight hundred to one thousand five hundred. (Nethercott 1961, p. 374)

She made lecture tours to America in 1891 and 1892, addressing large audiences on the aims of Theosophy and of the Universal Brotherhood, but which she now gave a particularly Theosophical slant.

At a mass meeting held at Fort Wayne, public interest was so great that over a thousand copies of Sinnett's *Esoteric Buddhism* were sold, while Besant's biographer, speaking of the Parliament of Religions, held in Chicago in 1892, and which Besant addressed, states that the American public were

> seemingly athirst for the message of Theosophy ... a vast audience of 3000 persons flooded into one of the two main halls to hear, 'the Exposition of Theosophy by its accredited representatives' ... so overwhelming was the response to her presentation that the managers of the Parliament itself suggested holding extra seminars. (Nethercott 1961, p. 406)

Besant's reforming zeal, ever practical, involved the T.S. in new directions of activity in an attempt to bring the concept of Universal Brotherhood closer to everyday experience. Hence a Theosophical Lending Library was established in the East End, and she used

> a donation of £1000 from a wealthy but anonymous Theosophist to establish a home for working women and put herself in charge of it. (Nethercott 1961, p. 350)

In the meantime the movement proliferated and many more Theosophical Lodges opened in the cities of Europe. By 1894 there were some 386 Theosophical Lodges worldwide and by 1904 the number had risen to 800 (Besterman 1934, p. 166).

In 1888 Madame Blavatsky had formed an Esoteric Section (E.S.) that was to be for 'the sincerest and most devoted of her Chelas'. The E.S. had strict rules, members having to swear solemn oaths of secrecy and being forbidden to divulge any of the activities of the E.S. The oaths they took bound them for life. Nethercott (1961, p. 344) observes that G.R.S. Mead, the reporter and editor, would not divulge the rites or occult experiments he shared, even after he had long split from the Society. In return the E.S. promised a change in personality and a great heightening of one's occult powers.

The creation of the E.S. was in part to counter the growing number of members who were joining the parent Theosophical Society, which, as a result, briefly threatened to become a mass movement. Nethercott (p. 383) mentions lectures in which Besant gave 'a simple elucidation of the tenets of Theosophy' before audiences that were 'unusually earnest and intelligent in character', and he mentions gatherings of up to 3000 at St George's Hall in London, and that such was the heat of public inquisition that even *The Times* was forced to yield and send a reporter.

The E.S. ensured that the intrinsically occult nature of Theosophy would not be submerged, as seemed possible when, at the height of its popularity, it was being harnessed to Annie Besant's pamphleteering energy. Even so the E.S. obviously proved to be insufficiently exclusive and an Inner Group (I.G.) was also formed to develop the occult powers of the elect of the elect.

Perhaps inevitably after the death of Madame Blavatsky there were internecine struggles and emerging factions, but after the secession of the American co-founder, William Quem Judge – which led to the separate establishment of an American T.S. and the founding of the Universal Brotherhood in California – Besant and Leadbeater dominated the remaining European and Asiatic lodges. Another break was to come later in 1906 when Rudolf Steiner led the German Theosophists into secession as a result of Besant's proclaiming that Krishnamurti was the new saviour. Steiner went on to form his own Anthroposophical Society, which modified Blavatsky's occult teachings with an occult praxis derived from Rosicrucian initiation.

'A SIMPLE ELUCIDATION OF THE TENETS OF THEOSOPHY'

The main teachings of Theosophy, at least in its post-Egyptian phase when the insistence is upon the revelations of the Masters in Tibet, are all found in the two volumes of *The Secret Doctrine*, and although after the death of Madame Blavatsky certain aspects of the teachings achieved a greater prominence than previously, the essential beliefs remained unchanged. It was an intellectually static organization, inevitably so since its position and propositions were said to represent eternal verities, whose proof was hidden from the uninitiated.

> This is the true reason, why the outline of a few fundamental truths from the Secret Doctrine of the Archaic ages is now permitted to see the light, after long millenniums of the most profound silence and secrecy. I say 'a *few* truths', advisedly, because that which must remain unsaid could not be contained in a hundred such volumes, nor could it be imparted to the present generation of Sadducees.   (Blavatsky 1888, vol, 1, p. xxii; italics in original)

The following are the main tenets, and are listed as bald statements, although it must be remembered that their exposition could take several pages of abstruse discussion that often cannot be penetrated by mere intelligence, as the number of Theosophical primers and textbooks serves to illustrate, and propositions will be quoted from such sources also.

1. There is an Omnipresent, Eternal and Immutable Principle that is the sole creator of the Cosmos and upon which all speculation is futile. 'The parent Space is the eternal, ever present, cause of all, the incomprehensible DEITY, whose "invisible robes" are the mystic root of all matter and the universe' (Blavatsky 1888, vol. 1, p. 35). This 'God' plays no active part in the universe, none in its development or evolution and is relegated to a mere cypher. Thus, in practice, Theosophists were largely to ignore such a deity in their speculations. 'The occultist accepts revelations as coming from divine yet still finite Beings, never from the Unmanifestable ONE LIFE' (Blavatsky, 1888, vol. 2, p. 9).

2. The world, indeed the universe as created, is a conflict of opposites. Good and Evil are not absolutes in themselves but contraries without which life cannot exist. This warring of opposing forces, of good and evil, is governed by the Universal Law of Polarity, and of Periodicity. Good and evil are not the only opposites throughout the universe, and at various levels opposing forces clash and resolve, no one force being ultimately triumphant.

What is evil? . . . Evil is only imperfection, that which is not complete, which is becoming, but has not yet found its end . . . Evil is not a positive thing; it is the absence of perfection, the state which is ever growing to perfection. (Besant 1912, p. 38)

and:

the war of the Titans is but a legendary and deified copy of the real war that took place in the Himalayan Kailasa (heaven) instead of in the depths of Cosmic interplanetary Space. It is the record of the terrible strife between the Sons of God and the Sons of the Shadow of the Fourth and Fifth races.

and:

Esoterically the *Asuras*, transformed subsequentially into evil Spirits and lower gods, who, are eternally at war with the great deities are the gods of the Secret Wisdom. (Blavatsky 1888, vol. 2, p. 500)

In this we see the relegation of evil, as presented in Christian thinking, although there is an implicit contradiction between the anodyne presentation of evil by Besant and the 'Spirits . . . eternally at war', in Blavatsky's depiction. None the less, the way is paved for freeing the Satan figure from his Christian role as the source of all ill, and the Manichean elements in Blavatsky's account, with the reference to wars in 'Cosmic interplanetary space', are obvious markers for later Techno-Occultist exegesis.

3. Theosophists believe that all created entities have, at some level, however deep, a living consciousness.

Matter is the vehicle for the manifestation of soul on this plane of existence and soul is the vehicle on a higher plane for the manifestation of spirit and these three are a trinity synthesised by Life, which pervades them all. (Blavatsky 1888, vol. 1, p. 49)

and:

Yet, this cosmic dust is something more; for every atom in the Universe has the potentiality of self consciousness in it: *IT IS AN ATOM AND AN ANGEL.* (Blavatsky 1888, vol. 1, p. 107)

4. However, all life forms possess a soul, or soul material, and share a fundamental identity with a Universal Oversoul. It is the destiny of the universe that all souls shall unite with the Oversoul in a final, stateless Nirvana. This destiny, however, will not necessarily be fulfilled.

Behind the organisms of the vegetable kingdom as a whole is the vegetable group-soul, an indestructible reservoir of those life-forces which are attaining complexity by building vegetable forms . . . The same is true of the animal kingdom; . . . With man too, the principle is the same. (Jinarajadasa 1938, p. 18)

5. Each soul is, in its life form, in but one stage of a long odyssey through a cycle of incarnations, of death and rebirth. Moreover, this cycle of incarnation is governed by the Law of Karma, which accounts for the quality of life that each soul inherits with its body at each fresh incarnation.

> Moreover, the secret Doctrine teaches: The fundamental identity of all Souls with the Universal Over-Soul . . . and the obligatory pilgrimage of every Soul through the 'Cycle of Necessity', or Incarnation, in accordance with Cyclic and Karmic law.   (Hillard 1907, p. 15)

6. The doctrine of Karma and the cycle of reincarnation are the vehicles that carry forward the full spiritual evolution of humanity and the universe, of which the materialist life evolution, as described by Darwin, is but an erroneous fragment. In this evolution all manner of detailed spiritual forces participate.

> Each part of a group-soul, each type of life, each group and class and order has this aim. (To manifest through such forms as shall dominate . . . all other forms while at the same time they shall be capable of the most delicate response to the inner prompting of life itself.)
>   When the fittest forms, for a given environment, have been evolved, then that particular part of the group-soul pours its life through them with a fullness and richness which mark an epoch in its domination. (Jinarajadasa 1938, p. 21)

Theosophical interpretation of evolutionary theory is particularly important when considering the response to Darwinian thought and the wide-spread influence of Theosophy upon Romantic Occultism. However, as can be seen from the above, Darwinian axioms, such as the survival of the fittest, could be contained within a Theosophical manifold, although the tenor of Madame Blavatsky's treatment of Darwinian evolution was one of scathing dismissal for its lack of spiritual insight.

> It has been repeatedly stated that evolution as taught by Manu and Kapila was the groundwork of the modern teachings, but neither Occultism nor Theosophy has ever supported the wild theories of the present Darwinists – least of all the descent of man from an ape.   (Blavatsky 1888, vol. 2, p. 186)

7. The soul in its incarnation passes through seven rounds. Each round is a passage round the seven planets, there being life forms on various (or each) planet.

> And when we say human, this does not merely apply to our terrestrial humanity, but to the immortals that inhabit any world, *i.e.* to those Intelligences that have reached the appropriate equilibrium between matter and spirit, as we have now, since the middle point of the Fourth Root Race.   (Blavatsky 1888, vol. 1, p. 106)

---

8. When in its round the soul is incarnated on earth, it is, in each successive round, incarnated into a body that has become, through spiritual evolution, increasingly corporeal. Thus in the first round on earth, over 18,000,000 years ago, humanity is relatively ethereal, super-spiritual, while the later rounds find the soul incarnated in bodies that get increasingly closer to our own understanding of the body. Although humanity is, in various rounds, different not only in degree of corporeality, but also radically different in biological organization.

> The little ones of the earlier races were entirely sexless – shapeless even for all one knows; but those of the later races were born androgynous. It is in the Third Race that separation of sexes occurred. From being previously a-sexual Humanity became distinctly hermaphrodite or bi-sexual; and finally the man bearing eggs began to give birth, gradually and almost imperceptibly in their evolutionary development, first, to beings in which one sex predominated over the other, and, finally, to distinct men and women. (Blavatsky 1888, vol. 2. p. 132)

9. Closely related to the concept of cyclic incarnation is the concept of the occult destiny of races and that of the 'Ages'. Briefly – for a complete exposition would take several pages since the system is exceedingly complex in detail – humanity has incarnated on this planet in previous ages (corresponding to the rounds of the individual soul). In the first humanity lived on an unnamed continent designated as 'The Imperishable Sacred Land', where life was lived as a kind of astral jellyfish. The second root-race, slightly more substantial, dwelt on an Arctic continent called Hyperborea. The third root-race was the hermaphroditic egg-laying Lemurians. The fourth root-race was the Atlanteans, with giant bodies and evolving intelligence. Humanity today represents the fifth root-race, though the sixth is soon to appear: it being the occult destiny of the sixth root-race to achieve a complete harmony of body and consciousness, whilst a seventh root-race will achieve a stateless Nirvana, which the present human mind is incapable of conceiving. The present fifth root-race is termed the Aryan race.

However, each root-race is divided into seven sub-races. 'A sub-race has the fundamental characteristics of the Root-race but it has some tendency of modification peculiar to itself' (Jinarajadasa 1938, p. 50). Of the first two root-races no trace has survived, they lived so long ago and their bodies were so ethereal. Of the third root-race, the Lemurians, whose type was the negroid race, the remnants of its last four sub-races survive, 'Negroes, Negritos and Negrillos and other woolly-haired peoples, represent the later sub-races of the Lemurian Root-race' (Jinarajadasa 1938, p. 50). However, it is from the seventh sub-race of the Lemurians that the MANU (i.e. the adept brother who directs the physical destiny of the root-race) of the next root-race is developed. Thus from the seventh sub-race of the Lemurians is developed the root-race of the Atlantean Age. The 'type' of the Atlantean root-race is the mongoloid. The Atlantean Age existed some 800,000 years ago, ending, as did the Lemurian Age, in continental catastrophe and deluge: 'and Lemuria was not submerged as Atlantis was, but *sunk* under the waves, owing to earthquakes and subterranean fires, as Great Britain and Europe will one day' (Blavatsky 1888, vol. 2, p. 266).

Of the seven sub-races of Atlantis few remain, although the fifth sub-race, the Semitic, evolved the MANU of the fifth and present Aryan root-race.

Those who incarnate in this age as the remainders of previous root-races are but senile representatives of archaic nations that will simply die out.

The concept of root-races was to provide a potent source of occult-political speculation, and as Webb has demonstrated helps to account for the permeation of racist doctrine in the twentieth century with 'illuminated' thinking. As will be shown, the concept of root-races has a significant role in the suppositions of Techno-occultism.

10. The depiction of human evolution through successive incarnations in a series of root-races requires that the following three points are accepted.

> A. The appearance of man before that of other mammalia and even before the age of huge reptiles.
> B. Periodic deluges and glacial periods owing to the Karmic disturbance of the axis.
> C. The birth of man from a Superior Being in what materialism would call a *Supernatural Being*. (Blavatsky 1888, vol. 2, p. 274)

Implicit in point B and underpinning all occult thinking is the fundamental concept that physical disturbances – deluge, earthquake, shifting polar ice caps, sudden climatic reversal, mass exterminations – are all the result of spiritual activity and brought about by moral decline and decay. This underlying concept is found in vestigial Romantic Occultism of the twentieth century as well as in Techno-Occultism, while in the late nineteenth century the theme was also represented in fictive texts, often on the theme of Atlantis.

11. Although all are equal in terms of possessing a soul, Theosophy accounts for the divisions and injustices of life by application of the laws of Karma, that is to say that the fortunes experienced in this life are partly a result of the quality of life that one has led in previous incarnations, and also, of course, to what particular sub-race one happens to belong to. There is also a sociology of soul types, to further complicate the system, and these are given as follows:

(1) *Adept* – Past need of reincarnation.

(2) *'On the Path'* – Reincarnates immediately under supervision of his Master. Renounces life in the heaven-world.

(3) *Cultured* – (a) Reincarnates twice in each sub-race. Average of 1,200 years in the heaven-world. (b) Reincarnates more than twice in the same sub-race. Average of 700 years in the heaven-world.

(4) and (5) *Simple minded* and *Undeveloped* – Reincarnates many times in one sub-race before passing to the next. (Jinarajadasa 1938, p. 69)

However, whether initiate, cultured or simple minded 'no Spiritual Entity can reincarnate before a period of many centuries has elapsed' (Blavatsky 1888, vol. 2, p. 303).

12. Satan–Lucifer is the bringer of light and power to humanity. His genealogy is traced through Prometheus, and the identification of Satan as the fallen angel banished by a jealous Jehovah is a calumny and a measure of the spiritual blindness of a hypocritical Christian religion, 'one of the most cruel as well as the most pernicious of all theological dogmas' (Blavatsky 1888, vol. 2, p. 231). Further, 'it is "Satan who is the god of our planet and *the only* god", and this without any allusive metaphor to its wickedness and depravity. For he is one with the Logos' (Blavatsky 1888, vol. 2, p. 234). The transmogrification of Satan had already been given in Volume One with

> *Demon est Deus Inversus*. The devil is now called Darkness by the Church, whereas in the Bible he is called the 'Son of God' (see Job), the bright star of the early morning, Lucifer (see Isaiah). There is a whole philosophy of dogmatic craft in the reason why the first Archangel, who sprang from the depths of Chaos, was called Lux (Lucifer), the 'Luminous Son of the Morning'. (Blavatsky 1888, vol. 1, p. 70)

13. Jehovah, the Christian god, is therefore demoted, no longer the omnipotent deity as depicted by Christian theology, but merely one of the Archangels, a spiritual enemy of Satan–Lucifer, and the real identification of the serpent-devil in the Old Testament. Thus:

> Jehovah – esoterically (as Elohim) – is also the Serpent or Dragon that tempted Eve. It was left to the early and ignorant Christian fathers to degrade the philosophical and highly scientific idea of this emblem (the Dragon) into the absurd superstition called the 'Devil'. (Blavatsky 1888, vol. 1, p. 73)

14. Jesus Christ was an adept, the true (i.e. esoteric) message of whom was not for the multitude, but for a small body of the Elect.

> For the teachings of Christ were *occult* teachings which could only be explained *at the initiation*. They were never intended for the masses ... and repeated to his disciples that the 'mysteries of Heaven' were for them alone and not for the multitudes. (Blavatsky 1888, vol. 2, p. 231, footnote)

Jesus was a productof the Essene School, a great teacher, on a par with Plato and Buddha, who represent models for the next root-race.

> Thence it follows that those persons who, like Confucius and Plato, being physically, mentally and spiritually to the higher planes of evolution, were in our Fourth Round as the average man will be in the Fifth Round. (Blavatsky 1888, vol. 1, p. 162)

15. Added to these tenets of belief there were frequently promulgated tenets of practice, which the Theosophical Society found necessary to issue. These were:

> To form a nucleus of the Universal Brotherhood of Humanity without distinction of race, creed, caste or colour.
>
> To encourage the study of comparative religion, philosophy and science.
>
> To investigate the unexplained laws of Nature and the powers latent in man. (Besterman 1934, p. 160)

It is clear from the above list of main tenets that Theosophy offered its adherents a belief system of startling originality. Its novelty lay in that it sought to replace the belief system of the Christian religion and the knowledge system of modern science, replacing both with a spiritual knowledge that was free from associations of guilt and which did not carry within it a moral imperative. Theosophy transmuted scientific knowledge into an echo of spiritual knowledge.

Theosophy thus offered a comprehensive and interacting series of pictures that encompassed the spatio-temporal expansion of the universe that scientific understanding had brought about. However, the plausibility of Blavatsky's cosmology (strictly speaking her system was conceived as cosmogony but presented as cosmology) was all the more pertinent for its time when it was set against the cultural crisis which Western society was experiencing in the late nineteenth century.

THE CULTURAL CRISIS OF THE LATE NINETEENTH CENTURY

If we are to understand the appeal that Theosophy held, albeit briefly, for so many in the late nineteenth century it will be necessary to examine the particularly potent complex of social and ideological features that, in total, provided a cultural crisis. The interaction of severe social change, challenged beliefs and new creeds provides the cultural historian with a complicated picture, but there can be no doubt that the most significant feature of the crisis was the reception of Darwin's theory of evolution and its later variants.

The publication of *The Origin of Species* in 1859 is one of the decisive events of Western intellectual history. The furore that followed publication, the Oxford debate between Huxley and Bishop Wilberforce, the notoriety of crude popularizations featuring such concepts as 'The Missing Link' and the numerous caricatures of men as apes have all been well documented. Yet such features serve, by focusing on local events, to obscure to some extent the full impact of evolutionary theory upon the late nineteenth-century mind and its cause of the disquietude that pervaded late Victorian perceptions. The acute reasoning of *The Origin of Species* could be blurred and blunted by dissemination, but as evolutionary notions settled upon the bed of popular perceptions they lost none of their potency, nor their ambivalence. Crucially important was the circumstance that Darwin's theory was readily intelligible to the lay reader, and as Gillian Beer has demonstrated in *Darwin's Plots*

> The common language of scientific prose and literary prose at this period allowed rapid movement of ideas and metaphors to take place. It is clear that Darwin spoke not only to the confraternity of scientists but with the assumption that his work would be readable to any educated reader. (Beer 1985, p. 46)[2]

That *The Origin* did reach the educated reader is undeniable; it was from the outset a sensational bestseller and all 1250 copies of the first edition were sold out on the first day of publication in November 1859, and there were several subsequent editions. Clearly, since it cost £1 a copy, the initial readership was probably wholly of the middle class and John Chancellor in his biography of Darwin comments that 'the masses could not have been expected to read a book ... crammed with fact and sustained reasoning' (Chancellor 1973, p. 173), but he adds that the popular dissemination of Darwinian ideas is undeniable when evolution was seen to be challenging biblical explanations of the origin of life and that 'the popular press saw that it was on to a good thing and alarmed and titillated its readers with Darwin's "Ape Theory"' (Chancellor 1973, p. 173).

But this view is rather dismissive of an increasingly literate public, and mere titillation worked up by perceptive editors would not hold the public attention for long. The success of Robert Chambers's proto-evolutionary *Vestiges of Creation* published anonymously in 1844 speaks of a public readiness for a purportedly scientific, if not agnostic, account of the development of life. In Chambers's *Vestiges of Creation*, 'Development' was the organizing principle that was elevated to the level of a natural law, its function as total as that of gravity in the ordering of physical bodies, or as that of natural selection in Darwin's later essay on origins.

Chambers's work was universally derided by the scientific orthodoxy and the author condemned for his amateurish presumption. Yet there was nothing to shock or titillate in *Vestiges*, it was a work with serious moral intent, avowedly so, though popularly presented. The work had undergone eleven editions by 1860, with later editions deliberately sold at a price acceptable to the working man.[3]

The undoubted success of *Vestiges of Creation* indicates that a serious reception for scientific (or quasi-scientific) accounts could be expected in wide reaches of society, and that biological and geological theory in particular, if presented in a format that was stylistically and financially acceptable, could arouse great interest. *Vestiges* also provides a marker for the later success of Theosophy, which adopted a quasi-scientific style for the presentation of its occult theses.

The cultural impact of Darwin's work was wide reaching, and Beer comments that just as today we live in a post-Freudian world and that our own thinking is 'charged with Freudian assumptions and patterns', even though we may not have read a word of Freud, so also to Darwin's and succeeding generations who

> found themselves living in a Darwinian world to which old assumptions had ceased to be assumptions. . . . So the question of who read Darwin . . . becomes only a fraction of the answer . . . *who had read what does not fix limits*. (Beer 1985, p. 56; my italics)

Yet the reading and reception of evolutionary theory led to various and often contradictory lessons. One aspect of evolution, for example, was that it reduced all creation to being no more than the product of chance, of a Natural Selection, which acted automatically, as some infernal gadget, perpetually organizing and dividing the Malthusian superabundance. Consequently, because Darwinian process stressed the role of blind chance as the only proponent of advancement – measured by growing organic complexity – it denied 'Man' his position as the unique creation of a God that acted through specific interventions. The origin of man was the result of the continuous action of natural laws and not by special creation. The mutability of the species, the distinction as of between humankind and protozoic slime being but the repeated intervention of accident over aeons of time, dealt a catastrophic blow to the traditional teleology of Christian thinking.

The result was that moral responsibility lost its divinely ordained basis in the freedom of the will. This, coupled with the circumstance that the individual life is at birth the product of evolution but that no amount of endeavour during that life can add a single jot to the received evolutionary script, meant that for many, Darwinism represented a loss of individuality and profound ontological fears.

Other readings of the theory were notable. Helen Lynd has observed a close and complementary development in the conception of economic theory,[4] and she concludes that:

> Belief in this kind of natural law, which had taken its character from an unwarranted extension of Newton's celestial mechanics, received a new lease on life from a similar embracing rather than understanding of Darwin. The Darwinians taught that free competition had not only built London but had built Man. (Lynd 1945, p. 71)

To others, not wedded to an economic perspective of the universe, Darwinism was spiritually shocking, and to a Victorian public that had been steeped in Biblical fundamentalism and creationist theology, its novelty was often personally distasteful in a manner not readily appreciated in the modern age, but captured in Ruskin's 'filthy heraldries which record the relation of humanity to the ascidian and the crocodile' (Ruskin 1873, p. 59).

The need for caution against over-stressing the shock of Darwin's thinking upon his contemporaries has been demonstrated by Robert M. Young in his challenging essay, 'The Impact of Darwin on Conventional Thought',[5] but what is being emphasized here is the variety of reaction to Darwin, not its uniformity. Other readings stressed quite different values. Darwin's evolution presented the reification of 'Nature': nature was now but the stuff upon which Natural Selection worked, and such a reading encouraged an exploitationary view of the world at the very time when capitalist endeavour was bringing about a global imperialism. Other derivations of evolutionary theory provided racial perceptions with a framework of logic that also underwrote and provided an apologetic for imperialist exploitation. If such readings represent the darker side of Darwinian adaptation, then the sunnier variants are to be found in the circumstance that evolution fostered a then novel concept of the future as being extrapolated from the past. That is to say the future would not be brought about by some unimaginable saltus – such as, ironically, Nietzsche required to posit his Superman – but rather by the continued application of those forces that in the past had created the present. All is process and the future, rigorously ordained by the past, is demythologized.

It was the extrapolative futurizers such as Wells, Verne and Bellamy who, in their fiction, were able to use the progressive, or, in their terms, optimistic aspects of evolutionary theory. So too the political determinists such as Marx, who wished to dedicate *Das Kapital* to Darwin, or Herbert Spencer, with a theory of evolutionary elites; both seized upon Darwin's theory to validate their quite different political prescriptions.

Clearly then, evolutionary theory, readily available as a narrative script, so easily rendered as popular tenet, offered a wide range of quite disparate readings, all equally potent in their adaptability. As Beer concludes in her introductory examination of Darwin's work evolutionary theory has functioned in our culture like a myth in a period of belief, moving effortlessly to and fro between metaphor and paradigm, feeding an extraordinary range of disciplines beyond its original biological field. (Beer 1985, p. 17)

and Darwinian variants spawned as if their appearance was in itself witness of evolutionary process.

But the varied Darwinian prescriptions were given an added potency due to the circumstance of their being received in a society that was undergoing profound social change. Historians have argued the issue of 'The Great Depression' at some length – whether in fact there was a depression at all when many industries continued to expand and new industries were established to meet the ever more varied demands of an expanding urban society. But to the historian of popular cultures contemporary presentations are vital. As L.C.B. Seaman in *Victorian England* tartly remarks:

Modern economic historians insist that the Great Depression of those years (1873–1896) is a 'myth'. ... But what most people believe and what most people suffer ... is usually more important historically than the long-term views of historians. (Seaman 1973, p. 264)

The main elements that constituted the 'Great Depression' have always been clearly defined. There was a collapse of the traditional wheat and meat agriculture and a lack of confidence in key sectors of the industrial economy – both brought about by overseas competition on an unaccustomed scale.

In agriculture it was the opening of the vast prairie lands to wheat cultivation and the importation of refrigerated carcasses from Australasia that, dealing a telling blow to the most powerful land magnates, ensured that the crisis in farming received the most telling portents of doom. 'The countryside lost its most respected figures. Those whose pride in and conscience towards the land was greatest suffered most', lamented Ensor, following with an apocalyptic note when he adds, 'Across the stricken fields strange birds of prey flitted; speculators' (Ensor 1936, p. 118).

The crisis in agriculture, economic in nature, was for the aristocracy a social crisis, and one that was not soluble in the old terms,

... the whole territorial basis of patrician existence was undermined and the easy confidences and certainties of the Mid Victorian period vanished for ever ... (Cannadine 1990, p. 27).

As Oscar Wilde commented in *The Importance of Being Earnest* 'Land has ceased to be either a profit or a pleasure', and for many an aristocratic family its financial future now rested upon its children's success in the marriage-cattle market so wittily, if tangentially, observed by Wilde. An *ad hoc* policy of permeation with the new rich of home and abroad inevitably ensued. Beatrice Webb noted in her diary that 'the new rich of the British Empire and the United States were assimilated by marriage, or by the sale of honours to persons of great riches but with mean minds and mediocre manners' (B. Webb 1971, p. 68).[6]

In the field of industry the emergence of rivals in Germany and America, whose crude output of industrial commodities gradually overhauled that of Britain, and who both played a prominent role in developing the key new technologies of the period, was the decisive factor. Britain often played only a slight role in the new chemical, electrical and automobile industries. Seaman comments that 'one reason why the progress of British industry slowed down after 1873 ... was psychological; businessmen thought themselves into a pessimistic frame of mind that inhibited growth and the ability to change' (1973, p. 270).

The same crucial psychological feature is given in L.T.C. Rolt's *Victorian Engineering*, when he speaks of the need for a fundamental theory to account for a 'mood of doubt and disillusionment ... which distrusted all further technical innovations' (Rolt 1970, p. 279).

The 'Great Depression', whatever its economic veracity, presents the cultural historian with potent psycho-social insecurities. The old certainties had crumbled, while to the social mix new ingredients were being identified: the working class, ever growing in numbers, presented itself as a new political force after the hiatus of the post-Chartist years. The social complexity of the new proletariat, its sudden organizing ability, its indifference to the artisanal traditions of the old craft unions, all assured that the new worker-voter could not be ignored – as the sudden progress to the palliative of state education indicated. 'Few of the intellectual and political elite looked forward to an age of mass politics without anxiety', commented Beatrice Webb.

These anxieties aroused by socio-political change were given a tight focus in the 'rediscovery of the city' – the inescapable reality of the enormous poverty and misery of the East End, which received several startling presentations in the 1880s.

Ever since the eighteenth century the city, ever growing, ever more complex, had ceased to inspire theological metaphor. Cobbett's metaphor for London, 'The Great Wen' consigned the whole of urban humanity to the level of a cancerous tumour. But this was the metaphor of a rural sentimentalist, and during the mid-Victorian period the problems of city life were encompassed within quite different metaphors. Even in the mid-century the attendant problems of poverty, prostitution and crime could still be embraced within the unitary metaphor of the family. Dickens, that most London of writers, could relate Little Jo, the crossing sweeper, to the landed gentry and bind him and his kind within a web of familial connections and responsibilities. So too George Eliot, who in *Middlemarch* could have Bulstrode's involvement in capital vice brought to life by

Raffles, a distant relation. This unitary metaphor of the family as embracing all human existence placed those problems, long acknowledged to be intrinsic to city life, within the range of solution by existing social structures. The price paid for this unitary metaphor was to see the problems of poverty, prostitution, crime and drunkenness as being an aggregate of individual problems, to be resolved by particular solutions: the passing of a law; the work of a society; or the acts of an individual philanthropist.[7]

But by the 1880s the situation had changed: now the problems of the city, almost exclusively seen as the problems of the capital city and its East End, were presented within quite different metaphors. Gareth Steadman Jones has graphically shown in *Outcast London* how a combination of cyclical trade depression, falling property prices, demolition and unemployment, created in the East End a vast area of deprivation and misery that was unique to Western civilization.[8]

By the 1880s the unitary metaphors of the mid-Victorian period could no longer cope with the situation as it was being revealed in the East End. Other, more disturbing metaphors began to emerge. These were not presented in the main by leading novelists constructing 'the great work', but rather by public figures: social researchers, evangelists, reformers and authors of vigorous reportage, and hence they more readily reached a wider public.

It was Walter Besant's novel *All Sorts and Conditions of Men* (1882) that first presented working-class life that was not in terms of individual poverty but rather as 'a generalised total impression . . . so much so that the East End is finally seen as one huge cultureless void' (Keating 1975, p. 590). But the most powerful metaphor of this totality of squalor and deprivation was furnished by the evangelist and founder of the Salvation Army, William Booth, with his *In Darkest England and the Way Out* (1890), in which he depicted the East End as being comparable to the equatorial forests of Africa.

> The Equatorial Forest travelled by Stanley resembles that Darkest England . . . alike in its vast extent, its monstrous darkness, its malaria and its gloom, its dwarfish de-humanised inhabitants, the slavery to which they are subjected, their privations and their misery.[9]

Though not new, this was a particularly telling image at a time when imperialist expanison was beginning to throw a light of sorts upon the vast interior of Africa. The same theme is found in Gissing's 1889 novel detailing life in the East End, *The Nether World*, and is yet again reiterated in Jack London's reportage of a decade later, *The People of the Abyss* (1902). Jack London builds upon Booth's metaphor and begins his account with considering a visit to Thomas Cook's to purchase guide and passage to the unknown world that lay just beyond Aldgate Pump. This city-continent of the poor was vast and its inmates trapped in a narrow life of casual violence.

At exactly the same time Charles Booth's monumental investigation into the statistics of poverty, the first volume of which was published as *East London* in 1889, made what Keating (1973, p. 595) describes as 'a culminating point in the discovery of the East End ... Booth set out to study not the poor but poverty, not the individual but the mass'.[10]

Throughout, it is the condition of the 'mass', not the individual man or woman that is constantly being reiterated. And significantly the problem was posed as being one beyond the reach of individual solution. Yet this 'continent' of misery was immediately adjacent to the city itself, 'not a mile from the General Post Office', and the daily injections of the dockers marching to the West End during the Dockers' Strike of 1889 confirmed the terrifying proximity. This was not the interpenetration of wealth and poverty of the mid-Victorian city, but the uncomfortable juxtaposition of two irreconcilable opposites, as if in geographical analogy of Stevenson's potent fable *Dr Jekyll and Mr Hyde* (1886): 'Henry Jekyll stood at times aghast before the acts of Edward Hyde; but the situation was apart from ordinary laws'.

The discovery and depiction of want and misery on such a scale gave ample cause for anxiety. George Sims in *How the Poor Live and Horrible London* (1889, p. 44) wrote 'This mighty mob ... of famished and filthy helots is getting dangerous, physically, morally, politically dangerous. The barriers that have kept it back are rotten and giving way.' And Toynbee's dramatic lecture to an East End audience, published in 1883, has him crying out, 'We have neglected you ... wronged you ... sinned against you grievously ... if you will forgive us ... we will devote our lives to your service' (quoted in B. Webb 1971, p. 195). Steadman Jones argues that 'the condition of the London poor ... now became the subject of urgent general debate from 1883 onwards ... and the press were full of warnings of the necessity of immediate reform to ward off impending revolutionary threat' (1984, p. 290). One such warning from *The Contemporary Review* (8 January 1885, p. 108) has one Samuel Smith writing, 'I am deeply convinced that the time is approaching when this seething mass of human misery will shake the social fabric'.

The Darwinian fount of prescriptive certainty was hydra-headed, and quickly ranged beyond the intrinsic concerns of the biological sciences. It was Darwinian formulations that underwrote the pseudo-science of eugenics: the term was first proposed in 1883 by Galton, a cousin of Darwin. Galton advocated in his *English Men of Science* (1874) the establishment of a 'scientific priesthood', whose duty it would be to ensure the 'health and well being of the nation in its broadest sense'. Galton and the eugenicists' concern, sharpened by the discovery of the nature of East End life, was that the denizens of 'Darkest England', whose reproductive proclivities were in no way diminished, as were those of the middle classes – by birth control – would overwhelm their social betters. Consequently the eugenicists argued that the unfit should not be aided by legislation and policy that, though well intentioned, was fundamentally misguided. The unfit should be eliminated by the intervention of the fit.

Concern for the role of the middle class is also found in the Spencerian variant of Darwinism, which proposed a bourgeois theory of elites which found ready application amongst apologists for the arrival of plutocracy and the adventures of imperialism, as well as those who sought to allay the fears over the growing proportion of the proletariat within the population as a whole. Thus the very anxieties aroused by the discovery of the poor were channelled and subsumed within variants of a biological theory that had itself been a major source of anxiety due to its denial of Christian belief. The symptom had become the cure.

The cultural fix becomes, therefore, strained and contradictory and the intellectual scene of the *fin de siècle* emphasizes paths that cross and recross as if in a detailed tapestry.[11] The individual or particulars cease to be important if set against the generalized theme, as expressed by W.H. Mallock when he remarked in 1878 'There are many about us though they never confess their pain ... whose hearts are aching for the God they no longer believe in' (quoted in Mackenzie 1979, p. 16). Or in the *Weltschmerz* expressed by William Morris when he wrote to Mrs Burne-Jones in 1885, 'I have no more faith than a grain of mustard seed in the future history of civilisation which I know is doomed to destruction before very long: what a joy it is to think of! and how often it consoles me to think of barbarism once more flooding the world.'

It was into this flux within the 'environment of ideas', at what Beatrice Webb termed the 'watershed between the metaphysics of the Christian Church ... and the agnosticism, deeply coloured by scientific materialism' (1971, p. 76), that the new variants of belief begin to appear. They present a panoply of secular or mystic creeds derived from diverse sources, but whose support, intellectual or irrational, was inherited from the wreckage of Anglican and Nonconformist evangelism. It was into this flux that the encyclopaedic cosmology of Madame Blavatsky's Theosophy sprang complete and ready-armed.

THEOSOPHY AS A RESPONSE TO THE CULTURAL CRISIS

The cultural crisis produced a number of clearly distinguished social and philosophical needs that are identified as follows:

(1) With the dissolution of traditional social hierarchies there was a clear, though variously expressed, desire to establish a new elite. Galton's hopes of forming a 'scientific priesthood' have already been noted, by no means an isolated example of trying to foist an intellectual aristocracy upon a disordered social scene. The same desire is found in Beatrice Webb's demand for a 'ruling caste' of intelligent spinsters. 'It will be needful for women with strong natures to remain celibate, so that the special force of womanhood ... may be forced into public work' (Mackenzie 1979, p. 125).

(2) In contradistinction to the old aristocracy, whose main function was to *be*, the purpose of the new aristocracy would be to *act*, and in such a way as to 'do good', that is to say to ease or resolve the crisis by strengthening the position of the bourgeoisie and remove the anxiety caused by the discovery of working-class life. Programmes for doing good ranged from the schemes of the eugenicists to Toynbee's impassioned expression of guilt or Beatrice Webb's ruling caste of devoted spinsters, 'forced into public service'. Anxiety could only be erased by a radical plan of action – the new elite would have a programme.

(3) There was a widespread desire for a new faith. This desire was founded upon the collapse of traditional Christian belief and sharpened by the new awareness of a profound social malaise. The eighties and nineties resound with the spiritual crises of those demanding faith but denied it in the light of the intellectual programmes advanced by science. Thus Harry Sidgwick's ten-year struggle with his faith before resigning his Cambridge professorship since he could no longer proclaim Anglican belief, and his subsequent membership of the Society for Psychical Research. Similar is the case of John Bruce Glazier, who had aspired to be a Presbyterian minister but lost his vocation after reading Darwin and went on to propose a religion of socialism, or his future wife, Kate Conway, who also came to socialism through a crisis of faith and saw in socialism a millenarianism that had its roots in Blake's vision of Jerusalem. These and many others attest in striking fashion, though by different routes, to Mallock's 'hearts ... aching for the God they no longer believed in'.

(4) Subsequent to points (2) and (3) this new faith would have to offer a cosmology as well as a programme for action. A cosmology, moreover, that could accommodate rather than deny the advances of materialist sciences.

It is in the manner that Theosophy was able to address itself to these four needs that its sudden popularity can be understood. At the very heart of Theosophy was a programme of social elites that had the unique advantage of being class-rigorous and yet individually flexible. Moreover, this programme of elites was embedded in a vision of humanity that did not seek to deny the portentous changes brought about by industrial advances and urbanization. Thus its programme of social elites could appeal to both aristocratic and bourgeois presumptions without the slightest hint of contradiction.

The core concept for the idea of individual elitism lay in the belief in reincarnation and the associated doctrine of Karma. Hierarchy is inseparable from occult thinking, and in Theosophy the hierarchy is of a spiritual nature, in which all humanity inhabits but a stage in the ladder of consciousness rising from matter to spirit. The *First Principles of Theosophy* explains that,

> All souls at any given epoch are not of equal capacity, for some are older souls and others are younger ... but it is found that while one soul has the ability of learning quickly from an experience, another will be extremely slow to learn, and needs such experience to be repeated over and over again. (Jinarajadasa 1938, p. 68)

The text continues to explain that it is the youngest souls that are those which are 'unable to control their violent and crude desires'. Such souls appear in 'savage and semi-civilized races and in criminal minded individuals in civilized communities'. Furthermore, there are 'souls who have passed beyond the savage state, but all are still simple minded, unimaginative and lacking in initiative'. Altogether such souls are held to comprise 'nine tenths of humanity', and a detailed chart is given to illustrate the difference in quality between 'types of soul that reincarnate'.

Clearly then, with spiritually determined elites and individuals bound by the law of Karma, unable to break out of the soul hierarchy, there is ample scope for the imaginative depiction of self, group or class as a spiritual elite and for the relegation of the working class, subject to 'their violent and crude desire-natures ... lacking in mental ability' to a lumpen spirituality, to be helped, shaped and guarded by the soul elites.

What imaginative programmes must have offered themselves to genteel souls of aristocratic or bourgeois persuasion that flocked to Theosophy. What fine paternalism must have suggested itself as in Lodge or drawing-room they contemplated their souls' superiority and the necessary social distinctions being reflected in the wider spirit world. And with what joy must they have learned that however 'dungeon dark' the present was with social problems, nevertheless 'Among the many startling ideas which confront the enquirer into Theosophy, one of the most significant is that there is an inner government of the world' (Jinarajadasa 1938, p. 315) and that 'the Hierarchy on our earth is known in tradition ... as ... "the Great White Brotherhood"' (*ibid.* p. 31). Therefore, ultimately, no reversible harm can be admitted to the spiritually authenticated hierarchy since we are told that, 'The "Everlasting Arms" of the Great Brothers enfold humanity, and while they labour to complete the Plan, no ultimate failure is possible for mankind' (*ibid.* p. 327).

The crisis wil be resolved, social hierarchy maintained and the gulf between the 'types of soul that reincarnate' remains unbridgeable. And abroad, according to the doctrine of the occult destiny of the races, those remnants of the third root-race, the Lemurians, an earlier and less differentiated form of evolution of soul matter in corporeal form, the 'Negroes, Negritos, Negrillos and other woolly-haired peoples ...' (*ibid.* p. 50), are even more divorced from the elites of Western civilization.

And yet, through the adoption of the Eastern doctrine of Karma, Blavatsky offered a most powerful anodyne – the awful inevitability of Darwin's natural selection, ceaselessly working like a blind automaton, is transferred in Blavatsky's cosmology to the working of Karma in the non-bodily stages of the soul's cycle. Now the onus is placed upon the individual to better his chances in the next incarnation by developing occult powers in the present incarnation. Thus the automatic quality of natural selection has been transferred to this Hindu doctrine. Inevitability is retained but – and this is crucial – unlike evolution, which took the individual to be but a product of evolution and unable to change the *spirit* after birth, Blavatsky's system provided the individual with the means of ameliorating his or her spiritual destiny. The significance of the individual in the greater scheme of things is thereby restored. This was a truly important innovation; humanity is restored to the centre of creation as a purposive being.

And of course Theosophy did offer a programme for social amelioration – it did provide a programme for action, and the mass meetings, lecture tours and Lodge discussions mentioned earlier clearly speak of the incorporation of evangelical zeal and the organizational energies of Nonconformism being carried over to the Theosophical Society.

A good example of how Theosophy provided bourgeois plans for mission and amelioration is found in the autobiography of Lady Emily Lutyens, *Candles In The Sun* (1957), largely devoted to her involvement with Theosophy, which commenced in 1910 when she was aged 36. A woman of intelligence and energy, she found that her marriage to the architect Lutyens did not provide the 'companionship I had hoped for, nor a release for my energies'. She explains how she was bored by Society and determined not to become just another Society hostess.

Her introduction to Theosophy came when one of her husband's clients sent her some of Annie Besant's works. On reading them she 'became so excited that I could hardly restrain myself from shouting with joy. It seemed to open up to me new vistas of spiritual understanding' (Lutyens 1957, p. 15).

She visited the Theosophical Society's headquarters in Bond Street and there met Mrs Maud Sharp, the General Secretary of the T.S. The meeting is decribed as follows,

> At the first moment of meeting her I loved her and felt that I could give her all my confidence. It made me more convinced than ever of the truth of reincarnation ... because I felt certain that we must have been close to each other in a past life (p. 16).

Lady Lutyens was determined not to play a passive role and decided to found her own Theosophical Lodge, the Central London Lodge, which would be 'specially devoted to the practical application of Theosophy to social problems' (p. 17). The example of Lady Lutyens provides a clear illustration of how Theosophy was able to provide both an acting elite and a meaningful role for individual action; she subsequently took lessons in public speaking in order to tour the provinces speaking to Lodge meetings.

The third and fourth needs produced by the cultural crisis were for faith and cosmology, and in both of these Theosophy was perfectly suited to meet the demand. It is easy to see the appeal of a cosmology that retained individual purpose, rewrote the Darwinian script, accommodated the vast aeons of time required for evolution to operate and could underwrite imperialist adventure with its occult doctrine of races. The need for a new faith is however a different matter, and the role of Theosophy here is best understood by considering the circumstances of its emergence, out of the recent proliferation of the spiritualist movement.

Spiritualism emerged in its popular nineteenth-century format in 1848, with the discovery by Mrs Fox of Hydesville, in up-state New York, that her two daughters, Kate and Maggie, then aged twelve and fifteen, were able to produce 'knocking sounds', or rather that such sounds could be produced as if out of nowhere whenever her two daughters were present. In her book *The Spiritualists*, Ruth Brandon argues that in the mid-nineteenth century New York state was the source of so many religious sects and revivals that it was referred to as the 'burned-over district' (1983, p. 8) and that consequently the tappings and knockings produced by the Fox sisters found a more favourably inclined audience than would otherwise have been the case.

The innovation at the heart of spiritualism, and its only innovation, lay in the situation that it would seem that the spirits were actually trying to communicate with the living – albeit in an extremely obscure and haphazard fashion. There was thus an urgency to spiritualist happenings that was missing from the traditional 'ghostly apparitions', and this undoubtedly did much to foster the rapid growth of all forms of spiritualist activity.

Within a few years spiritualism had spread throughout the Eastern states and across the Atlantic to Europe, with all the time ever more people discovering that they had mediumistic powers. Inevitably a large number of tracts and periodicals kept the psychic movement before the public eye, and Brandon records that 'By 1850, two years after the Hydesville happenings, it was estimated that there were a hundred mediums in New York city and some sixty private circles in Philadelphia. A decade later believers would be numbered in their millions' (Brandon 1983, p. 42).

However, the attention gained by spiritualism was often critical, as scientists began to investigate mediums and attend seances. In London in 1871 the young physicist William Crookes investigated the claims and activities of the most celebrated medium of his day, Daniel Dunglas Home. His report, which appeared in the *Quarterly Journal of Science* (July 1871) was entirely favourable. Other investigators working with other mediums were not so persuaded and many frauds were revealed and confessed. No matter, mediums, by now having moved on from table rappings to levitation, apportage, voices from the dead and the production of glowing ectoplasm, continued to prosper and proliferate: so too did the contraptions that were being used to simulate or stimulate etheric phenomena, and Brandon speaks of a situation such that 'quite a cottage industry arose' to cater for the needs of the spiritualists (Brandon, p. 45).

A distinguishing feature of spiritualism was that it was open to all. There was no formal institutional structure, it did not rely on a hierarchy of trained priests to interpret dogma – there was no dogma. The result was that spiritualism's crude, experiential mode, unfettered by any authorial sanction, gave it an availability that was denied to organized religions. Brandon observes that 'certainly spiritualism rendered heaven utterly democratic' (p. 40).

In crossing the Atlantic spiritualism inevitably underwent many changes. Its democratic nature, however, was retained, with many converts and adherents won to the cause from the lower classes. Spiritualism also became, particularly by the eighties, something of a drawing-room phenomenon, an after-dinner entertainment, in which a servant girl could usually be relied upon to go into a trance and amaze her social betters. Thus there is a situation that a new quasi-religious movement gained in popularity with both lower- and upper-class society: more earnestly so with the former, where an indigenous pre-American spiritualism was being supplanted by the American variant, more of a diversion with the latter.[12]

The movement acquainted its followers with a proposed world of 'spirit', yet provided no intellectual structure to advance the meaning of the random and frequently capricious communication received from that world. It was a movement, moreover, which kept itself firmly before the public's eye by frequent exposés and by the constant bickering debate within its own ranks concerning the advocacy by some of a belief in free love. On the other hand spiritualism to some extent welcomed scientific attention, 'its desire for new knowledge, its faith in science and progress, its fevered interest in new developments in religious or quasi-religious matters, all reflected the vital concern of the age' (Brandon 1983, p. 127).

However, spiritualism had one crucial drawback; what Brandon has termed 'the absolute stasis, the complete lack of progress on the entire subject' (p. 107). Without any intellectual structure, spiritualism remained experiential, its explanatory role limited to that of the individual communicants with the dead, and their commentaries. Perhaps without the frauds, revelations and confessions spiritualism would have withered. Certainly, whatever the veracity of phenomena and experience, spiritualism was unable to offer tenet or creed, except in adopting Christian belief and a modified order of service.

It was precisely into this gap and at a time, in the 1880s, that spiritualism was facing attack and ridicule over the free-love issue and the increasing number of mediums exposed as frauds, that Theosophy was to step, providing a splendid and detailed cosmology. Spiritualism prepared the ground for Theosophy – its experience and witness rehearsed the public mind for the acceptance of an occult system, particularly one that put spiritualistic phenomena into a context and moved on from the binding stasis of the spiritualist movement.

Having made this step, Theosophy, though it was never to deny spiritualism, relegated it to being the uncontrolled evocation of discarded astral bodies that had 'a curious vitality for a while . . . often attracted to seances, where they are mistaken for the true souls, of whom they are nothing more than mere simulacra' (Jinarajadasa 1938, p. 136).[13]

A further crucial feature of Theosophical cosmology is that it did not demand the rejection of any creed. It is significant that Theosophy was quite different from other, contemporary forms of occultism, which did of course demand many rejections, particularly of Christian belief. In fact Theosophy represented an immense break with all other forms of occult thinking and practice. This is shown by considering, for example, the occult society inhabited by the French novelist Huysmans, with its own particular insistence on personal modes of thought and behaviour.

Huysmans's brief involvement with Satanism in Paris in the late 1880s provides a cameo of the mode and manners of occultism at a time when it was undergoing something of a renaissance, quite independently of Theosophy. Huysmans's explanation of his fascination with the occult was that in its study and practice he hoped to find 'some compensation for the horror of daily life, the squalor of existence, the excremental filthiness of the loathsome age we live in' (Baldick 1955, p. 140). The same virulent misanthropy is found in letters that Huysmans wrote to friends in which he speaks of 'the streets . . . swarming with provincials trailing bewildered wives and squalling brats behind them . . . The need for a little wholesale slaughter becomes evident' and Baldick adds 'it was but a short step to the medieval concept of woman as an *instrumentum diaboli*; and Huysmans found it easy to accept this idea' (p. 147).

Huysmans's misanthropy is directed not only at humanity in the mass but also at those features of urban life that he took as attributes of mass humanity; his biographer comments that he 'spoke with loathing of . . .

pavements swarming with a hideous crowd in search of money, with women degraded by childbirth and worn out by hideous trafficking' (Baldick, p. 146).

This is the closed world of traditional occultism, of what may be termed Gothic Occultism, with its insistence on rite and ritual, its strict esotericism, its sadistic Satanism, culminating in the celebration of the Black Mass, that Huysmans claimed to have observed. In this evocation of an imagined medievalism, the occult movement, for all its late romantic literary trappings, remained but a pernicious reaction to modernity, a distorted project of the *Ancien Régime*.

The extent of Blavatsky's innovation is quite clear. Satan is rescued from Gothic presentations, from the paranoic misanthropy that led to sadistic ritual and the excremental desecration of religious artefacts. Instead Satan is now proposed as a progressive force, intellectually realized, that aims for human salvation in a world unfettered by religious dogma or ethical codes. The contrast between the morphine addiction, misanthropy and sacerdotal ritual of Huysmans's circle and the earnest young converts to Theosophy, as depicted by Lady Lutyens, could not be greater. The rites of Gothic Occultism are a world apart from the neat textbooks of Theosophy with their careful diagrams and lavish illustrations.

Theosophy presented the modern world with its own unique synthesis. It did not deny Christian belief, or evolution, or the atomic structure of matter – as then understood in its Daltonic form. Instead it relegated them; they were all depicted as features of a spiritual cosmology. In this manner Theosophy could resolve the main anxieties of the cultural crisis. It was no longer a case of Christian faith *or* scientific knowledge – rather an acceptance of both but on quite different terms. Blavatsky's evolution worked within a timescale that offered 18,000,000 years since the appearance of humanity, and those oceans of time required by the Darwinians could now be filled with progressive spiritual process, and that aspect of Darwin's evolution that caused so much distress, the common ancestry of man and ape is easily dealt with, 'As the embryo has no more of the ape in it than any other mammal . . . it seems as illogical to make him evolve from the ape as it would be to trace his origin to the frog or the dog' (Blavatsky 1888 vol. 1, p. 389).

The treatment of Christ, as indicated earlier, was equally radical, with the insistence that 'The teachings of Christ were OCCULT teachings . . . They were never intended for the masses' (Blavatsky 1888 vol. 2, p. 231, footnote) and that 'many were the good and holy men in antiquity who bore the surname or title of Chrestos before Jesus of Nazareth was born. The Christians . . . have tried to throw into the background all Chrestoi, who have appeared to them as rivals to their Man-God' (Blavatsky 1892, p. 169). The result was that *the* Christ was relegated to being but *a* Christ, part of a tradition of holy men whose message had an esoteric meaning that needed such as Theosophy to unravel the secret.

The features discussed above would be sufficient to explain the appeal of Blavatsky's system in the closing decades of the nineteenth century; but to that list needs to be added a number of factors whose addition briefly elevated it to being a *cause célèbre*. To concentrate on the purely structural features of Theosophic belief and to ignore the particular circumstances of the leadership of the Society by Blavatsky and Besant would be to omit important factors in explaining its success.

Both were forceful women and shaped the work and nature of the society to some extent to conform to their personalities. Of Blavatsky, Yeats, who briefly involved himself with Theosophy, wrote that she was 'A great passionate nature, a sort of female Dr Johnson, almost always full of fun that unlike the occasional joking of those about her, was illogical and uncontrollable' (Unterecker 1959, p. 20). There is ample evidence that she had a warm and lively personality. Even Solovyoff, who wrote a detracting account of her in *A Modern Priestess of Isis*, asked, 'How came it that this old and ill-favoured woman had such a power of attraction? How could this humorous good nature and simplicity be confined in her with the sort of painful mystery hidden in her wonderful eyes?' (V.S. Solovyoff 1895, p. 22). Her power of attraction it would seem lay in a curious mixture of personal charm, robust vulgarity and sheer tomfoolery. How else is one to interpret that in her New York study there had been 'stuffed baboons with white collars and cravats around their necks, spectacles on their noses, and bundles of manuscripts under their arms labelled "The Descent of the Species"' (Nethercott 1961, p. 334)?

The result has been that most commentators are as distrustful of the author as of her lengthy compilations. Ruth Brandon in *The Spiritualists* asserts that Blavatsky was quite insincere in the advocacy of her occult system: 'The disarming thing about her is that she saw Theosophy as a vast and delightful joke that she played at the world's expense' (1973, p. 86).

Also, it has to be admitted that Theosophy, whatever else it may have been, was also, at least in the eighties and nineties, quite simply good fun. Any creed that proclaimed 'it is but natural ... to view ... the Serpent of Genesis, as the real creator and benefactor, the Father of Spiritual mankind. For it was he ... bright radiant Lucifer, who opened the eyes of the automaton created by Jehovah' (Blavatsky 1888 vol 2, p. 243), could expect a certain acrimony and outrage. Ellic Howe, in his history of astrology, *Urania's Children* (1967), speaking of Theosophy, comments that 'The press in its turn, gave the Society an immense volume of publicity, since Theosophical personalities, wrangles and scandals provided editors with an almost perennial abundance of news-worthy copy' (p. 55). And Nethercott (1961, p. 326) instances Stuart

Cumberland, the editor of the *Mirror*, offering a wager of £1000 to Madame Blavatsky to produce occult phenomena which he could not explain and parallel. Shaw is quoted by Nethercott as saying that 'everybody who was anybody in London has been talking about Theosophy for the last four or five years' (p. 295).[14]

In spite of the novelty of her occult cosmology and the well-reported doings of the Society, Blavatsky almost certainly could not have maintained such a popular momentum for long, she was one of the 'topical lions', to use Beatrice Webb's term, with a strictly temporary ticket of admission for the season of their ephemeral notoriety, and in one sense her death in 1891 was timely.

FROM ROMANTIC OCCULTISM TO TECHNO-OCCULTISM

Blavatsky's Theosophy, for all its errors and borrowings, was finally a unity that transformed its constituent parts and which in total provided a syncretic system of startling originality. Proclaiming that the promulgation of its occult cosmology was *made necessary* by the advances of material science, in order to understand the nature of the forces being developed by that advance, it was resting its occult pretensions upon exoteric foundations as no previous occult system had done.

By the mid-twentieth century, those features that created a cultural crisis in the late nineteenth century and which had done so much to account for the advocacy of Theosophy no longer existed. Aristocracies had been abolished or rendered powerless and Darwinism had become an unquestioned orthodoxy. Furthermore, with its talk of angels, spirits and demons Theosophy was to seem particularly dated when, throughout the industrialized countries, both in peace and war, the dependency of society upon technology became a prominent theme of popular expression.

If a variant of occult expression was to achieve a popular credence it would have to lose its nineteenth-century imagery and gain one that was scientifically acceptable to the new century.

It was in the 1920s that occult thought began to extend its appropriative licence to technology. This occurs with the early development of rocketry, particularly in Germany, and through the advocacy of rocket travel by Max Valier, a builder of rocket cars and the author of several popular articles on rocketry. Valier, who later became the chairman of the Society for Spacetravel, founded in 1927, toured Germany giving lectures on Hoerbiger's occult cosmology – the Welteislehre, Atlantis and Lemuria.

Manfred Nagl in 'S.F., Occult Sciences and Nazi Myths' in *Science Fiction Studies* (1974, vol. 1, p. 185) has given a concise account of how Valier, Herman Oberth and other rocket engineers subscribed to occult doctrines connected with apocalypse and prehistoric cataclysms, and advocated rocketry as a liberating act if 'the fate of our fatherland, yes even of the entire world, is to take a turn for the better' (Nagl, p. 186). Here is a new development: technology, the rocket, as both inspiration for and the means of projecting occult programmes.

For reasons that will be detailed in the following chapters it was not until after the Second World War that a new variant of occult expression, one which depended upon presentations of technology, was able to achieve the status of a popular culture and produce a body of texts that share the same assumptions concerning an alternative cosmology that derived, in the main, from Blavatsky's secret doctrine.

Of course the later success of Techno-Occultism does not mean that Romantic Occultism has been completely superseded. The Theosophical Society continues to exist, publishing its texts and advocating the ideas of its foundress. Yet again the bookshop shelves bear witness to a growing interest in all forms of occultism, but in terms of texts and readership it was Techno-Occultism that from the fifties through to the early eighties became the most prominent variant of occult belief – sufficiently so for it to constitute a self-sustaining popular culture.

One theme of occult speculation that became relegated by twentieth-century developments and which Techno-Occultism was to rehabilitate was the ability to posit an absolute 'Elsewhere' – somewhere safe from the manifold of the mundane, everyday life.

The term 'Elsewhere' is used here in a specific sense and needs clarification. If we consider the late nineteenth-century story of adventure in far places it can be seen that two distinct traditions emerge. For instance, Jules Verne's *A Journey To The Centre Of The Earth* (1863) has its heroes journeying via an Icelandic volcano to the centre of the earth. The journey takes up some third of the account. The small band of explorers take scientific equipment with them. They have adventures and run risks but return to the surface essentially unchanged. Verne's subterranea is presented merely as a place, a backdrop for adventure and scientific endeavour, no different from the floor of the Atlantic, the surface of the moon or the Jurassic plateau in Doyle's *Lost World*, which also took a third of the book to reach. There is, however, another tradition of adventure story telling, represented by works such as Bulwer Lytton's *The Coming Race* (1871), W.H. Hudson's *A Crystal Age* (1887) or Cutclyffe Hyne's *Beneath Your Very Boots* (1889) and *The Lost Continent* (1900). These lesser-known works differ crucially from the Verne–Haggard–Doyle model of adventure tale. In this latter type of adventure, 'Elsewhere' is suddenly happened upon, there is no long odyssey. Further, the other world that is discovered is made to serve as an allegory or warning to the present, and the heroes' adventures in that world leave them permanently changed. The far places presented in this second tradition are of more importance than mere scenarios for scientific heroics and derring-do. They present an 'Elsewhere' whose location is not a matter of geographical reference but to present a warning or an alternative to the present. 'Elsewhere' is an imaginative escape from the all-pervading manifold of the modern world.

It is not surprising then to find that many of the texts within this tradition can be said to stand in a definite relation to occult speculation: to stand within an occult penumbra. Bulwer Lytton's *The Coming Race* depicts a subterranean race, the Vril-Ya, possessed of the force of the Vril, a fingertip power of wish fulfilment, whose advanced society is described in detail and who 'are destined to return to the upper world, and supplant all the inferior races now existing therein' (Lytton 1871, p. 106). Lytton's is an anti-Darwinist tract that advances occult speculation (strangely commentators upon *The Coming Race* usually categorize it as a text that advances Darwinian ideas, whereas in fact the text ridicules both evolutionary theory, 'Humble yourselves my descendants; the father of your race was a tadpole' (p. 120) and democracy, and represents an imaginative project at refuting the contemporary world). So too Cutclyffe Hyne's *The Lost Continent*, at Atlantean fable which is a warning of the dangers of both democracy and plutocracy and of the awful catastrophe that will ensue as a result of the move from an aristocratic-sacerdotal society.

With the coming of the twentieth century and the colonization of almost the whole of the globe by industrial development, the terrestrial sources of 'Elsewhere' become extremely limited. The evocative appeal of the Tibetan valley in which Blavatsky's Masters lived, 'an unknown valley, amidst the crags and glaciers of Terick-Mir – a vale never trodden by European foot since the day its parent was itself breathed out from within our Mother earth's bosom', does not hold when the world is criss-crossed by commercial airline routes and no country remains unmapped or out of radio contact. As will be seen, Techno-Occultism, by embracing the possibilities inherent in modern science and technology, will rework old myths to present new possibilities for 'Elsewhere', both terrestrial and extra-terrestrial, which will again serve as parable and warning against our present condition. Techno-Occultism is able to present *imaginatively plausible* 'Elsewheres' free from the enveloping manifold of mundane life.

2

VELIKOVSKY AND INCIPIENT CATASTROPHISM

Velikovsky's catastrophist theory was first published with *Worlds in Collision* in 1950. His thesis was that sudden and devastating catastrophes have repeatedly played a part in both the evolution of life on the planet and the cultural development of humanity within the historical era. The memory of such events is lost, although their cultural record is found in the literal reading of myth. The cataclysms were the result of both cometary and errant planetary movements.

On first examination Velikovsky's works cannot be said to be an example of Techno-Occultism. There is no appropriate connection with contemporary technology and Velikovsky does not draw upon any variant of occult speculation. But the matter is not that simple. There are important and distinctive features of Velikovsky's catastrophism that are shared with occult speculation. Both insist that humanity is living under the thrall of a monstrous heresy. Both insist upon the error of Darwinian evolution and propose their own variants; both rely upon the literal reading of myth; both demand a complete re-ordering of accepted ethical codes. These common elements ensure that Velikovsky's theories fall within the occult paradigm, and the nature and success of Velikovsky's text in 1950 will be shown to be clearly related to the success of flying saucer texts of the same period.

Indeed, Velikovsky does have a late nineteenth-century progenitor in Ignatius Donnelly, whose suppositional texts, *Atlantis: The Antediluvian World* (1882) and *Ragnorak: The Age of Fire and Gravel* (1882), were also heavily plagiarized by Blavatsky, although Donnelly himself disdained the occult and mystical Atlantean cults that welcomed his work.

In *Ragnorak: The Age of Fire and Gravel*, Donnelly argued that the earth's great deposits of sand, gravel and clay were not, as geologists had suggested, the result of glacial action, but rather the debris of a comet that had passed by, or even struck the earth. The catastrophe had occurred in prehistoric times, and knowledge of the event was still retained in the myths of various races. He argued that prior to the catastrophe there had been a Golden Age, 'a garden, a paradise ... with so mild and equable a climate that the plants we now call tropical flourished within our present Arctic Circle' (Donnelly 1882, p. 43).

This paradise was abruptly ended by the cometary cataclysm. Assembling evidence from a variety of sources, Donnelly provided a strong narrative that is constantly enlivened with imaginative interjections. 'But lo! through the darkness, the wretches not beaten down and whelmed in darkness, but scurrying to mountain caves for refuge, have a new terror: the cry passes from lip to lip, "The world is on fire"' (1882, p. 108).

Such a presentation, with its biblical undertones, undoubtedly helped to account for the work's popularity with the American public. Martin Ridge, Donnelly's biographer, records that '*Ragnorak* sold 3500 copies during its first five weeks on the market. Because these sales exceeded even the record for his *Atlantis*, Donnelly believed that the book was a great success ... and in April the entire first edition of almost 5000 copies had been sold' (1962, p. 208).

Final proof of his thesis is placed upon the interpretation of myth. 'But above all the legends prove the absolute fidelity of the memory of the races' (1882, p. 116). It is from the literal rendition of myth, a stance that is central to both Romantic- and Techno-Occultism, that Donnelly is able to deduce the cometary cataclysm and a subsequent reworking of ancient history, strongly prefiguring Velikovsky some seventy years later. Donnelly thus invests recognized palaeontological remains with his own value systems, for instance by equating Neanderthal Man with 'a Cain' (1882, p. 125).

In tones that anticipate Velikovsky, Daniken and Techno-Occultism in general, Donnelly admonishes the conservatism of 'Unthinkingness' that 'lies athwart the progress of mankind like a colossal mountain chain' (1882, p. 390), and he justified his cataclysm to his fellow man, when he maintains that after every cataclysm the world has risen 'to higher levels of development' and that modern humanity has nothing to fear unless it be that 'Sensual sins grow huge ... if Sodom and Gomorrah come again ... who can say that God may not bring out of the depths of space a rejuvenating comet?' (1882, p. 439).

The warning against profligacy and materialism is tempered by the need for a moral regeneration, and the moral eschatology adopted reverts back to a Christian fundamentalist interpretation of Genesis. But by using scientific evidence and by the introduction of non-Christian myth systems, Donnelly was welding together many of the tenets of occultism into a powerful yet secular form. As will be shown, Velikovsky's texts belong to the same world order as that propounded by Donnelly. In method and style Velikovsky owed much to *Atlantis* and *Ragnorak*.

There was also a distinct similarity between the circumstances out of which both writers constructed their theories, circumstances that indicate the function of occult (or in this case occultistic) works for the author. Donnelly was, at the time of writing *Atlantis*, a failed farmer and politician. He had been a strong advocate of 'The Patrons of Husbandry', or, as it was popularly known, 'The Grange', a MidWest organization that aimed to protect the farmer against capital and industrial growth, in the late 1860s and 1870s. His support for minority political causes continued with the Greenback movement, which worked for currency reform as a means of protecting the small farmer. His diary for 3 November 1880 gives expression to his despair:

> This is my 49th birthday and a sad day it is . . . All my hopes are gone and the future settles upon me, dark and gloomy indeed. . . . My life has been a failure and a mistake. My hopes have so often come to naught that I cease to hope . . .

Donnelly, witnessing the failure of the farming communities to withstand the advance of capital and the power of the railroad companies, and having failed in his own attempts as a farmer, wrote after the success of *Atlantis*, 'One thing is certain: my books have lifted me out of the dirty cess of politics, nasty enough at all times, but absolutely foul to the man who does not win.' The situation is clear, for the author constructing the theories of catastrophism was a liberating act of revenge against the encroaching new world order that is responsible for his failure.

There is a strong suspicion that in Velikovsky's case also, his catastrophism derived from a desire for revenge against an unheeding world. Velikovsky was born in Russia in 1895. After a period of study in France and brief travels to Palestine, he took up medical studies in Edinburgh until his progress was interrupted by the outbreak of war in 1914. He returned to Russia, completed his medical studies there and in the 1920s moved to Berlin, where, together with Heinrich Loewe, he founded and published the *Scripta Universitatis*, a series of volumes conceived as a foundation for a University of Jerusalem. By the end of the decade he had returned to Europe and undergone training as a psychoanalyst.

In 1937 his father died and with the money left him he planned to set up an Academy of Sciences. His studies and researches occupied most of the thirties, together with plans for a detailed work on the interpretation of Freud's own dreams and also a work on the comparative study of the lives of Oedipus, Akhnaton and Moses. Research for this work brought him to New York in 1939.

It was in the summer of 1940, while researching this work that he conceived of the possibility that the events of the Exodus were a literal account of an earth-shaking cataclysm. This was to be the core thesis of

Worlds in Collision and formulated in a text entitled *Ages in Chaos* which was completed in 1942, and subsequently published after the wider-ranging work, *Worlds in Collision*.

So Velikovsky, a Jewish scholar writing at a time when the Nazi grip on Europe was at its greatest extent and when the Jewish populations of Europe were being consigned to the death camps, develops the idea that the cataclysm described in Exodus was literally true and that it is suppressed fear that prevents humanity from recognizing the truth in the old texts. The theory functions as a liberating act. Exodus was literally true: its catastrophism can happen again. There will be revenge against an unheeding world.

Of course the subsequent popularity of a text has little to do with the personal circumstances of the author at the time of its inception and the success, and in Velikovsky's case, acrimony, that followed publication, was beyond both authors' expectations. Donnelly was actually elected to the American Association for the Advancement of Science, although scholars never took his work seriously; he became, as did Velikovsky seventy years later, '... probably the most discussed literary figure outside professional and intellectual circles' (Ridge 1962, p. 202). Atlantis became the theme for the New Orleans 'Mardi Gras' of 1883, and for the Baltimore 'Oriole' pageant of the same year. Velikovsky's success was of a different nature, but then his brand of Catastrophism was not solely located in a remote past, it placed contemporary humanity at the mercy of an erratic solar system and warned that cataclysms would happen again.

SUMMARY OF MAIN TEXTS: WORLDS IN COLLISION AND EARTH IN UPHEAVAL

On the 3 April 1950 Immanuel Velikovsky published *Worlds in Collision*, the first of what was to be a series of books that dealt with various aspects of one central theme, the all important role of catastrophe in shaping the history and *future* of humanity. Of all Velikovsky's texts, *Worlds in Collision* achieved the greatest fame and notoriety, the work managing to arouse both a storm of critical hostility in the academic world and enormous general interest, even before publication, as a result of previous part serialization in popular journals.

The main thesis of *Worlds in Collision* was both radical and innovative; it was that literally earth-shaking cataclysms had occurred in historical times; that the effects of such events had been recorded in myth and legend and that the agency of the cataclysms had been disturbances within the solar system. Furthermore it was claimed that though immediately before and after the cataclysms their nature as planetary dislocations was widely known, all memory of the disaster was soon lost to the survivors as a result of collective amnesia induced by the trauma.

The first edition of *Worlds in Collision* 'topped the best seller lists of the *New York Times* and the *New York Herald Tribune* for twenty successive weeks in 1950' (Alfred de Grazia 1978, p. 33). To understand why the text had such an impact demands both an investigation into the diverse and often contradictory influences to be found surrounding the work on its publication, and also an effort to relate the text to the powerful sources of anxiety in American society that were reaching a peak of ferocious intensity at precisely the time that *Worlds in Collision* received publication. To begin, however, analysis must start with the given text.

Worlds in Collision
(page references are to the Abacus 1972 edition)

The text is divided into two sections. Part One, entitled 'Venus', gives an account of the fifteenth century BC catastrophes caused by the close passage to the earth of a bright comet that had been emitted by Jupiter and which subsequently became the planet Venus. Part Two, entitled Mars, gives details of altercations between Mars and the still erratic Venus during the eighth century BC, altercations which caused Mars to change its orbit and the earth once again to be gravely threatened. The detection of both sets of events is derived from the literal reading of myth and legend from all over the world. The book opens, however, with a short Prologue which offers a stark and challenging statement of scientific honesty. Chapter One of the Prologue entitled 'In An Immense Universe' gives a brief picture of the solar system, as understood by science at the time, yet skilfully outlining the many gaps in our understanding of the system and arguing that theory cannot explain the multitude of irregularities that have been discovered, such as the retrograde motion of Venus.

Velikovsky's position is not to deny scientific knowledge but rather to illustrate the inadequacy of theory and the gaps in our knowledge of the system. This cold catalogue of omission and ignorance would have come as something of a shock in 1950 to anyone with even a slight interest in astronomy, for it was only in the previous decades that the multi-galactic, expanding nature of the universe had been revealed. And it was only in 1947 that the 200-inch Mount Palomar telescope had been commissioned, which gave unparalleled photographs of the moon and the distant and mysterious galaxies. After such heady optimism Velikovsky's catalogue 'here begins Homo Ignoremus' (p. 17) seems to run to every salient detail of the solar system . . .

Chapter Two of the Prologue, 'The Planet Earth' begins with a résumé of existing knowledge of earth structure and geological theory, readily pointing out yet again important gaps in the knowledge and discrepancies that are admitted in the theories. Velikovsky then claims that there is a respectable scientific pedigree to the notion that links catastrophe with sudden evolutionary leaps. He concludes with an argument for the universality of myth and thus introducing what is to be the methodology for the remainder of the work: a scientifically literal exegesis of myth systems and a system of synchronous datings of geographically dispersed myths on the insistence that they are relating to the same catastrophic events.

The account proper in Book One begins with the Old Testament account of Joshua ordering the sun and moon to stand still in the sky (Joshua x. 12–13). Arguably the most unbelievable story in the whole Bible, by taking this event as his starting point, Velikovsky is able to square up to his reader. The unbelievable nature of the account is admitted, but no possible exegesis begins to make sense unless we consider the impossible and regard the event as literally true. If so, he then argues, on the other side of the world we should find myths that relate to a correspondingly prolonged night, and the Mexican Annals of Cuauhtitlan are cited (p. 57) as just such evidence.

Having detailed the Joshua account in terms of physical catastrophe, Velikovsky proceeds to fix that upheaval into a cataclysmic system that began some 52 years earlier and covers the calamitous events related in Exodus. Again a literal reading of Exodus is maintained, with the events being the result not of a particularist divinity but of a worldwide catastrophe of enormous proportions. Again he adduces evidence from myth and fable from all over the world to argue for a common and unifying sequence of events, a worldwide cataclysm caused by the near passage of the cometary proto-planet Venus.

Reading Velikovsky's account one is struck by a feeling of inadequacy, so many myth systems are quoted, and without a thorough under-standing of text or its cultural context one is unable to qualify or deny the exegesis offered. This feeling of inadequacy communicated itself to his reviewers, and Eric Larabee writing in *Harper's Magazine* commented that 'Dr. Velikovsky's work crosses so many of the jurisdictional boundaries of learning that few experts could check it against their own competence' (Jan 1950, p. 20). This is the type of comment that undoubtedly served to add some acid to the notorious debate that accompanied publication of the work.

None the less, *Worlds in Collision* was aimed at the general reader. The narrative is taut, evocative and often gripping, and with frequent sideswipes at the scientific establishment, whose inadequacies have already been amply demonstrated, the result is inevitable; the reader suspends judgement and settles for a good read. And what a good read the book provides. Velikovsky astutely paints a picture of cosmic disasters, of sudden destruction, of awful portents in the sky as planets and comet career off expected courses, of crushed cities, of erased civilizations. It is the paintings of John Martin that are called to mind when he writes:

> The earth entered deeper into the tail of the onrushing comet and approached its body. This approach . . . was followed by a disturbance in the rotation of the earth. Terrific hurricanes swept the earth.

and

> At the same time that the seas were heaped up in immense tides, a pageant went on in the sky which presented itself to the horrified onlookers on earth as a gigantic battle.   (pp. 69 and 85)

It is a constant association in the imagination that links catastrophe and doom with guilt and retribution. The Mosaic Flood and the happenings at Sodom and Gomorrah are early examples, but the association is found later and forms a continuous strand in catastrophist literature of Romantic Occultism, Donnelly's *Ragnorak* being a prime example. Velikovsky is different; he is able to step away from the issue and argue not that the cataclysm was a result of moral excess, but rather that the peoples of the earth believed that was the case. Hence the important psychic development was the birth of a guilt–catastrophe association which was responsible for new socio-cultural constructs. Thus, for example, new laws were formed.

> Also, the day of the Lawgiving, when the worlds collided again, was according to numerous rabbinical sources, a day of unusual length: the motion of the sun was disturbed.   (p. 122)

He identifies the Day of Atonement, when the Israelites used to send their Scapegoat into the desert, as being the time when the periodic return of the comet caused diminishing but still destructive events in a 52-year cycle.

One benefit that he gains from arguing for the birth of a sense of guilt from global catastrophe is that he is able to present biblical and mythic material as being a literal truth to a wide and largely agnostic urban readership who would have turned away from straightforward fundamentalist readings of the Old Testament.

It is a measure of his skill as a writer that he can, while giving a graphic account of cataclysm and hoisting a wealth of mythic imagery before the reader, suddenly interpose queries and suggestions that seem sensible, fundamental even and without any apparent answer. Thus,

> why Jupiter, a planet which only a few persons out of a crowd know how to find in the sky, was the main deity of the peoples of antiquity.   (p. 363)

Yet the fascination of Velikovsky's work is that it retains its focus; implications, queries and suggestions are never allowed to deflect the reader from the picture of world cataclysm that is relentlessly built up and detailed in all its manifestations. The text continues, outlining how the comet, given the name Typhon by the ancient world, settles in an irregular orbit and becomes the planet Venus which, having a stretched elliptical orbit, eventually came to imperil the planet Mars so that by the eighth century BC Venus and Mars collided, creating a spectacle observable from earth. This collision became the subject of many myths as Ares (Mars) and Athena (Venus) career across the sky 'locked in combat' and endanger the earth. It is from this time, it is claimed, that Mars, which came perilously close to the earth, came to be regarded as the god of war and destruction.

In detailing the effect of these cataclysms Velikovsky makes several scientific assertions as to the planetary conditions, of Jupiter, Mars and, in particular, of Venus. Many of these assertions, necessary if his catastrophic thesis is to hold, were radical and completely at odds with contemporary depictions of planetary conditions. Thus Velikovsky claims that Mars has a heavily cratered surface, that Jupiter emits radio waves, that Venus has a surface temperature of hundreds of degrees Celsius. It has been the alleged accuracy of these and other related assertions that has served to keep the Velikovsky issue alive in some circles to this day, even though some of these claims have been refuted.[1]

With the eighth century BC cataclysms, as with the earlier disasters, Velikovsky argues that knowledge of the trauma was suppressed by a collective amnesia. This theorem allows him to square the circle; we cannot have literal, explicit accounts of the disaster because such knowledge has been driven into the 'unconscious strata of the mind', to emerge as mythopoeic account that requires a trained psychologist (which Velikovsky was) to interpret by freeing the essential package of information within the myth from its fear- and guilt-induced associations. It is of course an argument that cannot be countered, since to do so is to exhibit one's own guilt associations, one's own need to sustain the mythology of the ancient texts, because one is unable to face up to the fact of recurring disaster on an erratic and randomly destructive world. Humanity is at the mercy of an unpredictable and very dangerous local astronomy that is very different from the elegant dynamics of a galactic universe; this is the circumstance that humanity cannot accept and suppresses against all the evidence.

Worlds In Collision concludes with a short Epilogue in which it is argued that although focus has been maintained upon the cataclysms within 'two world ages', there have been cataclysms prior to these, and that these earlier cataclysms have provided a formative agency in the history of the planet and the evolution of life.

> The question before historical cosmogony is this: If it is true that cosmic catastrophes occurred such a short time ago, how about the more remote past? (p. 363)

Evidence for such cataclysms must be found in geological and palaeontological data and thus points the way to a further text, which is promised with

> The author feels an obligation to expand the scope of his work in order to include the problem of the birth of religion and of monotheism in particular. (p. 364)

That further work was *Earth in Upheaval*, first published in America in November 1955. It was not, however, Velikovsky's second title, that was *Ages in Chaos* (1952) which, being based on a more detailed reworking of his Exodus account, aimed at formulating a new chronology for Egyptian history. *Ages in Chaos* did not add to the controversy surrounding the publication of *Worlds in Collision* or advance the Catastrophist cosmology that would be developed in *Earth in Upheaval* and so need not be considered here.

Earth in Upheaval deals largely with geological evidence. Even so it does have an important sub-theme when it considers the sociological and cultural restraints that have served to direct the course of nineteenth-century science, when geological and evolutionary theory became so culturally powerful.

Although by the time of its publication in November 1955 much of the controversy aroused by *Worlds in Collision* had subsided, this later work is considered here because its arguments throw central features of the first text into a clearer light and help towards an understanding of the controversy surrounding *Worlds in Collision*.

Earth in Upheaval
(page references are to the Abacus 1973 edition)

Velikovsky's main concern at the beginning of *Earth in Upheaval*, on which he commenced work at the same time as he was completing *Worlds In Collision*, was to demonstrate that the evidence for cataclysm found in previous geological epochs is distributed all over the world. In Alaska, Siberia, South America and England, the witness of rock and fossil is to the result of enormous and repeated cataclysms.

> The animals could have been dismembered only by a stupendous wave that lifted and carried and smashed and tore and buried millions of bodies and millions of trees. (p. 4)

However, the point was made at the outset that what is being found in the fossil record is not evidence of one catastrophe, but of many, at different times, all of them global in nature. Thus already an important addition to the theses of *Worlds in Collision* has been made; catastrophe becomes Catastrophism, nature's agency for development and progression. This stance, implicit in *Worlds In Collision*, becomes central in *Earth in Upheaval*, and there are several passages detailing the turmoil and ravage within the fossil record of every landmass.

Velikovsky's next point is that since the fossil evidence of cataclysm is so widespread, so unmistakable, the question must be asked as to why it is that current palaeontology and evolutionary biology take no account of the selective and formative aspect of cataclysm. To answer this he launched on a brief historical and sociological survey of the development of geology and palaeontology in the late eighteenth and early nineteenth centuries. He argued that the early savants who developed these sciences did recognize the evidence for cataclysm and recorded their sense of enormity in their books and diaries. The effect is subtle; the feeling of awe, of inadequacy, of these early scientists, Cuvier, Buckland and Miller, writing in a direct and approachable manner in their journals and diaries, is communicated to the reader, who inevitably attaches their awe to the far more comprehensive and influential role for cataclysm demanded by Velikovsky.

In the third chapter, continuing his examination of the development of the earth sciences, he argued that the preponderance of the Doctrine of Uniformity, that

> Present continuity implies the improbability of past catastrophism and violence of change, either in the lifeless or in the living world   (p. 23)

is due to the political and social circumstances in post-Napoleonic Europe, when there was a universal desire for peace and tranquility. No wonder that in the climate of reaction to the eruptions of revolution and the Napoleonic Wars the theory of uniformity became popular (p. 22). Velikovsky claimed that the Doctrine of Uniformity still taught in all centres of learning has become a dogma, such that to question it is heresy (p. 23); a dogma, moreover, that can only be maintained by the rigorous suppression of the evidence to the contrary. Such evidence is manifest, but was suppressed by Lyell and Darwin because they could not face the necessary conclusions concerning man and his place in the universe. That courage is demanded of the modern reader.

> The past of mankind, and of the animal and plant kingdoms too, must now be viewed in the light of the experience of Hiroshima and no longer from the portholes of the Beagle.   (p. 227)

Uniformity can be maintained only by suppressing manifest evidence, and with Uniformity of course goes Darwinian evolution, with its requirement of steady-state conditions for the accretion of random survival-favouring mutations. This, therefore, leads to the final thesis of catastrophist cosmology, for such it has now become, that of 'cataclysmic evolution'.

> Therefore we are led to the belief that evolution is a process initiated in catastrophes. Numerous catastrophes or bursts of effective radiation must have taken place in the geological past in order to change so radically the living forms of earth, as the record of fossils embedded in lava and sediment bear witness. (p. 224).

It is with this final thesis that Catastrophism becomes the central feature of all living existence. Catastrophe and its results shape the planet, generate species, favour or doom civilizations and psychologically shape humankind, creating its culture, determining beliefs and knowledge.

One important feature in Blavatsky's Theosophy that had encouraged its reception in certain circles was that it had been able to present itself as a synthesis of sorts of both science and religion, both of which were depicted as being fundamentally flawed. The same position has been advanced by Velikovsky, and is made quite explicit in his final work, a collection of notes and commentaries made over the previous thirty years and published posthumously in 1982, under the title *Mankind in Amnesia*. In this the conflicting political systems of the modern world, the nuclear arms race and modern science and world religious systems are all depicted as the products of a catastrophe-induced collective amnesia. Subconscious knowledge of cataclysm is Velikovsky's 'secret doctrine', and conscious recollection of such knowledge becomes his initiatory process.

Unlike Donnelly, whose catastrophes happened at remote periods, only to provide the means of moral renewal, the exciting sense conveyed by a first reading of Velikovsky is that catastrophe has happened frequently in the past, as a result of the interaction of blind forces, and it could happen again. The resonances associated with Old Testament eschatology are transferred to the present world. There is also an unmistakable sense of imminence, which is then transferred through the concept of amnesia to the upheavals of the contemporary world. The catastrophe-induced amnesia has become a psychic lens for transforming all human activity, and any sustained criticism of his cosmology is open to the charge of being evidence of repressed thinking.

PUBLISHING HISTORY OF WORLDS IN COLLISION

The first introduction of the work to a popular readership comes at an early date when the *New York Herald Tribune* printed a consideration of

Worlds in Collision in August 1946, some four years prior to its final publication, by its science editor, John O'Neill, who wrote

> This magnificent piece of scholarly research raises world history to a level of superlative interest. ... Dr Velikovsky's work presents a stupendous panorama of terrestrial and human histories which will stand as a challenge to scientists to frame a realistic picture of the cosmos. (*New York Herald Tribune*, 14 May 1946)

The terminology is crucial; there is an explicit challenge and an implicit equation of Velikovsky's theories versus the whole of orthodox science. The same tone is found in Harlow Shapley's 'If Dr Velikovsky is right, the rest of us are crazy.' Shapley was Director of Harvard College and had been sent some of the radical predictions of Velikovsky's cometary theory to check.

Immediately before actual publication in April 1950 no less than three summaries or part-serializations of *Worlds in Collision* appeared in popular magazines. In *Harper's* of January 1950, in which Eric Larrabee, under the title 'The Day The Sun Stood Still' gave an uncritical summary of the work, then in April 1950 in the *Reader's Digest* Fulton Oursler gave a summary under the title 'Why The Sun Stood Still', and finally in *Collier's* a three-part serialization was begun, only the first two instalments ever appearing, as Velikovsky was so incensed by the treatment of his work.

Oursler's *Reader's Digest* article claimed that

> Leading critics have predicted that it may turn out to be as epochal as 'The Origin of Species' of Darwin or 'The Principia' of Newton (April 1950, p. 95)

and continued to set Velikovsky's work in a new perspective when he quoted from the famous Scopes Trial of twenty-five years earlier when he argued that *Worlds in Collision* could be seen as a vindication of the Bible. He concluded with:

> To science, *Worlds in Collision* opens a vast new debate: to millions of true believers in the Old Testament, it will come as an unintended and reassuring answer to the rationalist criticism of the last seventy-five years. (April 1950, p. 106)

Clearly Velikovsky's theories could also be seen as a validation of the most difficult Old Testament accounts.

Therefore by the time of publication of *Worlds in Collision* a mass readership was acquainted with its thesis, which could be made to support all manner of contradictory positions. And then in 1950, as Macmillan were going to press, attempts were suddenly made to prevent publication. Letters from Harlow Shapley at Harvard warned the publishers that

> It will be interesting a year from now to hear from you as to whether or not the reputation of the Macmillan Company is damaged by the publication of *Worlds In Collision*. (Juergens 1978, p. 28)

Extensive details of the subsequent controversy are given by Juergens, and the precise stance of publisher and academic critics need not be considered here, but what is important is that the general public were well aware that Velikovsky's work had aroused academic fury. *Science Newsletter* of February 1950 printed a denunciation of Velikovsky's ideas by authorities in five different fields: archaeology, oriental studies, anthropology, geology and astronomy. All this was but two months prior to publication. The controversy turned into outright confrontation, not just between author and critic, but between academe and publisher, and continued after publication against a background of enormous sales. Macmillan claimed that

> Professors in certain large universities were refusing to see Macmillan's salesmen, and letters demanding cessation of publication were arriving from a number of scientists. (Juergens 1978, p. 33)

The outcome was that publication was transferred to Doubleday and Co., which did not have a textbook department and was thus immune to the proposed academic boycott. The *New York Times* spoke of the publishing transfer as 'The greatest bombshell dropped on Publishers' Row in many a year.'

The controversy and acrimony did not end with publication but the point that is being emphasized here is that at the time of publication, in April of 1950, *Worlds in Collision* was widely known, its main theses were much discussed, and it was the subject of fierce controversy for both intra- and extra-textual reasons.

It is not surprising then that upon publication the book was enormously successful. Even the Larrabee article in *Harper's* led to the journal being

> sold out within a few days; so great was the demand that a number of dailies, here and abroad reprinted Larrabee's text in full. (Juergens 1978, p. 27)

The reviews of *World in Collision* also serve to indicate the extraordinary popular success of the work. Alfred Kazin, writing in *The New Yorker*, began his review with 'By this time, anyone who so much as looks at a newstand has heard of Dr Immanuel Velikovsky' (Kazin, April 1950).

It is not difficult therefore to account for the popularity of *Worlds in Collision*: the pre-publication build-up, the acrimonious debate, the academic pronouncements – often filled with 'parenthetical sneers' – all provided an intellectual circus, with the public able to sit back and watch. Within the text itself were several qualities that recommended it to a mass readership: the instant scholarship cutting across a host of disciplines, the fact that, as Harlow Shapley admitted, if Velikovsky was right then almost all science was wrong, and the gripping narrative with its imaginative portrayal of catastrophe. Even Velikovsky's name: Immanuel–imminent . . . Velikovsky–velocity–catastrophe, had properties of evocation that were strangely in keeping for a prophet of planetary doom.

SOURCES OF ANXIETY IN POST-WAR AMERICAN SOCIETY

It is intended to show that the popularity and notoriety of *Worlds in Collision* was due to far more than the qualities outlined above. The claim will be made that the popularity of Velikovsky's work was due also to the fact that it was able to act as a metaphor for identifiable anxieties that peaked in 1950, precisely the time of publication. In order to prove such a position it is necessary to delineate the sources and nature of those anxieties in American society when the country

> went through some of its most profound and disturbing changes of its modern history – changes that altered national direction, shifted the ideological mood, shifted and enlarged the nation's world role and redirected American consciousness. (Temperley & Bradbury 1981, p. 243)

Of course anxiety is a perennial feature of the human condition and it is dangerously easy to itemize specific features as sole sources of anxiety; what is being argued here is that within the narrow band of six years, 1949–53, it is possible to identify three specific themes that became foci for social and personal anxiety. These were: anxiety aroused by the Russian possession of the atom bomb; fear of communist infiltration into American public life; the realization that America could never again fall back into an isolationist stance and ignore its involvement in world affairs. Inevitably the tensions caused by these anxieties fluctuated during the post-war years, but they reached a peak that manifested itself in waves of public hysteria during the years 1949–53, at precisely the time that *Worlds in Collision* was being written up, published and debated.

ATOMIC WEAPONS

The emotions aroused by the development, use and deployment of atomic weaponry were obviously complex and changing. The baseline argument however is simply that from 1945 to 1953 there is a constantly high level of anxiety that is centred on nuclear weaponry. Howard Temperley and Malcolm Bradbury express the situation as follows.

> The new world order was based on tension and contained conflict, and over it all was the shadow of the 'bomb', the atomic weapon that had ended the Pacific war. The post war period was, indeed, for most Americans an 'age of abundance', and even an 'age' of equilibrium. But it was also an 'age of anxiety', and atomic anxiety at that. (1981, p. 244)

The projected public imagery of the atomic bomb was sustained in the same apocalyptic terms it had aroused in its begetters. Oppenheimer's recollection of the line from the Bhagavat Ghita, 'Behold I am become death, the destroyer of worlds', when he witnessed the first test of the bomb became the tone of public pronouncement and the *New York Herald Tribune*'s editorial on the dropping of the first bomb on Japan stated,

> it is an announcement more fateful for human history than the whole war itself . . . the practical unlocking of the inconceivable energy of the atom would stir history to its deepest depths. . . .
>
> The statement (Truman's announcement of the raid) is weird, incredible and somehow disturbing . . . one senses the foundations of one's own universe trembling a little. It is as if we had put our hands on the lever of power, too strange, too terrible, too unpredictable in all its possible consequences for any rejoicing over the immediate consequences of its employment . . . one must devotedly hope that mankind can . . . employ the powers he has grasped for some other end than self destruction.   (Tuesday 7 August 1945)

The editorial has been quoted at some length since its thematic richness indicates that from the very outset the mere fact of the bomb, independent of its deployment or counter-threat, was able to arouse a range of interlocking themes: death, destruction, extinction. Such imagery was not confined to the American press; the lead article in *The Times* of 8 August claimed

> The world stands in the presence of a revolution in earthly affairs . . . the new power must be consecrated to peace not war,

and the quasi-religious tone of such utterances served to heighten the sense of enormity and bewilderment that was aroused by the first public news of the bomb and its use. Paul Chilton in *Nukespeak: The Media and the Bomb* argues that in August 1945 there emerged 'a new consensus language, speaking of the atom bomb in terms of religious awe. . . . One useful consequence of such language, if not one of its actual motivations, was to appear to diminish human control, responsibility and guilt' (Chilton 1982, p. 98). Meanwhile *Life* for 29 October printed an article by three physicists entitled 'The Atomic Scientists Speak Up', in which the fears and concerns of the authors were clearly spelt out – could the bomb be kept a secret? Was there a possible defence against atomic weapons?

Writing a decade later Edward A. Shils commented that whereas initially the American people had embraced the bomb and peace together, nevertheless

> the bomb left in its wake grave apprehensions which soon became substantial. The faint trace of guilt which was tinting the outlook of some Americans has never really died away, but it has been greatly overshadowed by a far more widespread horror over any future use of the bomb.   (Shils 1956, p. 68)

Thus as early as 1945, physicists, politicians, editors and journalists were presenting the bomb to the general public in terms redolent of religion, divine power, apocalypse and world ending: a nexus of thematic associations that set up a cultural resonance that was henceforth always to be associated with nuclear weaponry. However, by 1950 popular concerns and attitudes to the bomb had been radically re-orientated. For 1949 had been a traumatic year in America's history: it saw the communist take-over in China, the beginning of the war in Korea and the explosion of the Russian atom bomb, announced by President Truman on 23 September.

The Russian atom bomb was a severe blow to American technological self-esteem, since it had been confidently believed that it would be at least another generation, perhaps another twenty-five years, before the Russians would have an atomic weapon capability.

By 1950 there were further disquieting developments, the hydrogen or 'super' bomb was now being openly bruited abroad. On 31 January Truman directed the Atomic Energy Commission to study the possibility of building hydrogen bombs and on 29 June the Commission disclosed that great steps had been achieved towards the development of such a bomb. And in the same period a nationwide programme of civil defence was being planned, publicized and implemented.

3 June 1949.	NSRB requested Federal Works Agency and Department of Defense to develop civil defense plans.
September 1949.	Department of Defense held 'Operation Lookout' in ten northeastern states to test air defenses.
December 1949.	First of a series of NSRB Civil Defense planning bulletins sent to state governors.
August 1950.	AEC issued Weapons' Effects handbook. (*Bulletin of Atomic Scientists*, August–September 1950, p. 270)

At precisely the time that Velikovsky's cataclysmic theories were being read and debated, the American public was thus experiencing detailed measures to combat and counteract the effects of an *expected* nuclear war. Further, it was just at this time, during 1949–50 that, as a result of the developments mentioned above, the concerns and attitudes to the bomb were being re-orientated. Now the average citizen 'every human being capable of comprehension' was no longer invited to stand back in awe before the unimaginable power of the bomb, but was made to confront the problem of personal survival in an *expected* atomic war. Now the population was being forced to confront the issue of national or civic survival. The result was that the undirected awe the bomb was made to evoke in 1945 became a vectored anxiety over personal, public and national survival. It was also, therefore, at precisely that time that interaction between bomb-induced anxieties and fears of communist infiltration and concern over America's unavoidable commitment to a global involvement became most complex.

The depth of the anxiety aroused by active consideration of an atomic war can be gauged by a review of the journals, newspapers and periodicals of the period. Details of civil defence plans were widely known and variously reported. The *Bulletin of the Atomic Scientists* in a special double issue for August–September 1950 gave a detailed account of the defence plans.

> New York city plans to enroll an auxiliary police force of 40,000 men and women.
>
> A plan calling for the construction of huge underground shelters in city park areas, roughly estimated to cost $450,000,000, was submitted in a report from the City Planning Commission and is under consideration. (p. 277)

In more popular journalism an examination of the articles in *Time* for the months of April 1950, the month of the publication of *Worlds in Collision*, through to December 1950 shows the regularity with which items on the atom bomb and the possibility of nuclear war occur. The list (see Appendix 1) amply illustrates the extent to which this traumatic issue was kept at the forefront of the public's consciousness.

The 2 October issue had as its cover a montage of the New York skyline, a Civil Defense logo and a mushroom cloud against which is set the portrait of 'Civilian defender Clay', under whom is written the chilling nostrum 'No one is safe, but some can be saved'. The lead article, entitled 'The City Under the Bomb' deals with a hypothetical raid on New York and argues that

> For the first time a great many Americans were beginning to realise that the United States had become the target of a determined and ruthless enemy

and under the subheading 'The Horrendous Hypothesis' continues with

> Suppose that an overcast, autumn morning, a Russian bomber carrying an atomic bomb ... swept through the stratosphere above New York and dropped its missile,

and sets out in some detail to outline what was then for the first time, the results of such an attack. It must be borne in mind that this was in a popular magazine with mass circulation figures, not in a politically committed minority magazine. Further, behind these novel scenarios there was a powerful sense of advocacy: atomic war was expected; America must prepare; there will be a sneak attack. The article confidently concluded with the fact that there were some 140 American cities that were potential targets and that

> this was the problem of survival which the U.S. had just begun to comprehend. U.S. citizens would have to face it and live with it for a long time to come.

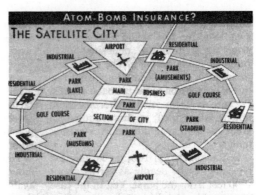

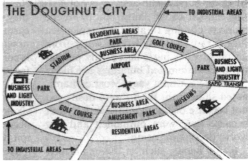

1 *Cities designed on a radial plan so as to be able to withstand attack with atom bombs. August 1949.*

A review of *Reader's Digest* shows a similar frequency of articles dealing with an expected atomic war. The August 1949 issue carried an article entitled 'New Facts About the Atom Bomb' which gave diagrams showing how cities of the future would be designed on a radial plan so as to withstand atomic bomb attacks (see illustration).

As the Civil Defense programmes got under way no citizen could avoid the preparations for war. On the main highways in and out of the major cities signboarding was erected stating that in the event of an enemy attack the road would be closed to all but military traffic. A recent account of a schoolboy's experience of war preparations during the early fifties was given in the *Bulletin of the Atomic Scientists*.

> Along with fire drills and occasional earthquake drills, we went through air raid drills every month or so. .... Children were to go quietly and directly to their lockers in the hall, take out their jackets and lie on the floor in the approved position. Heads should be next to the wall, face down to avoid the blinding flash, with the jacket covering the neck. .... Every year we also took home leaflets showing the best evacuation routes from the city, reminders that if the warning came we must go, and suddenly, to escape destruction. (A. Furtwangler, January 1981)

The young were particularly subjected to defence drills, and several educational films were made to give instruction in school and home on how to deal with the immediate results of nuclear detonations. The notorious 'duck and cover' exercises, rehearsed in classroom, school-hall and the streets were popularized by the cartoon character 'Burt the Turtle' as well as by realistic scenes of youngsters carrying out the 'duck and cover' procedure.

Concerning the effect of such exercises upon the young, Michael J. Carey, in an article entitled 'Psychological Fallout' in the *Bulletin of the Atomic Scientists* for January 1982, argues that

> Those Americans born between 1940 and 1950 were separated from preceding and following generations by the profound influence of Hiroshima, the cold war, the arms race and the rhetoric of annihilation that dominated international politics of the 1950s. (M. Carey 1982, p. 20)

Carey's method is to report findings from interviewees concerning their thoughts and feelings as a result of the bomb scare and war drills they experienced as children. The results were collected under three notions that epitomized such experiences: the atom bomb as 'the mystery of the age'; as the youngsters feeling that they were living in a 'world of victims' – no matter where you are the bomb will get you; and finally the notion of 'absurd death' – no desk top is going to stop anyone from being wiped out.

Carey's work was basically with Americans who were schoolchildren and teenagers during the forties and fifties; nevertheless, the response and memories that he chronicles are quite indicative and there are no grounds for supposing that these anxieties and images of death, cataclysm, extermination and nature in disorder, together with feelings of absurdity and guilt were not commonly experienced in the population as a whole. By the parents, for instance, who knew that their children were undergoing such drills at school and who read such tracts for parents as *Atomic Age. A Manual for Survival*, which demanded

> Can junior instantly fall down, elbow out, forehead on elbow, eyes shut? Have him try it tonight as he gets into bed . . .

and continues, explaining the effects of an atomic explosion, with

> Junior will feel the wind go by, the dirt and pebbles blow with hurricane force against his head . . . his playmates standing upright will be blown over like matchsticks. (Balderstone & Hughes, 1951)

The discrepancy between the efficacy of falling to the floor and placing a paper bag over one's head and the bruited power of the bomb heightened the sense of absurdity, and the official propaganda was forced to counteract with cartoon films such as that entitled *Nuclearosis*, which depicts an over-worried citizen getting good advice from an avuncular scientist, who proclaims that the symptoms of Nuclearosis – a form of nuclear blindness – are that

> All he can see is a mushroom cloud; he is blinded by the fire of it, deaf from the sound of it, there is a short circuit in his brain and all he can think of is the awfulness of the nuclear bombs.

Such snappy little cartoons speak of the official concern that all the exercises and civil defence preparations at the height of the cold war had produced anxieties which were common enough for the official propaganda to seek to remedy.

Snap-brim era of the Cold War before 'nuclear winter'. Richard Gerstell's government-sponsored *How to Survive an Atomic Bomb* (1950) advised hats for men, and stockings and long-sleeved dresses for women.

DIRECTION OF HEAT FLASH

If you are caught outdoors in a sudden attack, a hat will give you at least some protection from the 'heat flash'.

2   *One of the simple and immediately effective solutions.*

Reading the articles in the popular journals, watching the films of the official programmes of exercises, one senses the powerfully sustained logic behind the common scenario: atomic war is a probability as a result of Russian bad intentions and will come though a pre-emptive strike at several American cities. 'No one is safe, but some can be saved', therefore learn the drill, face up to the new reality, it won't be as bad as you think. This was the scenario that urban Americans had to accept in 1950 (see illustration).

FEAR OF COMMUNIST INFILTRATION

An examination of the fears inspired by the belief that communists were successfully infiltrating all sectors of American society shows that there are crucial points of contact with the fears and anxieties induced by the atom bomb. Clearly the issues are interrelated, though it would be wrong simply to assume that fear of communist infiltration was merely a direct consequence of the fact of Russia's possession of the atom bomb. Fear of a communist infiltration was a complex phenomenon born of varied socio-economic circumstances, and can be seen as a response to changing political factors as much as to the development of nuclear weaponry. It can nevertheless be demonstrated that there are important structural parallels in the manifestation of anxiety aroused by both issues.

The account of the communist scare has been written up on several occasions, and it is not the purpose here to attempt a further account or to add to the rationales that have been forwarded to account for the phenomenon; rather, simply to highlight certain developments and to indicate their impact upon public perceptions. As with the fears induced by atomic bombs, 1949 was to prove a climacteric year. In *The Crucial Decade* Eric F. Goldman wrote that

> August, the concession of China to the Communists; September, the announcement of the Soviet atom bomb; August and September and the months before and after, the explosive questions raised by the Hiss case – 1949 was a year of shocks, shocks with enormous catalytic force,

adding

> For Americans . . . the shocks of 1949 were the last straw . . . Western Europe may have been saved but what of the facts that vast China was now in Communist hands, that the Soviet Union could dangle an atomic bomb over American heads, that the Hiss case easily raised the question whether Communist infiltration into the American government was ended. (E. Goldman 1960, pp. 112 and 117)

The Hiss case had been 'news' since as early as August 1948, though Hiss was indicted to stand trial in December 1948. In February 1949 Cardinal Spellman, who as early as 1946 had been talking of the need to combat the aggression of enemies within, appeared in the pulpit of St Patrick's Cathedral to

> speak one of the most passionate sermons ever delivered from an American pulpit. America was in imminent danger of 'Communist conquest and annihilation . . . . Are we, the American people, the tools and the fools for which the Communists take us?' The situation called for an immediate end of all 'ostrich-like actions and pretenses', particularly in halting the 'Communist floodings of our own land'. (E. Goldman 1969, p. 131)

Goldman states that at times Catholic anti-communism took on an emotional tone that was close to being hysterical, and cites the example of the Catechetical of St Paul distributing a comic-strip tract entitled *Is This Tomorrow?* in which Communist mobs were depicted attacking St Patrick's Cathedral with torches and nailing the Cardinal to the door (p. 131).

A natural climax to these pressures and reactions came in 1950. In January of that year Hiss was proclaimed guilty on both counts of spying. Ten days later, on 31 January, Truman announced the decision to build the hydrogen or 'Super' bomb, and

> Twelve distinguished scientists immediately issued a joint statement which pointed out that, 'in the case of the fission bomb the Russians required four years to parallel our development. In the case of the hydrogen bomb they will probably need a shorter time'. (E. Goldman 1960, p. 135)

and thereby promoting the invidious situation that America must enter a race which, relatively speaking, it could only lose.

And then, on 3 February there was another disturbing development when the British Government announces the confession of Dr Klaus Fuchs. 'The last man in the world you would expect to be a spy', wrote Goldman, quoting an English journalist, an observation that highlighted another feature of the fear of Communist infiltration, that the agent is likely to be an ordinary, average-looking sort of person – the 'man next door', the unglamorous American quietly going about his daily business. Fuchs' confession that he had been spying for the Russians from 1943 to 1947 and his statement that he had 'complete confidence in Russian policy' and that he had 'no hesitation in giving them all the information I had' (Goldman 1960, p. 136) served to inflame American public opinion even further.

A speech by Senator Homer Capehart of Indiana welded all the American anxieties together in a cry of despair when he demanded

> How much more are we going to have to take? Fuchs and Acheson and Hiss and hydrogen bombs threatening outside and New Dealism eating away the vitals of the nation. In the name of heaven, is this the best America can do? (E. Goldman 1960, p. 136)

Such expressions indicate how anxieties born of the bomb and fears of communist infiltration were transpositional particularly at times of crisis, how they could both be placed in a context of American helplessness. *Time* for 2 October 1950, which has already been cited, spoke of America's cities as being 'pretty much defenseless and their populations naked under the enemy'.

Again popular journals served to keep the fear of communism and its intentions constantly before the public's eye. A list of all such articles in the *Saturday Evening Post* for the year April 1949 to April 1950 illustrates the prominence given to the theme (see Appendix 2).

It was on the same day that Britain announced Fuchs' confession that McCarthy delivered his speech before the Women's Republican Club in Wheeling, West Virginia, a speech that, together with a similar speech in Salt Lake City on 10 February, is generally held to mark the commencement of what is termed 'The McCarthy Era'. It was McCarthy's thesis that

> The communists within our borders have been more responsible for the success of communism abroad than Soviet Russia.

and that

> The writs of Moscow run to ... a good 40% of all living men ... this must be the product of ... a great conspiracy, a conspiracy on a scale so immense as to dwarf any previous such venture in the history of man. (Caute 1978, p. 46)

The universality of McCarthy's supposed conspiracy bears comparison with the destructive power of nuclear weapons; both are vast beyond imagination, both proclaim that no one is safe.

As a result of McCarthy's activities the crisis over fear of communist infiltration did not resolve itself, and tensions were maintained for the following two to three years. Thus for most of 1951 the bestseller lists included *Washington Confidential* by Lait and Mortimer, which gave a series of revelations about alleged communism in Washington. It was also in 1951 that Mickey Spillane's *One Lonely Night* was published. With sales eventually reaching over three million, its hero, Mike Hammer boasted

> I killed more people tonight than I have fingers on my hands. I shot them in cold blood and enjoyed every minute of it ... They were commies, Lee. They were red sons-of-bitches who should have died long ago ... they never thought that there were people like me in this country. They figure us all to be soft as horse manure and just as stupid. (Spillane 1951, p. 171)

Beyond the fantasy lies the circumstance, accepted as plausible for the fantasy to work, that communists are to be so readily found that a dozen or so can be disposed of in one evening's slaughter. The popular solution, then as now, was for the American guy to take matters into his own hands: the simple and immediately effective solutions – duck and cover, putting a paper bag over the head, 'Can junior instantly fall down?'.

There is no better illustration of how both sources of anxiety may be conjoined into an indissoluble whole than in an article by William L. Lawrence, 'one of the top authorities on atomic fission', entitled 'The Truth about the Hydrogen Bomb', that appeared in the 24 June 1950 issue of the *Saturday Evening Post*. The article was accompanied by photographs of physicists Bethe, Oppenheimer and Fuchs, and also by an aerial photograph of the New York area, on which circles were drawn to delineate the areas of complete destruction that would have been accomplished by the detonation of atom and hydrogen bombs. Again, as with the *Time* article mentioned earlier, it must be remembered that these were enormously popular magazines and that the destructive capacity of the hydrogen bomb, designated by Lawrence 'The Hell Bomb', was fearsome new knowledge presented to the public at a time when its use was expected.

In the course of the article Lawrence recalled a conversation he had had some years earlier at the Los Alamos installation with physicist Hans Bethe, when the theoretical possibility of a fusion bomb had been discussed. Would it be, he asked, as much as fifty times as powerful as the uranium or plutonium bomb? Lawrence gave an answer with

> I shall never forget his quiet answer as he looked away towards the Sangre de Cristo (Blood of Christ) mountain range. 'Yes', he said, 'it could be made to equal a million tons of TNT . . .'.
> The tops of the mountains seemed to catch fire as he spoke, my sense of shock was overpowering.

Lawrence continues with another anecdote

> I remember when Dr J.R. Oppenheimer . . . brought out . . . from a safe . . . a small vial of clear liquid that looked like water. It was the first highly diluted minute sample of super heavy water, composed of tritium and oxygen, ever to exist in the world. We both looked at it in silent, fearsome awe . . . . Here was something with the power to return the earth to its lifeless state of two million years ago.

The motifs proliferate: the destructive power locked deep in nature, the mountains turning red with blood, the Christ motif, emphasized by the anglicized name of the mountains in brackets, the vital fluid in the vial – and coalesce in what follows. How much greater would the author's sense of shock have been

> had I known that there, at Los Alamos, at that very moment, a spy was walking amongst us, collecting the secrets he would give to the Russians.

The spy was amongst them, seeing but unseen, stealing the 'Great Secret' that could produce the 'end of the world like thunder'. But if the bomb evoked eschatological imagery, the spy communist evoked the gospels, for Lawrence stated

> and there in our midst, as we learned only recently, stood a Judas, 'Klaus Fuchs', a name that will live in infamy. There he was, this spy, standing right there, in the centre of what we believed at the time to be the world's greatest secret. . . .
> It is no accident that President Truman's official announcement of the order to build 'the so-called Hydrogen or Superbomb' came within three days of Fuchs' arrest and confession.

The terms of the mythologism are quite clear; if the hydrogen bomb is an evil, it is an evil necessity, a 'Hell Bomb' that has to be brought into the world as a result of communist duplicity. And as a result of which America, instead of possessing the 'vital secret' that can give it world domination, is now engaged in a deadly race. If, as a result of treachery, America fails to win this race, it could lead to her virtual enslavement. The date of the article – 24 June 1950, at the time when the furore over Velikovsky's *Worlds in Collision* was at its height. What is significant about both bomb and communist infiltration anxieties is that though they were clearly defined fears the individual was quite powerless to do anything to remedy them, other than in the perceived absurdity of duck and cover exercises or in the fantasy indulgence of Mickey Spillane. It is in this gap, between anxiety and resolution that a function for the Velikovskian metaphor can be found.

AMERICAN LOSS OF ISOLATION

The idiosyncratic history of anxiety in postwar American society focuses naturally on the emotions aroused by bomb development and spy scares; these issues as generators of anxiety were episodic, responding to developments and manipulation, their impact being chronologically un-even. But these anxieties need to be set against the counterpoint of a more general, more evenly sustained source of concern, that which stemmed from the inescapable circumstances of America's post-1945 involvement in world affairs. After 1945, indeed after Pearl Harbor in 1941, America would never again be able to turn its back on Europe or the world and involve itself with exclusively domestic affairs. In their essay, 'War and Cold War', Temperley and Bradbury explain that

> What made Americans so surprised and angry was not just that Pearl Harbor came totally without warning or, as far as they could see, provocation: it was that nothing remotely like it had happened before. Since the founding of the Republic, they had believed that their geography provided a barrier against potential aggressors. (Temperley & Bradbury 1981, p. 247)

After 1945 the geopolitical reality made retreat from world affairs clearly impossible: the deployment of American troops throughout Europe and the Far East; the mutual vulnerability of both Russia and America, who had each been the target of initially successful, unprovoked, well-executed attacks; the technical reality brought about by the power of the atom bomb, which meant that but a single enemy plane – or later, missile – need get through to inflict enormous damage, when during the war literally thousands had got through the German defences. All of these factors secured the early recognition that times had changed and that henceforth America was inextricably involved in world affairs. Goldman in *The Crucial Decade and After* expressed the situation as

> The more Americans fretted over home affairs, the more plain a fact of fundamental importance became. For the first time during an American era of peace, it was next to impossible to discuss domestic problems coherently without having the points become entangled in foreign affairs. (E. Goldman 1960, p. 130)

The distance travelled can be gauged by the speech given by Arthur H. Vandenberg of Michigan, a senior Republican and a notorious isolationist who four weeks after Germany had invaded Poland proclaimed 'This so-called war is nothing but about twenty-five people and propaganda', but yet confessed to a friend as he stood and contemplated V1s landing on London, 'How can there be immunity or isolation when man can devise weapons like that?' (E. Goldman 1960, p. 131).

Since there was nothing that could change the new geo-technical reality, concern over American involvement in world affairs remains a constant, if muted source of anxiety. An article in the *Saturday Evening Post* of 23 April 1949, entitled What of Our Futures? asks

> Have we Americans taken on more than we can handle in sponsoring the North Atlantic Treaty? What will our vast world wide commitments do to our cherished way of life?

and goes on to complain

> The collapse of European power, the atomic bomb and other ocean shrinking weapons . . . have eliminated the buffer of time which cushioned our detachment.

Significantly, the editorial of this same issue is entitled 'Let's Not Carry On The War Of Nerves Against Ourselves' and argies that, 'One thing that would be of no use at the moment is an increase of public hysteria and frenzy' (*Saturday Evening Post*, 23 April 1949).

Anxiety aroused by loss of isolation had the unique component of national self-doubt; hence the plea in the editorial quoted above. If the nation could not retreat within itself, then its own 'Americanism' was held up to question and doubt; the traditional American values could not be relied upon, they were no longer efficacious in the post-war world, and the questions and doubts aroused were given a strident expression by Louis B. Seltzer, editor of the *Cleveland Press*, who wrote in an editorial

> What is wrong with us? It is in the air we breathe. The things we do. The things we say. Our books. Our papers. Our theater. Our movies. Our radio. Our television. The way we behave. The interests we have. The values we fix.
>
> We have everything. . . . We are, on the average, rich beyond the dreams of the kings of old. . . . Yet . . . something is not there that should be – something we once had . . . .

> Are we our own worst enemies? Should we fear what is happening among us more than what is happening elsewhere? No one seems to know what to do to meet it. But everybody worries. (E. Goldman 1960, p. 217)

Such was the response to the editorial, Goldman relates, that forty-one publications throughout America reprinted the piece and phone calls and letters flooded into Seltzer's office, with strangers stopping him in the streets to shake hands.

VELIKOVSKY'S TEXT AS METAPHOR

The foregoing analysis has concentrated on three complementary and mutually reinforcing foci of anxiety in post-war American society. It is not being suggested that these anxieties had a pure and simple genealogy: Senator Homer Capehart's linking of the Hiss trial, hydrogen bombs and New Dealism, in the speech quoted above, indicates a complexity at least in the sources of anxiety. So too does Seltzer's complaint that the average American was 'rich beyond the dreams of the kings of old'. Undoubtedly anxiety aroused over the issue of atomic war was able to subsume other, more generalized concerns within its powerful and publicly prominent expression. But even after making such allowances the situation was undoubtedly that in the year 1949–50 the popular perception was of determinate and interrelated anxieties; these were individually and collectively the topic of frequent public utterances. The *Saturday Evening Post* editorial for 23 April 1949, already quoted, spoke of there being 'some disquieting premonitory symptoms of hysteria here and there'. Harold Ickes in an article entitled 'National Hysteria' in *New Republic* of August 1950 called for sensibility and the realization that the American people had nothing to fear but fear itself. An article in the *Bulletin of The Atomic Scientists* entitled 'Panic, Psychology and the Bomb' argued that

> a huge fraction of the public, perhaps the majority, already displays clinical symptoms of hysteria and predisposing to panic.

and continues

> our public is already exhibiting on a massive scale a vast variety of 'symptoms' which, in clinical psychology, one knows to be the results of deeply repressed fear, and these symptoms, classical in nature, are called hysterias. (P. Wylie. *Bulletin of The Atomic Scientists*, February 1954, p. 37)

It is being argued that there are important extra-textual reasons that account for the popularity and notoriety of Velikovsky's works in the early fifties. The situation is that Velikovsky's cosmology, which is dependent upon multiple cataclysms that determine all aspects, physical and spiritual, of human existence, acted as a metaphor for the real anxieties that were shaping the psychosocial self-presentations of American society.

The events after 1945 meant that Americans were faced with apparent paradoxes. America could no longer ignore the outside world; it had to learn to live with communism, which it believed was dedicated to its destruction. The 'super bomb' was needed even though, by beginning its construction, America was embarking on a race that she could not win. Once built the 'super bomb' could not even guarantee the safety of her cities. The greatest civic danger was the spy, who though evil and treacherous was indiscernible from the average American going about his daily business. These were paradoxes that could not be resolved and which led to anxieties mounting at times to public hysteria. Just such a peak was reached in late 1949 and early 1950, the time of publication of *Worlds in Collision*.

Evidence of the extent to which Velikovsky's cataclysmic cosmology functioned as a metaphor is found in the juxtaposition of key elements or motifs in the given account of post-war anxieties with main themes or elements in Velikovsky's writing. These are identified as follows.

Universality

The bomb posed a threat to all humanity. Following Truman's announcement of the decision to build the hydrogen bomb, Einstein appeared on television and warned 'general annihilation beckons' (E. Goldman 1960, p. 136).

The communist conspiracy was organized on a worldwide scale: McCarthy's 'On a scale so immense as to dwarf any previous such venture in the history of man'.

Velikovsky presents a series of cataclysms that wiped out entire civilizations, decimated the earth's population and literally stopped the earth in its rotation.

The vital secret

The knowledge of the 'basic power of the universe', as Truman put it, partakes of a 'vital secret', one that means 'a new relationship of man to the universe'. In the words of US Secretary of War, Henry Stimson, something with 'the power to return the earth to its lifeless state of two million years ago'. One of Carey's interviewees remarked that 'the bomb was the mystery of the age'. The Russian achievement in building nuclear weapons before it was believed that they would have the capability was as a result of the loss of knowledge, of what Caute in *The Great Fear* terms

'The myth of the vital secret'. In this case it was not the key to unlocking the wonders of the universe that was lost, but more prosaically the blueprint, a far more suitable image for the traffic of spies and traitors than the metaphysical speculations as to harnessing the secret powers of nature that were the currency for Western scientists. Caute writes that

> The notion of the Vital Secret – the fantasy of the 'haves', whose nuclear monopoly was threatened, hypnotised Congressmen, newspaper editors and radio commentators. (Caute 1978, p. 54)

For Velikovsky the 'vital secret' is the recognition of the role of catastrophe in all things, knowledge of which is denied to humanity because of the cultural amnesia and can only be represented symbolically

> I ask the reader, what would he make of the following? The five-pointed star – the ancient symbol of the planet Venus adorns the head gear of every American, Soviet and Chinese soldier. (Velikovsky 1982, p. 201)

and he speaks of the knowledge as to how some archetypes enter the human mind as being 'The sublime question, almost the awful quest' (1982, p. 23).

Omnipresence

The bomb is omnipresent as a threat, its mere potential raised as a Sword of Damocles over all humanity. But it is omnipresent also in its effects: one of Carey's interviewees states

> It's like a bomb could go off hundreds of miles from here . . . and I don't know if we would feel anything *but* maybe a day or two later, these little things we couldn't see – we'd suddenly be breathing them, and a couple of days later we'd be nauseous and pretty soon dead. (M. Carey 1982, p. 22).

With the anxiety aroused by fear of communist infiltration it is the communist agent who is omnipresent and undetectable, and there was no area of American life that was free from the danger of a communist plant. Harold Ickes in *New Republic*, in the article already cited, entitled 'National Hysteria', wrote that

> Mighty America is afraid . . . so afraid of intangible but possible infiltration of communism that we try to erect pretended barriers that are in fact futile. (Ickes 1950, p. 24)

In Velikovsky's works the theme of omnipresence is found in the evidence of rock, fossil and artefact, evidence that is literally worldwide and yet 'beneath your very boots' as it were. The evidence is so 'omnipresent' as to be unavoidable. The early savants in the earth sciences recognized such evidence, so too did the young Darwin, as shown by his journals, though he repressed such evidence as could not be accommodated within the Uniformitarian doctrine. As with radio-activity or the communist agent the threat is lethal, for acceptance of the omnipresent evidence of cataclysm inevitably leads to the embrace of Catastrophism and hence the overthrowing of existing scientific, religious and social orthodoxes.

Inescapability

As far as the threat of the bomb is concerned, the *Time* cover quotation to the effect that 'No one is safe but some can be saved' amply reflects the fears that the threat of nuclear war aroused in many. Carey's interviewees speak strongly of the sense of living 'In a world of victims: no matter where you are, it will get you' and that 'It was just going to kill off everything, man'.

In terms of the communist infiltration, McCarthy's 'There is only one real issue for the farmer, the labourer, the businessman – the issue of Communism in government' (Bovere 1960, p. 38), speaks eloquently of the sense that no American citizen could afford to ignore the danger of the supposed communist infiltration into American society.

In Velikovsky's world view the sense of inescapability cannot be clearly differentiated from the sense of universality. It is again the impact of catastrophe that is worldwide and repeated, even at 52-year intervals, so that, rather like the effect of radiation, catastrophe and its results stalk the future generations. 'No one is safe, but some can be saved', would serve as a motto for the inescapable quality of both communist infiltration and the Velikovskian Catastrophe.

There was thus a crucial congruity, exemplified in the reiteration of key motifs, between Velikovsky's Catastrophism and the powerfully aroused anxieties of the years 1949–55. It was this close congruity that enabled Velikovsky's cosmology to function as a working metaphor for those anxieties, and thereby help to sublimate them in the debate, rancour and popularity that surrounded the texts and their publication. Consideration of the reviews of *Worlds in Collision* goes part way to supporting the metaphor thesis, in that his reviewers often sensed an ulterior motive for the marketing of *Worlds in Collision*. J.B.S. Haldane, writing in the *New Statesman and Nation* gave the work a hostile review, but suggested an ulterior purpose for its publication. From a distinctly British perspective he concluded that

> I regard the wide sale which this book has had in the United States as one of the most alarming symptoms of our times. The journals ... in which it was boosted are those which may urge the use of Britain as a base for atomic warfare. A large section of the American people is dreaming in terms of world disasters, and Velikovsky will certainly encourage them to do so. (11 November 1950)

Alfred Kazin in the *New Yorker* of 29 April 1950 gave a review entitled 'On the Brink', which spoke of the thematic equivalence of cataclysm in the text with the fear of nuclear annihilation. He wrote

> a pathetic, ominous and superstitious piece of work by a man whose thinking is completely dominated by cataclysm . . . The book fits only too well into the intellectual melodrama of the period.

In a quite different tenor, Eric Larrabee's synopsis in *Harper's* of January 1950 made a similar point of association when he wrote

> In view of the cosmic upheavals of the past, our own time of troubles is dwarfed. There is also a hidden purpose in Dr Velikovsky's book, a warning to the world that threatens to explode with hatred among the nations; the cosmic catastrophes may repeat themselves . . . therefore, sirs, cultivate friendliness, cultivate compassion.

Velikovsky's metaphor has become a parable for a secular age. His Catastrophism offered a cosmology which ignored the recently discovered expanding galactic universe and concentrated upon a solar universe, the local universe, which was characterized by unpredictable events which had shaped and would continue to shape human destiny. Velikovsky's bleak vision offered but a single programme, to recognize the likelihood of future annihilation, and its brief popular notoriety indicated its success as metaphor for tapping those profound anxieties within American society in the post war decade.

Velikovsky had rescued Catastrophism from its association with Romantic Occultism, which had seen it as the act of an avenging God in a remote age (*qua* Donnelly) or a result of decline within a process of spiritual evolution (*qua* Blavatsky). Instead, in an *'atomic age'* the situation is reversed, all moral codes are a product of catastrophe, a force that is as secular as it is random. Destruction has achieved a blind omnipotence, far more determining, far more disruptive than the neat method of Natural Selection. Further Velikovsky's Catastrophism was incipient: cataclysm was a frequent event, it had happened in recorded history, it could happen again, without warning . . . in fact it was only a matter of time. It was this sense of incipience that helped to guarantee the associative readings of his parable and ensured the popularity of *Worlds in Collision* as America prepared its citizens for a pre-emptive Russian attack with atomic weapons.

If Velikovsky's Catastrophism provided a grim metaphor of the Cold War anxieties, with Old Testament warnings to a humanity conditioned and made ignorant by cataclysm, then those same anxieties also produced redemptive parables as the skies suddenly became host to those enigmatic messengers from Elsewhere, the flying saucers, a variant of the unidentified flying object that now assumes, in its new guise, a global significance. A New Testament, with its promise of salvation to Velikovsky's Old Testament of universal destruction

3

FLYING SAUCERS: THE MESSENGERS FROM ELSEWHERE

IN THE BEGINNING

The reportage of unidentified objects in the sky has a long history, and texts on flying saucers will often emphasize this point, listing accounts that range over a period of several centuries. What is significant is that the interpretations given to sightings by their contemporaries are culturally fixed by the epoch in which they are observed. Medieval accounts adopt a spiritual or religious interpretation, while in the modern age it is a technological presentation that is overwhelmingly preferred.

The cultural fix is fine-tuned. The observation of unidentified aerial objects that were perceived as technical artefacts begins in the 1890s when airships were reported over the American Mid-west. The mystery ships were described as being cylindrical or cigar-shaped and driven by propellors. The crew were human and the vessels were reported to have frequently stopped for provisions. On one occasion a crew member explained that the vessel was powered by 'highly condensed electricity'.

Then in the early thirties there were several accounts in Scandinavia of 'ghost planes' – which were described as monoplanes, grey in colour and having the ability to switch off their engines and glide for long periods. Sometimes it was reported that they would shine a powerful searchlight upon the ground below.

In both instances the presentation consists of a technical artefact that was at, or just beyond the horizon of the technically feasible at the time – electrically powered airships in the 1890s or fast monoplanes in 1933. In neither of these presentations do we find that so characteristic behaviour of the flying saucers – inertia-free acceleration and manoeuvrability.

Such motion was beyond the realm of the technically feasible and was simply not observed; indeed the airships were often described as being ponderous.

The history of flying saucer observation begins on 24 June 1947, when Kenneth Arnold first reported what immediately came to be termed as flying saucers and unwittingly brought into being a new area of popular cultural expression that still flourishes some forty years on. The 'Arnold sighting', detailed in several saucer texts, can be seen as an archetype for the thouands of later saucer encounters, and the salient details, taken from *The Encyclopaedia of UFOs*, edited by Ronald Story (1980, p. 25) are as follows.

On 24 June 1947 Kenneth Arnold, a civilian pilot, was flying his own plane over the Cascade Mountains in western Washington. An experienced pilot, he was taking part in the search for a missing US Marine C46 transport plane, a $5000 reward having been offered for its location. As he approached the vicinity of Mt Rainier, with the sky clear and visibility good, he was suddenly blinded by a brilliant flash which lit up the surface of his plane. He searched the immediate sky for the source of the light but found no answer. There was another craft in sight, a DC4, but too far away to his rear to have been the origin of the strange light. Then the flash occurred again and he saw nine brightly illuminated objects flying in formation from north to south. Arnold, described as a 'solid citizen and a respected businessman' estimated the sighting to have lasted between two and three minutes, during which time the objects kept close to the mountain tops, swerving in and out of the highest peaks. As a result of such manoeuvrings Arnold was able to estimate their speed to have been above 1600 miles per hour. He observed that the objects seemed to have wings but no tail, that their shapes varied, with one being 'crescent shaped with a small dome between the wingtips', but that others were 'flat like a pie pan' and so shiny that they reflected the sun like a mirror. Their motion he described as follows: 'They flew like a saucer would if you skipped it across water', a phrase that was misquoted by the news agencies so that the following day the American press spoke excitedly of 'flying saucers'. The misquote stuck, and 'flying saucers' became the designation that was to encapsulate a wide, varied and energetic range of popular cultural expression.

The term has never been completely replaced in either cult or common parlance by the rather awkward acronym, UFO. Perhaps the polarity of domestic to other-worldly serves to focus public imagination as much as do the events of saucer reportage. Back in 1947 even mocking detractors unwittingly popularized the saucer concept.

Ever since the cliché 'flying saucer' was coined, the greatest and most exciting mystery of our age has been automatically reduced to the level of a music hall

> joke. The comics of Vaudeville and the comedians of State and Science banded
> together . . . to encourage humanity . . . to laugh at what it does not understand

complained Desmond Leslie in *Flying Saucers Have Landed* (Leslie and Adamski 1977, p. 13), writing in 1953. Within weeks thousands of sightings were being reported from all over the world.

Since 1947 the subject of flying saucers has produced hundreds of texts, many of which largely consist of series of hermetic accounts of sightings, contacts and encounters. These accounts are then fitted into one or more of a wide range of suppositional theories in order to develop a meaning or pattern for all saucer activity. Throughout the forty years since Arnold's sighting, though there have been peaks of perceived saucer activity, and equally, peaks in the rate of publication of saucer texts, there has always been a continuum of both sightings and texts, while the advocacy of the 'ufologists' has remained insistent.

Thus we are presented with a novel cultural expression that is popular, enduring and diverse. Examination of flying saucer texts is helped by making a differentiation between what is termed the **mode**, of these texts and their **domain**. The **mode** is simply the feature of presenting lists of varied accounts of flying saucer encounters. The **domain** is the extent of the cosmic theory which is being used to give meaning and intention to saucer activity. Saucer texts present both of these features but work by fusing them, in that individual accounts of flying saucer encounters are slotted in with, and thus given meaning by, some overall cosmic design, as presented by the cosmology being adopted by the particular author. The system works well. No matter how diverse or strange the encounter, it can be given relevance by referral to the **domain** of the text. And it is within the **domain** of saucer texts that we find the revitalized theories of Romantic Occultism, and of Blavatsky's Theosophical cosmology in particular (though modified by the use of relativistic space–time concepts and technical extrapolations) being used to explain the relevance of saucer sightings.

In the following discussion of flying saucer literature the distinction between **mode** and **domain** must be kept in mind, for it is in the conjunction of the two that saucer literature gains its particular potency, rendering reported individual experience as a cultural artefact that is capable of appropriating a complex of values and meanings and presenting itself as component of a viable sub-science, complete with its own terminology and laws. The flying saucer is a means of reviving the late-nineteenth-century search for 'Elsewhere' in a particularly potent form.[1]

Any study of flying saucer phenomena – and in what follows that term will be used to refer to the reportage of experience rather than the experience itself – must of necessity be selective. The texts are too numerous, too repetitive for a comprehensive survey. Thus texts will be examined that either mark new developments within the genre, or else are quite typical of dozens of others being produced at the same time; the purpose being to establish a pattern of development and to relate that pattern to contemporary cultural expressions in order to cast a light on the dynamics and connections made by a remarkably energetic genre.

An important early text is *The Flying Saucers are Real* by Donald Keyhoe (1950). Typical of the early texts, Keyhoe, who is described on the title page as a graduate of the US Naval Academy at Annapolis, concentrates entirely on what may be termed 'official sightings'; that is, sightings made by trained observers: airline pilots, airforce pilots, test pilots, control tower staff, aero-research scientists. In most cases the experience and qualification of the observer are carefully noted.

> Highly trained test pilots and ground officers had seen two fast moving silver-colored discs circling over the base. (Keyhoe 1950, p. 170)

Significantly there is little scope in these early texts for sightings made by the ordinary citizen. What civilian sightings there are are usually presented in the context of mass sightings, 'Switchboards at the Pima County Sheriff's office ... were jammed with inquiries. Hundreds saw the object (Keyhoe 1950, p. 9). Common humanity plays the role of the corroborative mob consigned to it in the science fiction films of the period. This is so because flying saucer phenomena are seen to exist only at the interface between new technology and establishment concerns over the use and deployment of such technology. One of the starting points for *The Flying Saucers are Real* is with USAF documents entitled *Project Saucer* which are quoted to the effect that 'The mere existence of some yet unidentified flying objects necessitates constant vigilance ...' adding that 'The saucers are not jokes. Neither are they a cause for alarm' (Keyhoe 1950, p. 3).

Thus the saucer problem is an official problem a military establishment problem in which the public has a passive role as vigilant observer. Moreover it is the military establishment, not the public, that first points out a reason for a supposedly extraterrestrial intelligence to concern itself suddenly with earthly affairs, by linking saucer phenomena to nuclear weapons. Still quoting from the *Project Saucer* documents, Keyhoe states

> Such a civilisation might observe that on Earth we now have atomic bombs and are fast developing rockets. In view of the past history of mankind, they should be alarmed. We should therefore expect at this time above all to behold such visitations. (Keyhoe 1950, p.3).

The idea that it is the development of nuclear weapons that has alerted the extraterrestrials to humanity's existence is a suggestion that was eagerly seized upon by later writers, and the connection is made frequently. Usually it is atomic or hydrogen bomb tests, sometimes also the rocketry that is to carry the bombs, that serve to alert the alien intelligence; later, in the sixties, it was the first space probes that fulfilled the role. Keyhoe has his doubts, however, and is quick to enter the field with

> Just the idea of gigantic flying discs was incredible enough. It was almost as hard to believe that such missiles could have been developed without something leaking out. Yet we had produced the A bomb in comparative secrecy, and I knew we were working on long range guided missiles . . . Our supersonic planes had hit around two thousand miles an hour. Our two stage rockets had gone over two hundred miles high. If an atomic engine had been produced it could explain the speed and range of the saucers. (Keyhoe 1950, p. 23)

So the suggestion is that the saucers are one of the latest weapons, produced by either the Americans or the Russians in great secrecy, and that the extraterrestrial claim is merely a cover story. Saucers are an establishment problem and equally an establishment answer. There is therefore much equivocation in these early texts between flying saucers as truly extraterrestrial phenomena and their being part of an elaborate cover story to conceal a military superiority.

This equivocation is due to Keyhoe's difficulty in accepting the extraterrestrial premise: 'I had grown up believing the earth was the centre of everything – life, intelligence and religion. Now for the first time in my life that belief was shaken' (Keyhoe 1950, p. 65); and also to his firm belief in the possibilities of the post-war military technology in which America had a manifest superiority. Quintessentially a cold war writer, Keyhoe does not, as do later commentators, consider the flying saucers as a possible redemption for humanity under the threat of nuclear annihilation or ecological disaster. Instead flying saucers are merely a possible means of ensuring America's continued domination in the arms race, even a means of putting America into an unassailable lead. Thus

> If American scientists and engineers can learn the source of the space ship's power and adopt it to our use, it may well be the means of ending the threat of war. . . . The secret of the space ship's power is more important than even the hydrogen bomb. It may some day be the key to the fate of the world.   (Keyhoe 1950, p. 188/9)

And, having decided that the saucers were indeed extraterrestrial, a notion that at first his mind had rebelled against, he concludes that nevertheless the military authorities have recognized the problem and are firmly in control. Speaking of *Project Saucer* of 1949 he writes that it was set up to investigate and at the same time to conceal the truth from the public about the saucers, but that 'In the spring of 1949 this policy . . . underwent an abrupt change. On top level orders it was decided to let the facts gradually leak out in order to prepare the American people' (Keyhoe 1950, p. 189).

Although the **mode** of *The Flying Saucers are Real* is essentially that of later saucer texts, though only 'official' sightings are listed, most of these being air-to-air sightings, the **domain** of the text belongs completely to the cold war period of its publication. Having accepted the extraterrestrial premise, the significance of knowledge of alien spacecraft lies solely in the military secret of their atomic engines. Such engines, if gained by either superpower, would give it an immediate superiority and the means to world domination. Though he does admit that knowledge of the extraterrestrials would cause confusion, 'Unprepared we would be thrown into panic', this is no more than would result from a public awareness that the UFOs were secret Russian weapons. 'If it were Russian, the Air Force would of course try to conceal the fact for fear of public hysteria' (p. 47).

In the previous chapter it has been argued that in the late forties and early fifties, with cold war pressures reaching a climax, Velikovsky's theories were able to provide a metaphor for those anxieties located in nuclear weaponry, fear of communism and American loss of isolation. These fears centred upon the fact that by 1949 Russia had the atom bomb and an atomic war was feared to be imminent.

An inevitable consequence of such a development was that American defence concerns would be concentrated on missile systems, American or Russian, which could reliably deliver the atom bombs to their target. American military research was therefore directed to the development of reliable missile systems and the American public kept well informed, at a popular level, of such advances as were made. *Time* (17 September 1951), for example, gave a popularized but relatively detailed account of the Air Force's latest missile, the Matador, which it called 'the first operational pilotless missile which can plant an atomic bomb in support of US troops in the field', adding that mass production at the Martin plant was ready to commence and that if war came 'the deadly Matadors would be ready for action'.

Yet the Martin Matador, rocket-launched and jet-powered, is but mundane technology compared to the missile systems that the article promised, 'Bigger and better guided missiles on the drawing board, huge missiles with longer range and much greater speed'. The article continues to boast of the capabilities of 'a huge V2 sized supersonic rocket that . . . can deliver an atomic warhead within five hundred feet of target almost one hundred miles away,' and of anti-aircraft missiles designed to knock down enemy bombers at great altitude.

The celebratory and boastful style of the article, almost unknown today when the military establishment is somewhat more circumspect in claiming achievement for its latest weaponry, needs to be set against the manipulated but real fears of the American public at the time. The naïveté of 'pilotless missile' and the fact that in spite of the achievements of the new missiles the war was still partly conceived of as happening on

American soil 'within five hundred feet of target almost a hundred miles away' speaks of the very real fears aroused by the presented possibility of what would nowadays be termed a Russian first strike.

An article in *Time*, but a month later (15 October 1951), cited the chairman of the Atomic Energy Commission as promising that it was working on atomic artillery shells, guided missiles, rockets and bombs for ground support aircraft 'big ones for big situations and little ones for little situations'. He then concluded his article with

> Millions of people throughout the world ... have feared the only two alternatives left to mankind are gradual submission to persistent communist encroachment ... or atomic obliteration. We now have the third possibility of being able to bring to bear on the aggressor himself – at the place of his aggression ... a firepower that should cancel out any numerical advantage he might enjoy. ... We will have done much to bring stability and a sense of security back to an uneasy world.

The formula is identical to that advanced by Keyhoe; success with the latest technology as the only key to establishing American superiority over Russia. And yet if the development of an advanced missile system was portrayed by the government as being crucial to American survival, then any Russian advances in the same field, particularly if they were advances on the American state of the art, made the USA doubly vulnerable. Psychologically, by bruiting the advances of its own missile technology and endorsing America's dependence for survival upon such technology, the government and the military authorities were in effect doubling the odds in the propaganda campaign being waged upon its own population. If America were to lose the missile race her cities would be open to unprovoked attack. The 'missile race' placed American survival as being dependent upon the prowess of its military missile technology.

Against this background Keyhoe's text takes on a clearer meaning. Keyhoe equivocates in his interpretation of saucer phenomena because he cannot rid himself of the fear that they are Russian vehicles, which would be unthinkable. The alternative is the hope that they were American or even British vehicles, for he has been told that 'The first British types had been developed secretly in England', but that following erratic tests these saucer-shaped missiles had been 'launched from a British island in the South Pacific' (Keyhoe 1950, p. 129). It is because of his concern that the saucers are advanced military vehicles that his sightings are pre-dominantly from within the vicinity of airports and military installations. On page 143 he gives a list of some thirteen such locations, including a 'super secret research base near Albuquerque', locations that would inevitably lend a military interpretation to the sightings.

Some forty or so years on, the notion that flying saucers were advanced military craft of either the West of the East may seem rather naïve, but such an interpretation was then far more plausible, and not only due to the nature of the anxieties induced in the American public by the post-war developments in military technology. The plausibility of the 'saucer-as-weapon' hypothesis at the time is demonstrated by consideration of such magazines as *The Aeroplane Spotter*. This magazine, a British wartime illustrated publication, had served to educate the British public on the need for vigilance. The experience of the Blitz had convinced the government that its people, if informed about enemy and allied plane silhouettes, could perform a useful function in alerting the authorities of details of incoming and outgoing waves of planes. *The Aeroplane Spotter*, which incorporated the Royal Observer Corps clubs and the National Association of Spotters' Clubs, encouraged a new habit in the British public, of which the 30 July 1942 issue wrote

> Apart from Industrial Raid Spotters, the clubs have been formed also in the Air Training Corps, among Air Scout troops and at many public schools. Such enthusiasm and purely voluntary effort augur well for the airmindedness of Great Britain in the future.

The Aeroplane Spotter was always at pains to demonstrate the importance of the spotter and his semi-official status. Other publications appeared: handy pocket books giving numbers, specifications and details of all aircraft of the warring nations. Inevitably such wartime-engendered habits persisted into the post-war years, and *The Aeroplane Spotter* continued in publication beyond 1947. Commencing in January of that year there was a new regular feature article entitled 'New Shapes in the Air'. The first of these articles illustrated and discussed such novel aircraft as the Bell XS1 rocket-powered plane and the Armstrong Whitworth jet-powered 'Flying Wing'. Number VI of the feature has the Douglas D558 Skystreak, with which America was hoping to achieve supersonic piloted flight, and the French Leduc 010, a plane-launched jet that was also attempting supersonic flight.

Even more significant was a parallel series of articles entitled 'German Aircraft in Detail', of which article IX shows a bizarre trefoil-shaped, delta-winged craft powered by refined coal (*sic*). Article number X in the series shows the Gotha GO 229, a 'swept-back all-wing design for high-speed flight'. The appearance of the Gotha resembles nothing more than 'a tailless crescent with a dome midway between the wingtips', as Arnold described the leading saucer of the formation he observed. Indeed, the Gotha has inspired cover illustrations for later saucer texts (see illustrations).

The types mentioned and others in the series were all of them either craft at the limit of the aero-technology of the day or, more significantly, examples of new thinking in aerodynamics and aero-structure as engine power greatly increased and craft speed increased accordingly. Of the

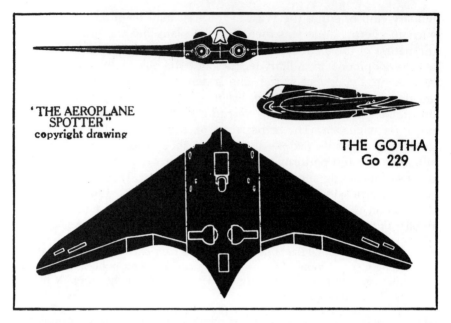

'THE AEROPLANE
SPOTTER"
copyright drawing

THE GOTHA
Go 229

3 *'Secret' German aircraft that could promote the Flying Saucer as a weapon hypothesis:
The Gotha 229*

plane shapes experimented with, only the delta wing configuration is familiar today, but back in 1947 all variants and bizarre shapes were known to a not inconsiderable air-minded public. Further, many of these exotic aircraft had been developed in Nazi Germany as the regime's aircraft industry attempted to make a quantum leap in aero-technology to answer the allied devastation of German cities, and it was these craft, like the V1 and V2 rockets, that were taken to America, together with their engineers, for research and development, including incidentally the crescent-winged Gotha GO 229.

It is not being suggested that what Arnold saw was actually an American version of the Gotha, but that what was more likely was that unable to define what he had seen, Arnold fixed the objects as craft at the very forefront of the aero-technology of the day, craft that exist at the interface between imagination and technical reality. Such an interpretation would have been made by Keyhoe, for instance, whose mind rebelled against an extraterrestrial interpretation. Such a possibility was not lost on the editor of *The Aeroplane Spotter*, for the cover of the 9 August 1947 number shows unusual Russian and American prototypes, the latter being saucer-shaped, and the quote beneath the pictures entitled 'Seeing Things' reads 'One of the fascinations of the aircraft industry is the diversity of ideas, designs and resultant shapes. Small wonder the uninitiated are occasionally taken unaware and see things like "Flying Saucers".'

The notion that Arnold and others witnessed flying saucers as ultra-advanced craft of their time accords with the cold war hysteria and the posture being developed in America that it was only by being at the very forefront of plane and missile technology that America could ease the threat posed by the Russian bomb and usher in a period of security. Even more so when the Nazi connection is taken into account. Keyhoe makes his readers repeatedly aware that 'Nazi' scientists were helping the Americans with their missile programme and with other more advanced craft that had first been attempted in Nazi Germany; 'the saucers . . . were rotating discs with cambered surfaces . . . originally a Nazi device. Near the end of the war the British seized all the models along with German technicians and scientists who worked on the project' (Keyhoe 1950, p. 127). The Russians however had seized the German rocket plant at Peenemunde, bagging the majority of the scientists and their plans, one of which was for

> a huge earth satellite . . . which would circle the earth . . . and from which . . . enormous mirrors would focus the sun's rays on any desired spot. The result, swift, fiery destruction of any city or base refusing to surrender. (Keyhoe 1950, p. 106)

Keyhoe's dilemma is clear: America has placed enormous confidence in its ability to maintain a technological superiority over Russia; upon this superiority depends America's survival. But this superiority is now in doubt, given the Russian achievement of the atom bomb. Doubly doubtful with thousands of Nazi scientists now working for the Russians on weapons that would render America's cities 'naked under Russian attack'. Hence anxiety deepens and seeks release in wishful rendering of the very artefact that could demonstrate an unassailable technological superiority.

Inevitably Keyhoe reaches for what must seem the only tenable conclusion, the only solution that is psychologically acceptable; that the craft are extraterrestrial in origin. If they were American craft they would have been flaunted before the public, as were the Martin Matador missiles, and they would not cause American aircraft to crash. On the other hand, if they were Russian they were effortlessly patrolling American skies and America's vulnerability was total. Therefore the saucers must be extraterrestrial, though their presence is as a witness to the arms race.

> It is Commander McLoughlin's opinion that the saucers come from Mars. Pointing out that Mars was in a good position to see our surface on 16 July 1945, he believes that the flash of the first 'A' bomb at Alamagordo . . . was caught by a giant telescope. (Keyhoe 1950, p. 158)

Because the arms race could not be ignored and because so much depended on its outcome, the saucers became that which could win the weapons race, hence the suggestion, quaint to later saucer interpreters, that the military authorities are party to a benign conspiracy, are in control of the situation and that the essential prize to be won from the saucers is not spiritual, cultural or scientific, but mere engineering – a knowledge of how their atomic engines work! *The Flying Saucers are Real* is a cold war text, founded upon the particular and well-articulated anxieties of the period. Anxiety is eased by a belief in the extraterrestrial nature of the saucers, and a symbol of hope begins to evolve with the patient but benign aliens who observe with a competence borne of great technological skill and refrain from direct intervention.

Such a symbol was obviously capable of far richer readings than that of mere technological artefact, and saucer literature flourished well beyond the early cold war period, which was determined by the joint superpower accomplishment of nuclear and missile technologies. There soon emerged other saucer texts that were to make quite different claims from those that are central to *The Flying Saucers are Real*.

THE CULT DEFINED

In the *Bulletin of the Atomic Scientists* (February 1954) Philip Wylie, in an article entitled 'Panic, Psychology and the Bomb', spoke of a 'neo-religion' surrounding flying saucers which he located as originating in the atomic bomb-induced 'hysterias' of the time, stating that saucer believers regarded the saucers as 'Saviours to rescue us from ourselves'; (Wylie's comments concerning public 'hysterias' over the threat of nuclear war have already been noted above (p. 70)).

It would seem apparent that even by the early fifties flying saucer phenomena, seen as 'Saviours to rescue us from ourselves', were failing to accord with the rather narrow semi-establishment prescription that had been outlined by Keyhoe. Flying saucers were being perceived as redemptive symbols according to Wylie, and not just as a possible means of winning the arms race. Keyhoe himself had widened the scope of interpretation by considering the range of anomalous sightings of objects in the sky that had been recorded in the hundred years prior to 1947, giving quotes from articles in newspapers and journals.

However, the scope of flying saucer advocacy is widened considerably with the publication of *Flying Saucers Have Landed* (1953) by Desmond Leslie and George Adamski. The text is in two sections: part one by Leslie widens the scope of saucer interpretation enormously by establishing the

domain of saucer advocacy as modified occult cosmology, and part two by Adamski consists of a detailed account of how he met and conversed with a saucer-borne Venusian in the Californian desert. Though simple-minded to an astonishing degree, Adamski's account serves to further establish the characteristic **mode** of saucer texts, namely the accounts of sightings and contacts reported by ordinary citizens, as opposed to those of the authorities as favoured by Keyhoe. *Flying Saucers Have Landed* is thus a seminal work in the genre and deserves discussion in some detail.

The opening paragraph of Leslie's foreword immediately lifts saucer phenomena out of Keyhoe's restricted cold war context. It reads:

> About eighteen million years ago, say the strange and ancient legends of our little planet, at a time when Mars, Venus and Earth were in close conjunction, along a magnetic path so formed came a huge, shining, radiant vessel of dazzling power and beauty, bringing to earth 'thrice thirty-five' human beings of perfection beyond our highest ideals; gods rather than men; divine kings of archaic memory, under whose benign world-government a shambling, hermaphrodite monster was evolved into thinking, sexual man. (Leslie 1953, p. 9)

So at one fell swoop the range of saucer interpretation has been dramatically widened. Keyhoe set saucer activity within a 150-year period and related their presence to America's role in the cold war. Leslie sets saucer phenomena within the occult timescale of Theosophy and yet retains their technological, as opposed to spiritual, nature. The saucers bring god-kings who evolved the distinctly un-Darwinian proto-man. Thus the Theosophical theorems of occult evolution, miscegenation, root-races and divine messengers from Venus are all immediately brought to bear upon flying saucer phenomena, but through the medium of an advanced technology, not through spiritual realization. Here is the fusion of Theosophical occult cosmology with perceptions of an advanced technology: a fusion that enables all the themes of Romantic Occultism to be re-vitiated, once de-spiritualized, and set within a technological context. Speaking of his intentions, Leslie writes that 'it is the purpose of this book to find out just what that something could be that authorities do not wish us to know' (p. 10).

Here there is no equivocation, no suggestion of a benign conspiracy by the government and the military authorities. Here the conspiracy is quite simply the blatant attempts by the establishment to ridicule, obfuscate, deny or ignore the greater reality the saucers represent. Here the notion of establishment is meant to involve the government, orthodox science, religion, military and technological research bodies. With a more radical and wider interpretation of saucer phenomena the scope of the conspiracy is widened, in fact widened to the limits of the conspiracy proclaimed by occult belief.

The theme of conspiracy is maintained, consequently chapter one, entitled 'What The Saucers Are Not', lambasts the 'semi-scientists and self-appointed "experts" who have simply failed to study the facts', and a catalogue of 'official' explanations are all listed and dismissed with contempt: 'too many glib pontifications have been issued to the Faithful by those who should have known better' (p. 13).

Even the language, with its use of ecclesiastical terminology reminds one of Madame Blavatsky at her most vituperative, and Techno-Occultism retains the invective style and vocabulary of the founder Theosophist.[2]

Following in Keyhoe's footsteps, Leslie retrospectively finds evidence for saucer sightings in the past. His list though goes back to 1619, when he interprets the experiences of the celebrated mystic St Teresa of Avila as being evidence of motion occasioned by her intellect having latched on to the 'wavelength' that causes 'opposite forces to the earth's magnetism to come into play' (Leslie 1953, p. 74). At the same time he extends the scope and scale of flying saucer phenomena as he casually introduces the reader to the main tenets of Theosophy as rendered in its new form. The source of such ideas is acknowledged, though their nature is not, except with 'The sacred Stanzas of Dzyan, said to be of Atlantean origin'.

In page after page the ideas and beliefs of Romantic Occultism are mentioned: Blavatsky's cosmological constructs, Scott Elliot's details of Atlantean life and Bulwer Lytton's Vril Power, as detailed in his novel *The Coming Race* and often mentioned by Theosophists. All these notions are introduced with the purpose of creating a matrix of supposition into which the concept of flying saucers in the expanded presentation being offered can fit. At the same time lists of 'inexplicable facts', feats and artefacts, such as the erection of various megalithic temples and obelisks, are given as necessary significations, showing that orthodox science is unable to begin to explain how such achievements were realized. Only the evidence of an Atlantean super-science, in the possession of an initiatory priestly cult which guards its knowledge on pain of death, can explain the achievements of ancient civilizations and societies.

The catalogues of inexplicable artefacts and events which are to become characteristic of the genre serve to create a suppositional matrix in which the occult theorems become more plausible. At the same time these mask their nineteenth-century character, which is then lost in the fusion with contemporary technology.[3]

The contrast between Leslie's cluttered but thematically rich text and Adamski's account of his meeting with a Venusian in the Californian desert is striking. Adamski introduces himself as a 'philosopher, student, teacher, saucer researcher', and adds that for most of his life he had believed that 'other planets are inhabited. And I have pictured them as "class rooms" for our experience and development' (Adamski 1953, p. 189).

Adamski was not the only person to have claimed to have met extraterrestrial beings in the early fifties. Orfeo Angelucci, a Lockheed aircraft worker, claimed to have met a 'superhumanly splendid man and woman bathed in light who had come by saucer from another world', on 23 May 1952 (R.D. Story 1980, p. 20). But Adamski was the first and most persistent of the contactees, claiming several later contacts and trips in the saucers.

As with Velikovsky, the onomatopoeic qualities of his name – a foreign Adam – undoubtedly helped in popularizing his case, as did the assumption of the title of 'professor', which he said was 'bestowed upon him by his students' (R.D. Story 1980, p. 20). So too the erroneous belief that he worked at Mount Palomar Observatory. In fact, Adamski variously worked a hamburger stall and a café on the road to the observatory, and his home address of Mount Palomar Gardens helped in the casual assumption that he was a professional astronomer. In his account Adamski does not deny any professional association with the staff at the observatory but explains that he is an amateur astronomer with two telescopes, through which he takes astronomical photographs.

It was from his own home that he saw, while observing a meteorite shower in October 1946, 'a gigantic spacecraft hovering high over the mountain ridge', a sighting that pre-dates that of Kenneth Arnold, but lacks the ambiguity of Arnold's sighting. Adamski himself plays down his 1946 sighting with the claim that he did not realize at the time quite what it was that he was seeing. However, when later discussing the incident with a group of people from San Diego, who had also seen the same craft, Adamski relates how six military officers overheard their conversation with interest, and how one of them later approached to tell him, 'It's not as fantastic as it sounds. We know something about this' (Adamski 1953, p. 190).

Later in 1949, Adamski is approached in his café by four men who are electronics experts and associated with the armed forces, one of them being a major. They ask him to take photographs through his 15-inch telescope of 'strange craft moving through space' since his smaller instrument is far more manoeuvrable than those at the 'big observatory'. He readily agrees and without any difficulty succeeds at once in getting pictures of 'what I deemed at the time to be . . . an object moving through space' (p. 193). As a result other 'government men' approach him regarding saucer landings reported in Mexico and he takes further daytime pictures of 'endless numbers of strange flashes that looked to me to be very far out from earth' (p. 195).

But it is on the 'memorable November the 20th . . . in the noon hour' that he first makes contact with 'a man from another world'. The meeting takes place in the Californian desert during a trip with the café proprietor and friends, its purpose being to make contact with a flying saucer. The details of the excursion are given at length, even as to the meals they ate, until suddenly, out of the blue, a spaceship appears in the sky, 'riding high and without sound . . . a gigantic cigar shaped silver ship', a sight unseen by any other of the passing motorists since 'comparatively few people have ever learned to look up. Especially is this true, and rightfully so, of cars travelling down an open highway' (p. 205).

From the spaceship a scout vehicle descends, and it is from this vehicle that the space traveller emerges. Of this visitor Adamski writes:

> The beauty of his form surpassed anything I had ever seen. I felt like a child in the presence of one with great wisdom and much love and I became very humble within myself. (p. 210)

Conversing in sign language the visitor indicates that he is from Venus, that the purpose of his visit is friendly but that he is concerned with 'radiations going out from the earth' (p. 213). Adamski, still in sign language, asks if these radiations were due to 'the explosion of our bombs with their resultant radioactive clouds?' and is answered in the affirmative, the Venusian adding, by the use of 'boom' sounds that the atomic explosions endangered all of the earth. He also told Adamski that once his race had lived on the earth but that now space was their real home.

The interview over, the spaceman returns to his scout ship and departs. At the time of the interview Adamski had been alone with the visitor, although observed at a distance by his friends, one of whom had conveniently brought along some plaster of paris and made a cast of the spaceman's footprints.

At first reading the juxtaposition of Leslie's far-ranging advocacy of a newly fashioned occult cosmology sits awkwardly with Adamski's naïve account of his desert meeting with the Venusian, but on further consideration the accounts are fundamentally complementary. Leslie's theorizing lifts saucer advocacy out of direct entanglement with the technology of the arms race, *qua* Keyhoe: the meaning and purport of the saucers transcends the immediate problem of America's superiority in modern weaponry over Russia. Perhaps this is possible because by 1953 America's missile superiority seems to have been established beyond doubt. Hence the disbelief and outrage that greeted the news of Russia's Sputnik in 1957. A further important factor was undoubtedly the circumstance that in the three years between Keyhoe's text and *Flying Saucers Have Landed*, both America and Russia had gone beyond the atom bomb to develop and deploy the hydrogen bomb as a usable weapon.

The potential of the latter represented far more than just an escalation of explosive power: it raised for the first time the threat of global extinction – Einstein's 'annihilation beckons'. Adamski's Venusian visitor was concerned over the threat of radiation to the earth, even to space itself.

While the technologies associated with atom bombs and missiles could be used to whip up hysteria over the possibility of a sneak Russian attack upon selected American cities, the thermonuclear hydrogen bomb raised the prospect of global catastrophe. So, if the flying saucers are to remain viable as anxiety-releasing events, as redemptive symbols, they must now be placed in a context that lies quite outside the seemingly suicidal production and deployment of thermonuclear weapons. Further, it must also be made clear beyond any doubt that flying saucers do not fit within a cold war context. Hence the direct contact by the Venusian with his message of planetary concern. Hence also the theorems of Romantic Occultism being revitalized within a technological guise, providing a post-thermonuclear context for flying saucer advocacy: a context that gains in validity since, in common with the prescriptions of Romantic Occultism, those of Techno-Occultism are shunned by the establishments of their day, by the very political–military authorities that were producing nuclear weapons.

Such hostility could only serve to endorse the new saucer theory by providing ample evidence for a conspiracy theory, essential for occultism of any guise to flourish. Additionally the doctrine of a technologically advanced Atlantean civilization which had perished in a cataclysm millions of years previously becomes a far more persuasive parable for late twentieth-century civilization, which was beginning to have its grave doubts over the untrammelled development of nuclear technology. That there are, in the Atlantean parable, a few survivors who manage to gain a foothold on a ravaged earth to develop a new society accords well with the imaginative scenario of a post-nuclear holocaust in which everyone sees himself or herself as a survivor.[4]

The dimensions of the conspiracy are now simplified and global to match the threat of thermonuclear weapons. With all humanity threatened there is now no talk of Russian weapons; the poles of the conspiracy are those of governmental–military authority against the rest of humanity, represented by the 'average' citizen. It is this polarity, between establishment power of all advanced industrial countries and the common man that gave such a strong cult credibility to the Adamski narrative. If there is a world-wide conspiracy to prevent humanity from knowing about the saucers and their purpose, then those conspired against form a global Third Estate. This is quite different from the pilots and technicians in Keyhoe's text who were the objects of a benign conspiracy.

Adamski's self-presentation as an enthusiastic amateur, capable of using technology, cameras, telescopes, etc. and as an honest citizen seeking the truth and not out to make a 'fast buck' from his experiences, undoubtedly gave him a kind of credibility that by 1953 an air force pilot or test engineer could not have established.

With global annihilation threatening it is now the voice of the honest, naïve, ordinary citizen that achieves recognition.

HERMETIC STORIES

The hundreds of saucer texts of the later decades all show, in the main, a remarkable similarity of style and content. Although interpretations of flying saucer phenomena vary to a degree, all, except those dealing with official refutation, fall clearly within the **domain** of Techno-Occultism established by Leslie. The variations do have some significance and will be discussed later, but the most arresting experience when reading a number of saucer texts is their **mode** – the method of fitting individual accounts within an occult theory. Again and again the texts detail accounts of saucer phenomena as incidents experienced by individuals or small groups. Frequently whole chapters are given over to what are no more than end-on lists of reported incidents. There is no analysis or explanation, just the crude account as detailed by the author or his source.

A quite typical example of such listing is taken from *The New U.F.O. Breakthrough* by Brad Steiger and Joan Whritenour (1986). It is an average saucer text, and chapter four, entitled 'Recent U.F.O. Landings, Contacts and Hostility' gives brief synoptic accounts of varied saucer phenomena as experienced by some thirty different people. Over twenty separate narratives and all presented between pages 39 and 51. (See Appendix 3 for selected extracts.)

Faced with such a welter of detail, none of it corroborated, none examined in any depth or given variation by second witnesses, the reader's critical faculties become blunted; one either accepts or dismisses these accounts, there is no half-way measure. The phenomena detailed in these narratives range from the observation of strange and erratic lights in the sky to having 'globs of a purplish substance' ejected from a hovering light on to the arms and face, or horses and cattle being killed and eviscerated.

Presented with such a variety of bizarre events and such a profusion of sightings, the reader becomes more susceptible to the suppositional matrix of occult speculation that is offered on previous and later pages. The chapter characteristically concludes with a series of unanswered questions.

What are the ufonauts covering up? What plan of action is so top secret that a knowledge of such maneuvres has proved fatal to hundreds? Why are some UFOs hostile and some indifferent, even benign? (Steiger and Whritenour 1973, p. 55)

The purpose of such lists of sightings and contacts is to create the impression of saucer phenomena as being intense and almost omnipresent, so that the concluding list of questions serves to underline the failure of reason to deal with these events. The sense is created for the reader that events are happening all around him, on a world-wide scale; that something significant is happening to humanity, here and now; and that the authorities, unable to read the signs, react by simply ignoring the insistently presented phenomena.

Again it is the average citizen that witnesses the events described. Reading through the pages of assorted accounts of saucer phenomena, the feeling grows that if one reads long enough, events from one's own neighbourhood will be reported; also the reader begins to feel left out, not having witnessed any of the range of events and contacts. If so many are witness to the phenomena that have no official explanation, then, as the chapter concedes

> We shall examine some of the keys that have been offered to those who investigate the flying saucer enigma. Only time will tell whether or not any of them opens a proper door to a complete understanding of the mystery. (Steiger and Whritenour 1973, p. 55)

So there grows a desire to verify, as much as to witness for oneself, the saucer phenomena. On reading a typical saucer text the reader is gradually induced to wish for that which the text seeks to prove. The mind becomes less critical, given the repetitive and episodic nature of the **mode**, which imparts a sense of omnipresence of the saucers, of their immediacy, and instils a sense of importance to all those listed events. There is somewhere a message to be read, or a 'key' to unlock an understanding of the bizarre phenomena that have been presented. All will, in due course, be provided by the authors.

The hapless reader, without any experience of saucer phenomena, reading long lists of accounts of contactee experiences, is left without a formal framework for meaning or criticism until a thematically coherent structure is provided; one that is acceptable provided all the basic premises are ignored. For example, if it is accepted that flying saucers are extraterrestrial spacecraft, then their presence on the earth must have some meaning and their many points of contact must have some relevance. The 'mission' of these craft, for such it must be, will have some hidden design or purpose.

It is worth considering briefly at this point the form that the reportage of saucer sightings almost invariably takes. The claim was made at the outset that such accounts are hermetic in character. That they are so is obviously crucial for the text's methodology, since corroboration or denial by independent witnesses would demand investigative exposition and prevent the repetitive **mode** from being maintained.

Taking the Arnold sighting considered at the outset, an early but much-repeated account that is found in several saucer texts, it can be considered as being typical of the form in which sightings are presented. In the Arnold account the following points are important but ignored. (1) Arnold reported that there was another plane in the vicinity, a DC4, but no mention is ever made as to whether the crew of that plane reported seeing unexplained aerial phenomena. (2) Neither is any further mention made of the missing military transport. Why was it lost? If it was found, why had it crashed? (3) Reference is never made to Arnold's opinion as to the wrong description and appellation of the events that henceforth came to be designated as 'flying saucers'. Details such as these are never given with the story, yet they are relevant and could even serve to endorse the account. Their discussion is denied. The 'story', for that is what is given, is self-contained, sealed off from all other considerations.

The same quality can be seen to apply also to the vast majority of later saucer stories. Those experiencing the sightings are presented outside any personal, social or historical context; they are just citizens, and if any office or rank is given, it is but as a label to emphasize the normality of the witness. Those experiencing the saucers are never ill, worried, ambitious, suicidal; they are simply citizens involved in the mundane routine of daily life, tending livestock, driving cars (a particularly frequent circumstance), returning home or going for a walk. There is never any mention of abiding preoccupations or generalized social tensions, no reference to political or economic life. Quite simply details are rarely given that lie outside the timespan of the saucer phenomenon, and the lives of those undergoing the experience are depicted as being value-free.

Casual consideration of the hundreds of accounts in several saucer texts leads to the observation that there is a loose structure to these hermetic stories. The accounts usually begin wih a statement of the everyday activity of those involved: Mr and Mrs Russell Carter were returning from visits to relatives, Steve Michalak was looking at land, Mrs Funk had been simply travelling north. When the story commences everything is functioning normally; there is neither tension nor diversion. Then a magic event takes place, magic in that it is inexplicable, falling outside all normal frames of reference or meaning. A bright light follows the car, a miraculous rainbow-reflecting spacecraft lands in a field, a bright light flares within the car and Mrs Funk loses consciousness, though the car does not crash.

But with the magic event having taken place, all quickly returns to normality. The lives of those who have experienced the event are rarely changed. If any tangible evidence is left behind, it too is magically transformed. Thus, for example, Steve Michalak's hat and undershirt with a geometrically burnt hole in it, or the eviscerated corpse of a gelding.

These accounts, or rather stories, proceed from the normal to the magical and then back to the normal. If there are any traces of the magical happening retained afterwards they are never presented as evidence upon which to base a logical deduction that may serve to demystify the event. The results of the magical events are never subjected to forensic enquiry; indeed the value of any such remnants is precisely as evidence that cannot be processed by orthodox science. Such magically transformed artefacts as Steve Michalak's hat and undershirt do not even form a basis for occult speculation, but then they need not, for the match between experience and speculation is associative, not deductive.

Thus the **mode** of flying saucer texts (hermetic stories, encapsulated experience, the mundane enriched by the magical) and the association, at a suppositional level, with occult speculation and theory, serves to link micro with macro, the everyday with the cosmic, the personal with the universal. As a result flying saucers are able to retain their essential qualities as redemptive symbols that are for ever beyond the reach of establishment agencies that would seek to appropriate them, to process them. The **mode** of the saucer text is thus essentially that of the fairy story.

The hermetic account begins with a contemporary paraphrase of 'Once upon a time', and though the magical events are bewildering, even frightening, as in a fairy story, their meaning is subsumed within a wider magical cosmology: in the fairy story a belief in a Manichean spirit world, in the flying saucer theory a belief in a neo-Blavatskian cosmology that is vitiated by being presented in a technical guise. The end, if not 'happy ever after', at least returns to the continuum of everyday life.

However, it is clear that these later saucer texts, presenting stories in which the saucer event interacts with observers in an obscure and highly personal fashion, demand a very different reading from the early texts by Keyhoe, Leslie or even Adamski. In those texts the saucers have a global significance. With the later texts the flying saucer is used to signify a range of concepts that have universalist connotations: extraterrestrial power, ultra-powerful technology. In those texts the significations are confused and the connotations restricted. Ultra-powerful technology does not fit in with burnt undershirts and eviscerated horses.

In these later texts the 'meaning' of flying saucer events is not to be read as a cosmic opposition to man's nuclear capability, nor as an invitation to join the 'Brotherhood of the Stars'. Instead the contactee experience injects mystery and doubt into individual lives. The events presented cannot be 'explained' though an attempt must be made if one wishes to refute the existence of flying saucers. And yet the detailing of such confusing events has severe consequences for the genre, as the next section explains.

BEWILDERING PROLIFERATION

When reviewing the developments in the literature on flying saucers in the sixties and seventies, it is the varied and capricious nature of the saucer phenomena that becomes the most striking feature. Mrs Funk's shiny, black object, 'the size of a soft ball', the emitted 'gobs of purplish substance' which dropped on to Mr Fletcher's arms and face, the eviscerated corpse of Harry Kine's gelding, all bear witness to such variety. Other texts detail similar events by the score. John Keel's *Visitors from Space* gives accounts of a family being plagued by 'Beeps and loud garbled noises, like a speeded up phonograph record' (1976, p. 67) and of animals being killed, their carcasses drained of blood, 'The wounds don't bleed. No blood is in evidence in the grass or dirt where the victims lay' (1976, p. 107).

What we have here is the 'maleficium' that was an important feature of the European 'witch-craze' of earlier centuries. Phenomena that were particular, local, trivial and frequently purposeless.

Given such a diversity of phenomena and a proliferation of contacts (Rex Dutta in *Adastra* for October/November 1978 estimates 100,000 contacts since 1947) the established **domain** of Techno-Occultism begins to break down.

One of the inevitable features of all occult cosmology is the existence of superior powers or entities whose purpose and method, though infinitely beyond humanity's grasp, can yet be believed to adhere to some cosmic ground plan or destiny. But with such trivial and purposeless events as have been indicated above, it is not possible to equate such behaviour with a grand cosmic design. So it is that with proliferation and diversity of saucer phenomena the Techno-Occult **domain** established by Leslie fails to contain and structure the phenomena. Therefore alternative occult variants appear, and subgroups emerge within the genre. Thus it is that Steiger and Whritenour in *The New U.F.O. Breakthrough* argue that

> Most of the experiences recounted in this chapter document aggression and hostility on the part of certain UFOs. Admittedly, the negative aspect of flying saucer research is not pleasant to consider, for its implications are far-reaching – possibly deadly. (1973, p. 53)

Indeed, for if flying saucers are hostile and the extent of their hostility is the playing of cruel and capricious tricks upon people selected at random, then the saucers can hardly be presented as manifestations of some great cosmic destiny or design. Further, the saucers are no longer to be seen as redemptive symbols, or even the vehicles for benign interplanetary visitors. This development serves to arouse the hostility of certain saucer advocates, and Steiger and Whritenour claim that they have been

> Steadily harassed for accenting the 'hostile' approach to certain facets of the flying saucer enigma, & there are many persistent critics of our 'menace' interpretation of certain UFO activity. (1973, p. 53)

clear evidence of divisions within the cult. Therefore John Keel in his *Visitors from Space,* a text that is subtitled 'The Astonishing, True Story of the Mothman Prophecies', details phenomena that are quite beyond the interpretative reach of Techno-Occultism and which hark back to the myths and symbols of Romantic Occultism.

For example Keel details how two teenagers, out courting in the car, see what they describe as a being . . .

> shaped like a man but bigger . . . maybe six or seven feet tall . . . red eyes and big wings folded against its back . . . which spread its batlike wings and took off straight up into the air. (J. Keel 1976, p. 60)

This creature followed their car even at speeds above a hundred miles an hour. Called 'Mothman' by Keel, the creature becomes the subject of a host of sightings as he plagues a local area for most of 1966.

Obviously such a being with self-contained powers of winged flight has no need of spacecraft. Keel therefore develops a suppositional matrix of Romantic Occult association to accommodate his beast. It has, for instance, a thoroughly nineteenth-century penchant for cattle's blood. Keel argues that

> my long and very expensive excursions into the borderland where the real and the unreal merge have failed to produce any evidence of any kind to support the idea that we were entertaining shy strangers from some other galaxy. (John Keel 1976, p. 47)

and he argues for the existence of 'Ultraterrestrials', beings and forces that co-exist with mankind, but who can switch within a spacetime continuum to other frames of reference. He therefore concludes that 'The UFO phenomenon is only one trivial fragment of a much larger phenomenon' (Keel 1976, p. 46).

Interestingly the language and conceptual framework – Ultraterrestrials and the Einsteinian spacetime continuum – belong to Techno-Occultism, but the contents are decidedly nineteenth century and the book's cover shows a figure derived from Gustav Doré's Satan. Such a departure from the extraterrestrial doctrine obviously leads to dispute. Keel argues that 'Few modern UFO enthusiasts have the educational background' to understand the ancient texts, and he goes on to claim that the solution to the mystery of unidentified flying objects was made over 3000 years ago by scholars such as Xenophanes.

The intrusion of Romantic Occultism into Techno-Occultism is taken a step further in *The Dark Gods*, whose authors, Roberts and Gilbertson, dedicate their text to H.P. Lovecraft and John Keel, 'who has helped to throw light on the Dark Gods'. Though Keel retained the vocabulary of Techno-Occultism, Roberts and Gilbertson maintain a rigidly pre-Copernican stance.

> All of the psychic, paranormal and UFO phenomena related in this book have been presented and interpreted in a basically earthly context. (Roberts and Gilbertson 1980, p. 179)

and they argue for a continuity of fable, folklore and UFO phenomena. These they set in a Manichean context of a struggle between Luciferic forces, the development of which was the real, and genuinely esoteric, purpose of Blavatsky and Steiner and their movements as against the Christian force of truth, and of 'Spiritual growth back towards the Godhead' (p. 240).

UFOs are therefore simply a contemporary dressing for an age-old phenomenon, which under various representational guises depicts the evil elements in the on-going Manichean struggle. The flying saucer is but one contemporary aspect of an ancient experience, Keel's Mothman yet another, though in a traditional guise.

The successful intrusion of Romantic Occultism with its pre-technical myths and motifs into the **domain** of Techno-Occultism established by Leslie and maintained by dozens of other saucer advocates is a complex phenomenon. Romantic and Techno-Occultism co-exist uneasily, hence the comments of Steiger and Keel as given above. The origin of such a development, though lying in circumstances outside the genre, served to modify the interpretative range of flying saucer advocacy. The question then arises as to why we get this regression to Romantic Occultism. The most important factor in explaining the situation was undoubtedly the developing space race in the fifties and sixties. The increasing use of satellites and space probes, the much more detailed knowledge of planetary local space that such developments brought and then, finally, the moon landings themselves, all crucially affected flying saucer advocacy.

It has already been argued that the perception of flying saucers as Cold War artefacts was essentially modified by the development of thermo-nuclear weapons and of reliable missile systems – a tandem technology whose potential relegated the particular threat of a Russian attack beneath the greater threat of global destruction. Hence, following the precedent set by Adamski, the personal account of the 'ordinary citizen' becomes the **mode**, setting individual hermetic accounts in contradistinction to a cosmic plan. Inevitably proliferation followed. Dutta's 'one hundred thousand contacts', for instance, meant that by now saucer phenomena were the possession of the average citizen. Flying saucer witness provided a readily available contemporary folklore that was resistant to all establishment explanation. This resistance was due in part to the adoption of a rhetorical strategy that actually embraced obfuscation by presenting a twentieth-century maleficium. The result was that interpretation lay solely in the hands of self-proclaimed 'ufologists', who interpreted saucer phenomena through occult cosmology and were generally unchallenged outside the genre.

Yet with the technical achievements of the space programmes becoming ever more confident and newsworthy, the interpretative role was being taken away from the saucer advocates and appropriated by the practitioners of establishment science. Given the moon landing programme with its mega-technologies, which were extensively previewed on television, and the myth-assumptive powers of such technology being eagerly seized by numerous commentators, the **mode** of saucer literature was being denied relevance. The witness of strange lights in the sky by Mr and Mrs Russell Carter of Pierre, South Dakota, on 5 March 1967 fades into insignificance when compared with the much-vaunted moon programme, which was presented by the establishment as being tantamount to the next evolutionary step – 'a giant step forward for mankind'.

There is thus a very real dilemma facing flying saucer advocacy. The **domain** of occult cosmology can quite easily accommodate and absorb those features that it found relevant in the space programme, but the **mode** of the genre is unable to make this accommodation. So the result is a distinct division within the genre. Those saucer advocates whose texts could absorb the possibilities offered by the moon programme continued to place those possibilities within their occult matrix. Indeed, they proved to be quite unintimidated as they cannibalized the NASA culture package to suit their own ends. For example, Brindsley LePoer Trench could produce texts such as *Secret of the Ages: UFOs from Inside the Earth* (1976), which covered the old stamping ground of inexplicable events and artefacts and lost civilizations, to argue for a hollow earth theory using NASA's global photographs of the earth's polar regions as evidence for polar tunnels leading into the hollow earth, wherein the flying saucers were said to be stationed. Thus also Walter Sullivan's *We Are Not Alone* (1966), which offered a then novel mixture of popular science and UFO speculation on the theme that by reaching into space humanity is coming of age and can expect to make contact soon with extraterrestrial life.

Also new variants of conspiracy theory emerge, a sure sign that the occult is alive and kicking. Don Wilson in *Our Mysterious Space Ship Moon*

(1975) argues that American astronauts saw strange structures on the moon and that the lunar expeditions were constantly shadowed by flying saucers. George Leonard in *Someone Else is on Our Moon* (1978) 'Fights the veil of secrecy'; by studying NASA photographs and 'talking candidly with dozens of officials' and 'listening to hours of the astronauts' Apollo tapes' concludes that the moon is occupied by at least two different forms of intelligent life.

All of these works fall within the **domain** of Techno-Occultism, and old themes from Romantic Occultism are actually revitalized by association with space technology and the adoption of circumstances and evidence offered by that technology. And yet, in all the above-mentioned texts there are no hermetic accounts of the experiences of the average citizen. Establishment science and technology have again become the medium for occult speculation. At the same time popular science was itself producing a new range of suppositional literature Exo-Biology. Carl Sagan published *Intelligent Life in the Universe* (1966) and *Communications with Extra-Terrestrial Intelligence*, a little later in 1972. In November 1974 a life-seeking probe was sent out from the Arecaibo radio telescope in Puerto Rico. This new science, popularized with perhaps the suggestion of convincing the taxpayer of the worthwhile cost of the NASA programme in its post-lunar hiatus, briefly fused with the more respectable areas of saucer advocacy. Texts such as *CETI*, an acronym for 'Communications with Extra Terrestrial Intelligence' by Jack Stoneley (1976) deal equally with popularized science, Doomsday concepts and UFO supposition. Chapter 26 is entitled 'Can We Ignore UFOs?', and Chapter 28 'We Belong Out There', and the text represents a complete fusion of the popularized establishment-offered neo-science of Exo-Biology with saucer specula-tion. As also do magazines such as *Adastra* and *Omni*, which offer a mixture of science, speculation, science fiction and UFO supposition. Sagan himself entered the UFO controversy with *UFOs, A Scientific Debate* (1972).

It is against this background that the re-emergence of Romantic Occultism in the field of Techno-Occultism has its meaning, and hence John Keel's complaint that

> In recent years a new element has been added by the few scientists being pulled into the controversy. This is the tiresome use of probabilities to explain that there must be zillions of other planets and therefore there must be uncounted numbers of inhabited places in the universe. In the early 1060s exobiology became the new scientific rip off. (John Keel 1976, p. 144)

Keel's subtext is quite clear: Ufology is not the territory for science and those scientists that are 'pulled into the controversy' can offer nothing of value and their purpose is suspect – 'a new scientific rip off'. By reverting to the prescriptions of Romantic Occultism the experiences of the everyday contactee retain significance and are pertinent to saucer advocacy. Thus Keel's Mothman, a defiantly terrestrial, oxygen-breathing creature. And so there is a further range of books that use the **mode** of lists of contactee experiences and manage to conflate more familiar mythic creatures – the Loch Ness Monster, Abominable Snowman, Yeti, Big Foot – with saucer advocacy. The connection between flying saucers and, for instance, the Loch Ness Monster, is not thematically obvious, and the reason for the conflation lies in the convolutions within the genre as it seeks, with success, to defend itself from being appropriated by establishment science.[5]

Another development in saucer literature, and one that also served to rescue 'ufologists' from the fatal embrace of management science, was the conflation of saucer phenomena with the system of ley lines first proclaimed by Watkins in *The Old Straight Track* (1925). One advocate who has been prominent in this development is the French mathematician Aimé Michel, who developed a theory called Orthoteny, that argued that UFO sightings that occurred on the same day are often arranged in straight lines. His *Flying Saucers and the Straight Line Mystery* (1958) argues that the notion of extraterrestrial life as being in the form of an advanced civilization is

> an anthropomorphic idea which supposes that the human level is the final one in the evolution of every intelligent species. (Ronald Story 1980, p. 232)

This view places Michel aside from the nuts and bolts of saucers as spacecraft advocacy, and Michel's ideas gained in popularity with the publication of texts by the English 'ufologist' John Mitchell that argued specifically for a connection between the ley line system that linked all the old religious sites and the occurrence of flying saucer phenomena. His *The Flying Saucer Vision* (1964) is complemented by later works like *The View Over Atlantis* (1965) and *City of Revelation* (1973), which argue for there being evidence in the topology of Glastonbury and the megalithic sites of Britain for an advanced geometrical system that was the product of 'a golden age of perfect spiritual knowledge' (J. Mitchell 1973, p. 31). He claims that the fragmented geometry he deduces from the ruins and the remains of the old ley system represent the traces of a gigantic work of prehistoric engineering, the remains of a once universal system of natural magic involving the use of polar magnetism together with 'another positive force related to solar energy'.

The works of Aimé Michel and John Mitchell establish what may be termed 'ecological ufology', a further variant of a most adaptive genre. The parallel contemporary cultural developments upon which ecological ufology feeds are quite obvious. A growing awareness of the techno-scientific threat to the pattern and order of life on the planet has become an ever more popular theme within the presentations of popular science by the late 1960s. The terms whole earth, eco-system, greenhouse effect and future shock enter common parlance.

The impact of these developments upon texts that serve to present a popularized but quite orthodox scientific view of the world can be measured by contrasting the title and contents of two works that both deal with the idea of world's ending. Kenneth Heur's *The End of the World* (1953), subtitled 'How it will end – if at all', receives an acknowledgement by Einstein on the cover and carries chapters on star collisions, the explosion and death of stars, atomic wars and cometary collision – this with but a passing, dismissive reference to Velikovsky. All of the scenarios presented are astrophysical in nature, with the sole exception of that dealing with atomic war.

On the other hand, Fred Warshofsky's *Doomsday: The Science of Catastrophe* (1979) offers a far more varied range of threats. Exploding stars and planetary collisions are included, but to the list are now added geological disasters, returning ice ages and biological or ecological scenarios for catastrophe.

From the late 1960s, with NASA photographs of the earth as seen from space becoming popular as Athena wall posters and with a number of popularly available concepts entering the language, ecology enters the field of popular culture, as a safely radical opposition to establishment science, as a financial impetus to the chains of 'whole food' stores, as an inspiration for television sitcom series, and as a new construct for flying saucer theory. Thus John Mitchell in *View Over Atlantis* can proclaim

> As everyone knows, the earth is slowly dying of poison, a process whose continuation is inevitably associated with many of the fundamental assumptions of the modern technological civilisations.   (J. Mitchell 1965, p. 200)

The saucers are now 'connected in several ways with Druid magic' (J. Mitchell 1965, p. 189), and those who see them 'experience the sensations of a vision as if what they are seeing has not only a physical form, but also some further existence as an object already familiar, encountered in dreams' (J. Mitchell 1965, p. 189). And the flying saucer–ley complex represents evidence of global society with no political antagonisms and a perfect economy. Hence their continued visitation and their witness by contactees in the twentieth century serve as a redemptive hope that the threatened ecological disasters may never happen, and that humanity, initiated in the lost wisdom deduced from geomancy, can overcome its nature and save itself from destruction.

The lights in the sky have come a long way from the cold war artefacts with atomic engines of the fifties.

The publication of works such as *Stonehenge Decoded* by Gerald Hawkins (1966) as a work of popular archaeology and the discussion of the theories of Professor Thom served to popularize the notion that Stonehenge and other megalithic sites functioned as primitive astronomical computers for Stone Age humanity. Ideas such as these encouraged the reception of Mitchell's mystic geometry based upon the use of ley lines, and the latest saucer advocates maintain the stance, or even go a stage further. Paul Devereux in *Earthlights* (1982) argues that 'the starting point for the study of UFOs has to be the UFO experience itself' (p. 11), and he complains that the old concepts of flying saucers as spacecraft have so conditioned the current cultural outlook that such a depiction 'actually effects the perception of the phenomenon itself' (p. 58). Devereux concludes, in a chapter entitled Geo-Epiphany, that the flying saucer, now devoid of content is of ecological rather than technological significance and is but an 'earthlight' to be seen under certain conditions at megalithic and ancient sites.

Given the adaptive and imitative nature of the genre, the persistence of its adherents, its cohesive clubs and journals, it would be rash to assume that ecologically benign earthlights appearing at selected spots on the earth's surface will be the last in a range of interpretation. Or that the genre, currently quiescent, will not achieve fresh popularity as a response to future techno-political developments.

Indeed, the recent publication of Whitley Strieber's *Communion* (1988) presents a radical departure in both tone and content from previous contactee accounts (the cover blurb notwithstanding). *Communion* relates, in considerable detail, the bewildering and disturbing 'events' that the author experienced in the mid-1980s, some of which had to be uncovered through prolonged periods of hypnosis with a trained psychotherapist. The main body of the text relates Strieber's attempts to verify and understand these experiences of contact with and abduction by alien beings. The aliens are described as being, 'little bitty people. I feel I could pick one of them up with one hand' (p. 80). One in particular who meets him and who he feels to be female, is described as looking like, 'a little person made out of leather' (p. 82). Later she seems to have inserted a penis into him, an operation that occasions a feeling of disgust and dismay. Strieber remains confused about the nature of these aliens, who have taken him up into their craft. He feels that they are 'insect-like', yet is at pains to point out that they had 'no feelers, no wings, no tangle of legs . . .' but that it was 'the way they moved – so stiffly – that suggested the insect world to me. That and their enormous, black eyes' (p. 96). In their behaviour we are forcibly reminded of the maleficium of the seventeenth-century witchcraft craze while Strieber repeatedly makes the point that what he is describing suggests the 'long tradition of fairy lore' (p. 95) and he entertains the novel notion that if his abductors were extraterrestrial or extratemporal, then they may be attempting to 'hide themselves in our folklore' (p. 96).

Strieber's text is so different from what has gone before in close encounter texts as to place it outside of the genre of Techno-Occultism as discussed above and in the following chapters. In his attempt to understand, or at least to come to terms with the disturbing and often distinctly unpleasant experiences he has undergone, the manner is one of a rational enquiry and there is no sense of advocacy and little of the suppositional matrix that has sustained so many of the previous texts. His insistence upon relating the unpleasant, absurd, nature of these experiences places any interpretation beyond the classic variants of the previous thirty years, as he recognizes when he gives a brief summary of the development of UFO sightings over the previous forty years and concludes, 'Now, in the mid-eighties, I and others – for the most part independent of one another – have begun to discover this presence in our lives' (p. 100). This is not Techno-Occultism, and the 'leatherlike', seemingly insect people who inhabit dirty and foul smelling craft offer little by way of signification of technological mastery. No, Strieber's conclusion, wittingly or otherwise, offers the possibility of a resurgent Romantic Occultism, complete with rites and sacerdotal trappings and the 'Bestseller' tag on *Communion* should ensure that the new priests will not be long in proclaiming their message.

In the meantime, in England at least, the recent spate of baffling and elegant circular patterns of cereal crop flattening has led to the production of texts such as Ralph Noyes' *The Crop Circle Mystery* (1990) which presents fresh evidence of the elusive visitants, albeit in coffee-table format.

CONCLUSIONS

Flying saucer literature constitutes a well-defined popular cultural expression that has been shown to be highly productive, adaptive and energetic. Consideration of the texts leads to the identification of basic subdivisions whose development reveals something of the inner impetus of the genre and also of the interaction and cross-referencing with parallel cultural expressions.

Nevertheless, in spite of deep divisions within the ranks of saucer advocacy and the occasional sniping between proponents of different interpretations, the genre viewed from without retains a conspicuous homogeneity. The cultural and methodological parameters that define the genre and the unitary power of the saucer symbol are far stronger than any internal divisions. Hence, for example, though there has been a fusion of ufology and exo-biology, the saucer texts that take material from the space programme still retain the occult **domain** established by Leslie.

For instance, Don Wilson's postulation that the moon is a creation of alien intelligence in *Our Mysterious Spaceship Moon*.

On the other hand the exo-biologists who, as Keel scathingly comments, express their ideas in probabilities, offered only a generalized expectation of extraterrestrial contact, subverted to some extent to the purpose of underwriting NASA's budgetry demands.

It is worthwhile pausing at this point to consider the distinction, referred to in the introduction, between *popular* culture and *popularized* culture. The two concepts are presented as opposite ends of a continuous spectrum, in the sense that any cultural expression that is deemed to be 'popular' will have within its presentation elements that are *popular* and elements that are *popularized*.

Consider a television soap series. Initially the acclamation of such a cultural product will be totally *popularized* – it will have no existence beyond its presentation in the media, its cultural expression will not have grown out of the experience of those who receive its presentation. Conversely the origins of football show a quite different pattern; the game, its rules, role and presentation derive from working-class experience in the late nineteenth century. Its presentation is therefore said to be *popular*.

It is also obvious that the two examples do not maintain a polar insularity at opposite extremes of the spectrum. The soap series soon establishes a 'fan club' (trips to meet the Archers in Ambridge) and such activity grows out of the experience of those receiving the presentation. Conversely it is equally obvious that football maintains its position as being pre-eminent in world sport due to its presentation on television, due to its *popularization*.

If we now turn to flying saucer literature we find the same polarity and shifts within the spectrum between *popular* and *popularized*. Saucer literature forms a *popular* cultural expression, manifested in books, clubs, journals, societies, etc.; exo-biology, on the other hand, is a *popularized* expression, issued by the media – with the blessing of establishment science. Once the media ceased to purvey exo-biology as the spotlight of media attention moved on from the space programme, its popularity waned. Exo-biology could at most modify attitudes and provide a climate more favourable to certain variants of saucer advocacy. But having neither the diversity nor the dynamic of saucer literature and having no cultural existence *sui generis*, exo-biology soon fell by the wayside.

When one considers flying saucer literature as a totality, one of the more persistent features that emerges is the varied conception of conspiracy that is developed. Conspiracy theory is endemic in all occult thought, and so the presence of some form of conspiracy in saucer literature is only to be expected. Yet what differentiates conspiracy in saucer literature from that in other expressions of Romantic or even

Techno-Occultism is the ability of the conspiracy to validate experience, rather than just underwrite belief.

As has been discussed, it is only in saucer advocacy that an experiential **mode** is developed: experience is the raw material of the saucer texts. This is not the case with other variants of Techno-Occultism, and the only comparison is to be found with spiritualists of the nineteenth century. Spiritualism did provide an experiential raw material which, as with saucer phenomena, soon developed until it produced a bewildering and apparently purposeless proliferation of events.

The extension from table rapping and voices from the dead to ecto-plasmic materializations and psycho-transportation is matched by the extension of saucer experience from that of the witness of weapons through to winged figures, or products of ancient geomancy or 'blobs of purplish light'. In both sets of extension there is profusion and bewilder-ment, and the annals of spiritualist experience bear a remarkable parallel with the accounts of saucer contactees.

There are other, distinctive similarities between the two cults. As has been noted in Chapter One, there was a democratic aspect to spiritualism in that it rendered 'heaven ... accessible to all' and did not rely on the authority of dogma or priesthood. Logie Barrow's *Independent Spirits* shows the association of radical, anti-establishment attitudes with plebeian mediums in the late nineteenth century. So too with saucer experience, there was no official dogma to shape contactee experience and the saucer advocates were not, as has been seen, particularly selective in their presentation of contactee experience.

Both cults were to share a certain radicalism, inherent in the circum-stance that at the centre of both is the sole authority of the untrammelled experience of the ordinary citizen, a situation that fostered a healthy disregard for establishment prescriptions and admonitions.

But where saucer advocacy does depart from spiritualism is in that the spiritualists did not need a conspiracy theory to validate their experiences, which were made relevant by mundane personal relevation. Saucer phenomena, on the other hand, largely derive their meaning by reference to impersonal constructs: military establishments, state control, state technology and science, all of which were seen to be threatening, destructive or enveloping. Therefore in saucer literature conspiracy becomes a means of validating the contactee experience.

The sighting of strange flashing lights can adopt the meaning of an alien spacecraft because this is precisely what the establishment could not admit the lights to be and still retain its authority and prestige. That there were already space stations on the moon, that extraterrestrials were patrolling the skies in atomic-, sonic-, magnetic- or psychic-powered craft, that ordinary citizens were being contacted by representatives of advanced other-worldly civilizations, were all possibilities that the establishment had to refute or ignore if it was to retain its power and authority.

An establishment that loses these attributes provides a powerful catharsis for those who feel themselves to be threatened or made simply insignificant by the works of the establishment. So, to protect itself the establishment has to deny the reality of the saucers, to present them as something socially and scientifically mundane such as a weather balloon or unusual cloud formations. Conversely, the contactee's experience endows him or her with a self-significance, a potency even, vis-á-vis the establishment that seeks to ridicule or make mundane the experience.

However, if saucer advocacy moves into areas that do not challenge the role of the establishment, by, for instance, realizing such phenomena as the winged Mothman, or purplish blobs of light, or eviscerated horses, then the establishment will not corroborate in providing a conspiratorial role. It will simply ignore the phenomena being presented. It will not and need not concern itself with such harmless trivia. The danger then for saucer advocates is that saucer phenomena were becoming insignificant. Consequently it was in the early 1960s, just at the time that saucer phenomena were becoming increasingly bizarre, that the genre produced out of itself its own internal conspiracy, the 'Men in Black'.

In 1953 Albert K. Bender, the then Director of the International Flying Saucer Bureau, reported that three men dressed in black suits called on him at his home and revealed to him the frightening answer to the whole flying saucer mystery. Soon afterwards Bender closed down his International Flying Saucer Bureau and, in what was to be the last issue of the organization's publication, *Space Review*, he wrote detailing his experience of the 'Men in Black' under the heading 'A Statement of Importance'. He wrote, 'We advise those engaged in saucer work to please be very cautious' (Ronald Story 1980, p. 50).

The first book to detail the Bender affair came some years later with Barker's *They Knew Too Much About Flying Saucers* (1956), but it was not until 1962, when Bender announced that he was ready to reveal all and published *Flying Saucers and the Three Men*, that the 'Men in Black' became a persistent feature in the genre. Although the book was a disappointment, few being able to accept Bender's account of the message given him by the 'Men in Black', the concept was to prove popular. Keel in his *Visitors from Space* details several 'Men in Black' contacts, the salient details always being fixed by the Bender experience.

Three men, dressed in black suits of a 1950s fashion and driving a black 1950s saloon, usually a Cadillac, call on someone who has recently had a saucer experience. The three visitors are thought to be slightly 'oriental' and in some way sinister. They present themselves as agents and deliver a cryptic message, usually warning the person visited to keep quiet about the flying saucer they have recently witnessed. The details of dress and transport, and that the visitors' questions indicate an ignorance of world events after the 1950s, suggest that the phenomenon is time-fixed. The interpretation of such visitors that is usually given by saucer advocates is that they are members of 'the phantom police arm of the (U.T.) Ultraterrestrial phenomenon' (Roberts and Gilbertson 1980, p. 42). The situation is that with the establishment showing no interest in the increasingly capricious and bizarre behaviour of the flying saucers, a necessary validating conspiracy is created from within.

The radicalism of the genre is shown in its ability to relegate orthodox symbols of cultural authority. 'All the jobs for the boys abolished: no more Popes, Califs, High Priests, Archbishops, Rabbis, Cardinals, Fakirs, Saddhus and the rest', wrote Rex Dutta, and he concluded 'We too are Space Peoples on our Space Earth ... we are growing up. ... We can progress. We need truly to open our Mind. Let's start now' (Rex Dutta 1978, p. 13).

Yet by refuting established authority and by wielding a variant of conspiracy theory at every turn, the genre was able to create its own experts and authorities. Crucially, their authority and expertise derived not from dogma but from their interpretation of contactee experience, and this authority is not directed at, but derives from, the assembly of contactees and is set against the various establishment authorities.

Rex Dutta, the author of the article quoted above and also of twelve books on saucer advocacy, is himself the 'Director' of *Viewpoint Aquarius*, a leading British UFO magazine. The penchant for directorships or presidency of impressively named organizations is a distinctive feature of the genre. Leonard Stringfield is described as 'Director' of Civilian Research on Interplanetary Flying Objects (CRIFO) and Johannes von Buttlar is described on the flyleaf of his *The UFO Phenomenon* as being the 'Director' of the Central European department of an international scientific centre. W.H. Andrews founded the Mutual UFO Network (MUFON), of which he was described as the 'International Director', and the British saucer advocate Brinsley LePoer Trench is 'Founder President' of Contact International, while Bender's directorship of the International Flying Saucer Bureau has already been noted.

The whole genre, for all its profusion of titles, is largely dominated by some two dozen experts (see Appendix 5), who each produce several volumes and are frequently found to quote each other in respectful terms. It is worth noting here that though the significations of such organizations are taken from within the genre, the metonymy belongs to the establishment, with its research organizations and bureaucratic structures.

The early texts in particular did struggle to gain a readership, the later texts to gain an identity amongst the veritable welter of books on flying saucers that began to appear on the market. As a result one comes across a frequent use of strongly insistent titles, *The Flying Saucers are Real*, *Flying*

Saucers, Serious Business and *Flying Saucers have Landed* being but three examples from many with abrupt, urgent, factual titles and an imperative tone that seems to shout for attention and to proclaim that the text is not fiction and convey more than a hint of being an official report. Neither were the covers reluctant to make establishment connections, provided they could be used to reinforce the idea of flying saucers being beyond reach or control by government powers. Hence Buttlar's *The UFO Phenomenon* provides under the large lettered title the snap comment that '"The Existence of these Machines is Proved", Air Chief Marshal Lord Dowding'.

A much repeated cover design is to give a juxtaposition of flying saucers hovering in close proximity and at an angle suggesting descent above an urban landscape, often New York or a Manhattan-style townscape, or in British texts, above London, the Houses of Parliament featuring prominently. Thus Steiger's *Gods of Aquarius*, Stringfield's *Situation Red; UFO Siege*, Keyhoe's *Flying Saucers from Outer Space* and Chapman's *UFO*, all show saucers that are huge and menacing, often in formation, posed above identifiable cityscapes.

Having established its own recognized experts, self-ordained in directorships of grandiosely titled organizations, it was not long before saucer advocacy developed its own vocabulary and accredited itself with a corpus of dedicated knowledge. Thus with texts such as *UFO Study*, subtitled 'A Handbook For Enthusiasts' by Jenny Randles (1981) and *The UFO Guidebook* by Briazack and Mennick (1978), which its cover claims 'Covers every aspect of ufology, from ACONIN to ZEROID' a scientific aura was created for the listing of numerous cult words. For example *The UFO Guidebook* gives a scientifically acceptable definition for Electromagnetism, and then adds

> Ufologists believe that electromagnetism may be one of the key elements in the propulsion of UFOs.   See: Electricity. EM Interference. Magnetism.

This cross-referencing of cult and scientific terms is used to endow the cult terms with an authority and an official quality. EM Interference refers to 'The large body of data which indicate that UFOs have the ability to interfere with electrical circuits'. Neologisms abound, always redolent of a scholarly, technical vocabulary. For example, 'Nebecism – a naphological theory that there are other advanced beings in the universe that have landed on the earth in the remote past'.

This chapter has outlined the major interpretations to be found within saucer advocacy and has tried to show how these different interpretations result from an often complex mix of external and internal factors. Flying saucer advocacy is the most prolific variant of Techno-Occultism, and though currently quiescent there is no reason to assume that a new wave of sightings will not produce new texts and fresh interpretations.

4

THE DAWN OF MAGIC: A NEW SYNTHESIS

The previous two chapters have dealt with variants of Techno-Occultism that were essentially American phenomena – Velikovsky exclusively so, flying saucers, in spite of several European texts and ufologists, predominantly so. Both of these variants were basically monothematic. Velikovsky offered a particular brand of Catastrophism, and the flying saucer texts, for all their variety, concentrated on the sustained observation of contemporary humanity by non-human visitants.

The subject of this chapter is different on both counts, for *The Dawn of Magic* by Jacques Bergier and Louis Pauwels (1963) is a product of the French-speaking world that achieved a European popularity before its success in America. Further, *The Dawn of Magic* was not in any way monothematic, it encouraged the acceptance of a variety of theories, it promoted an understanding of recent history that relied on the depiction of occult forces and it argued for a past that was far remoter than allowed for by orthodox archaeology, a past in which there existed highly accomplished civilizations which have been lost to recorded history. This variety of claim and theory was unified by the Techno-Occultistic assertion that it is only through the espousal of the possibilities inherent in contemporary science and technology that we can begin to understand the consciousness or the powers of those archaic civilizations. Finally, the text argued that it is the mission of some within 'mass society' to develop a new consciousness and herald a new world age.

The Dawn of Magic encouraged several kindred texts; René Noorbergen's *Secrets of the Lost Races* (1978) and Pauwels and Bergier's own later texts, *Impossible Possibilities* being examples.

The success of *The Dawn of Magic* may be attributed to several factors. Extrinsically, the situation that the 1960s saw a marked expansion in paperback publication with ample evidence of a growing readership of books in general is obviously of some importance. It is also probable that the fast-developing 'space race' between America and Russia fostered an interest in a book that prominently featured a distinctive evocation of all aspects of rocket and space technology. The same would apply to nuclear technology, which was both awesome and prestigious in the 1960s, and which was presented by Pauwels and Bergier as the key to developing the new consciousness.

For the present these external factors are merely noted, a fuller discussion on these grounds is reserved for the final chapter, and it is the internal features of style and content that will be considered.[1]

For all that the authors claim that *The Dawn of Magic* is a book to be read in any order and preferably by 'a reader in a hurry' (p. 9) and although there is no list of contents or chapter headings provided at the beginning of the book, the work does develop its argument in an ordered pattern that requires a consecutive reading if the complete thesis of the work is to be understood. The text is divided into three sections, each subdivided into headed chapters, each of which is further subdivided into numbered sections that each carry a synoptic list of contents; a curiously detailed form of address for a text to be read in any order.

Part One introduces and develops the main thesis of the work. In the opening section, entitled 'The Future Perfect', the reader is introduced to a set of values proposed in a deliberately abrasive manner. The full opening passage is given to illustrate the highly individual flavour and tone of the writing.

THE FUTURE PERFECT

1

Salute to the reader in a hurry—A resignation in 1875—Birds of ill omen—How the nineteenth century closed the doors—The end of science and the repression of fantasy—Poincaré's despair—We are our own grandfathers—Youth, Youth!

How can an intelligent man today not feel in a hurry? 'Get up, sir; you've got important things to do!' But one has to rise earlier every day. Speed up your machines for seeing, hearing, thinking, remembering and imagining. Our best reader, the one we value most, will have finished with us in two or three hours.

There are men I know who can read with the greatest profit one hundred pages of mathematics, philosophy, history or archaeology in twenty minutes. Actors learn how to place their voice. Who will teach us to 'place' our attention? At a certain height everything changes speed. So far as this work is concerned, I'm not one of those writers who want to keep their readers with them as long as possible and lull them to sleep. I'm not interested in sleep, only in waking. Get on with it quickly; take what you want and go. There's plenty to do outside. Skip chapters if you want to; begin where you like and read in any direction; this book is a multiple-use tool, like the knives campers use. For example, if you're afraid of arriving too slowly at the heart of the subject that interests you, skip these first pages. You should understand however, that they show how the nineteenth century had closed its doors against fantasy as a positive element in man and the world and the Universe, and how the twentieth has opened them again, although our morality, our philosophy and our sociology, which ought to be contemporary with the future are nothing of the kind and remain attached to the out-of-date nineteenth century. The bridge between the era of muskets and that of rockets hasn't yet been built; but it's being thought about. And the object of this book is to make people think about it harder. If we're in a hurry, it's not because we're crying over the past but are worried about the present and getting impatient. There you have it. You know enough now to be able, if necessary, to skim through this introduction and push on further. (p. 9)

The passage is rich in meanings. The text is obviously addressed to a clearly delineated readership: male, educated, youthful and techno-literate – 'Speed up your machines', etc. Writing in the early 1960s, the authors are specifically addressing the generation born during or just after the war, the generation that had recently completed its education and whose memories and experiences do not go back beyond the war. The first generation to have reached maturity in a consumer society, given the protection, in Europe at least, of certain welfare entitlements, and benefiting in much larger numbers than previously from extended educational possibilities. A generation that was above all increasingly techno-literate.

To this readership is emphasized the importance of the 'here and now' and of a decisive break with the past. Hence the discarding of tradition – for example of a detailed and sequential reading of the text, or the introduction of such novel concepts as the book being a 'multiple-use tool'. These notions are closely reinforced by the highly distinctive style of the writing, the urgent staccato of the clipped sentences, the series of injunctions and imperatives and the rapid change of focus. Moreover, the style conveys a sense of movement, providing a jerky dynamic, impelling the reader ever forward. Its flow makes against consideration of the subject matter and favours the reception of ideas and statements as being merely components of some grand construct, of relevance not as isolated entities whose veracity may be questioned, but as components of a greater unity that lies beyond the reach of analysis and doubt. Clearly here is a close, detailed and persistent harmony of style and content. Equally clearly the reader is being hurried and harried into a position that is radical and uncompromising.

The position is that the present time of the 1960s presents a new age with new possibilities, totally different from the possibilities of previous decades. The mid-twentieth century represents a decisive break with the past. It is an age that due to its scientific and technological accomplishments and their potential can dispense with its history and which must fashion its future out of some remote, mythical past – an as yet undiscovered past. 'The bridge between the era of muskets and that of rockets hasn't been built yet: but it's being thought about.' And herein lies the programme that will be developed in the text, which outlines the task that will be taken up by the new generation.

> Our literature, our philosophical discussions, our ideological conflicts, our attitude towards reality – all this is still slumbering behind the doors that have been burst open. Youth! Youth! go forth and tell the world that everything is opened up and already the Outside has come in! (p. 14)

The text continues to argue that the legacy of nineteenth-century science was that of a rigid determinism which could only stultify the imagination and hinder scientific creativity by presenting a doctrinaire orthodoxy that drove so many of the greater spirits of the age either to despair or out of science altogether. Numerous instances are cited, and the position is developed that writers such as Jules Verne and H.G. Wells, as much as the practising scientists who dared to break with orthodoxy, were the true progenitors of the new age.

For the rest of nineteenth-century science it was simply a case of 'From now on there's no mystery about the universe'. Pauwels and Bergier are arguing that by the late nineteenth century most scientists had lost the faculty of 'dreaming', since dreams found no place in nineteenth-century science. The argument is that it is men (*sic*) of vision, men who dream 'great dreams' who are the men of the future, no matter whether these dreams appear but as marginalia to a scientific treatise or as a fictional short story. The quality of mental activity that is being espoused is that of the free-ranging imagination where scientific speculation can be rendered in an available popular form as with Verne and Wells.

The result of such speculation is that everything is 'opened up' and the whole universe becomes available, 'one could visit the farthest star in the course of a lifetime' (p. 18).

The section then closes with a comparison between the narrow determinism that is held as being characteristic of the nineteenth century and the prospects opened up by contemporary science and technology, prospects that are amenable to 'all forms of imagination'. And we are told that

> suddenly the doors so carefully closed by the nineteenth century in the face of the infinite possibilities of man, of matter, of energy, of time and space are

about to burst asunder. Science and technical skills will make enormous progress, and a new assessment will be made of the very nature of knowledge.

Not merely progress this, but a transformation. In this new state of the world, consciousness itself acquires a new status. Today, in every domain, all forms of imagination are rampant – except in those spheres where our 'historical' life goes on, stifled, unhappy and precarious, like everything that is out of date.   (p. 14)

The phrase 'historical life' is ambiguous, as is a phrase that is used later, the 'old sociological order'. Both terms come to represent any form of orthodoxy, any activity or attitude that brings questions to bear upon free-ranging supposition, or checks the flow of the imagination rampant; in fact the same orthodoxies of religion and science that Romantic Occultism attacked in its day and then used to form the basis of its conspiracy theories.

And indeed the passages given do seek to convince by suggesting conspiracy. The reader is told that he is living at a most propitious time, in an age that must dispense with its history and traditions. He is about to witness the birth of a world consciousness and, crucially, may even participate in such a development. So, 'all forms of imagination are rampant', while the narrow necessities of daily life, of 'the historical life' may be discarded. To be a part of this new age, as collaborator, as joint author, the reader need only use his imagination, and should this fail the authors will provide a heady diet for that faculty to feed upon. In the light of what follows later in the text, the sentence, 'An immense gulf separates the man of adventure from humanity, and our societies from civilization' (p. 14) is crucial, for the men of adventure and the 'societies' are all, it is claimed, imbued with esoteric knowledge and powers.

The following sub-chapter opens with an attack upon the literature of 'soporific pleasure and bourgeois delights' (p. 15), seemingly any literature, at any level of cultural address that concerns itself with the relationship between individual and society or the evaluation of individual or societal mores. Of such literature, 'we workers of the earth, devotees of intellectual enlightenment, are well aware of all they contain in the way of insignificance, decadence and rottenness' (p. 15). The equivalence of 'workers of the earth' and 'devotees of intellectual enlightenment' is intentionally provocative but also revealing, for the hard-headed sensibility of proletarian approaches to bourgeois culture is appropriated and welded to the masculine discipline of analytical science. The literature of 'soporific pleasure and bourgeois delights' is characterized as being effete and female and soft. The masculine, productive, imaginative world of ideas is 'a thousand times stronger and more *real* than the world of the heart and the senses' (p. 15 – emphasis in original).

Already the 'we' of the conspiracy becomes a very large minority which, in its struggle to define the new reality, can claim sense and reason to its aid. Here is a significant and radical departure from previous occult speculation. Blavatsky considered her occult theorems to be beyond the reach of the materialist science of her day. Her revelation was of a complex cosmology of spirit. Technology played no role and had no depiction in the Theosophical scheme of things. With Pauwels and Bergier, technology, or rather specific technologies of rocketry and nuclear artefact, are conflated with pure science and made significant by evocation 'as we watch rockets rising to the sky and feel the ground vibrating with a thousand new radiations' (p. 14), illustrating both the conflation and the use of evocation. This evocation, however, is said to define a new reality, one that is at one and the same time a product of the 'imagination rampant' and yet also severely practical, a product of worker and intellectual, that will define new societal values. In the meantime any concern over the unbridled advocacy of science and technology is dismissed as evidence of 'A philosophy of despair ... which appears to be at once sinister and profound ... a temporary sickness of mind amongst civilized people who have not adapted the ideas they have inherited about such things as the freedom of the individual, human personality, happiness, etc., to the new set of values envisaged by the civilisation of the future' (p. 23).

Unlike Blavatsky, Pauwels and Bergier are not proclaiming an initiation, a secret knowledge; on the contrary they are announcing the birth of a new world order, witnessed in the evocation of science and the quasi-sacerdotal role of the scientist. Their safeguard is the certainty of advances in the techniques of science and technology, so that the narrow horizon of an extrapolative future can always be safely drawn. Technologies *will* proliferate, advances in technique *will* be made, scientific understanding *will* change. These are the presentations that secure the vision of Techno-Occultism, that give it the purchase on a self-evident common sense that Romantic Occultism could never achieve.

Consequently all that has been excluded from the evocation – the mundane life, long-standing social norms, traditional cultural presentations – can now be dismissed as being effete, sinister, tired and feminine. The following passage illustrates how this range of values and presentations can be scanned while subtly illogical connections are made, once the suppositional matrix is firmly established. Consider the following:

> While millions of civilized people read books and go to the cinema or the theatre to see how Françoise can be in love with René and yet, through her hatred of her father's mistress, revenge herself by becoming a lesbian, there are scientists, making a celestial music out of mathematics, who are speculating as to whether space does not contract around a vehicle. The whole universe would then be accessible; one could visit the farthest star in the space of a lifetime. If equations like these could be verified human thinking would be revolutionized. If mankind is no longer confined to this Earth new questions

will have to be asked with regard to the deeper aspects of Initiation and the possibility of making contact with intelligent beings from Beyond.   (p. 18)

The passage presents the equation of

MASCULINITY = TECHNO-SCIENTIFIC CONTROL = THE 'REAL' REALITY,

a theme that is prominent throughout.

Conversely, the representation of cultural values and social norms is given a distinctly female orientation in the quoted passage, a self-contained set of sexual–romantic interactions, an irrelevance when compared with the reality of a masculine super-science that can define a new reality and hold out the possibility of prodigious use.

From this new reality spring two imperatives: that the 'deeper aspects of Initiation' be examined and that contact with 'intelligent beings from Beyond' be considered. The suppositional matrix having been established, this kind of connection can easily be made. The reader does not stop to ask what is meant by Initiation, why it has a capital 'I' or what the connection is between higher mathematics and the necessity for an initiatory principle. Similarly the casual assumption of some other form of intelligent life is given the obscure location of 'Beyond', again with a capital letter.

What has happened is that the premise of scientists engaged in advanced mathematics has led to a specifically occult conclusion, that Initiation must be studied. At the same time there is little doubt that by 'intelligent creatures from Beyond' the authors do not have in mind the bug-eyed monsters so familiar in certain strands of science fiction. The quoted passage has moved from derision of cultural norms to evocation of science and then to advocacy of occultistic ideas.

Later in this section Pauwels and Bergier suggest that a quasi-Einsteinian conception of time, space and consciousness is tantamount to a state of consciousness achieved by ancient mysticism. Indeed, it is the 'new world of physics' that 'explicitly contradicts the philosophies of despair and nonsense' (by this is meant those who express concern over the dangers for humanity in the manufacture of hydrogen bombs – p. 23). The section then concludes with a further synthesis between the nature and behaviour of particles in the subatomic world and the nature of human psychology: 'the ultimate secrets of the elementary particles will be revealed to us by what takes place deep down in the brain' (p. 20).

Clearly the authors may, to a certain extent, be seen as precursors to the school of 'New Physics' as exemplified by Fritz Kapra and, more recently, Paul Davies in his *God and the New Physics*. There are fascinating parallels between the two, in their similar system of ordering, their initial assumptions and the common conviction that the mundane world is transcended by a deeper actuality, known only to physicists and mystics.[2]

The concluding sections of the chapter issue an imperative to the imagination

> We must therefore proceed by projecting ourselves farther and farther into space and time instead of making trivial comparisons with an infinitely small period where the past we have just being living in bears no resemblance to the future, and where the present has no sooner come into being than it is swallowed up by this unusable past. (p. 23)

The notion is original but obscure. The imagination must no longer be predicate to its own history. A radical caesura must take place, to prevent the imperialism of the past from colonizing the future. Clearly this past that is being referred to is more than the personal history of each reader, and presumably something more than the spirit of nineteenth-century conformity and determinism that was delineated at the beginning of the chapter. The following parable makes it quite clear in what sense and to what extent the term 'past' is used.

> Once again it's a question of saving the Holy Sepulchre–spirit weighed down by matter–and repulsing the Infidel–everything that is unfaithful to the infinite might of the spirit. It is still a religious question: making manifest everything that binds man to his own greatness, and that greatness to the laws of the Universe. We should have to show our Crusader a world in which cyclotrons are like cathedrals, and mathematics like Gregorian plain-chant; where transmutations take place not only in matter, but in the brain; where human beings of all races and colours are on the march; where man in his quest for knowledge extends his antennae into cosmic space, and where the soul of our planet is awakening. Perhaps then, our Crusader would ask to go back to the past. Perhaps he would feel at home there, but placed as it were on a different level. Perhaps, on the other hand, he would march eagerly toward the future, just as long ago he marched to the east, inspired once again by faith, but this time of a different kind. (p. 24)

What is significant about this passage is not that it is forwarding a new project for masculine endeavour based upon a synthesis of the spiritual and the material, but that it is a Luciferic crusade that is to be mounted; it is also now quite clear what is meant by the term 'past'. The authors are arguing against far more than the stifling atmosphere of nineteenth-century science and literature. *The Dawn of Magic* has wider horizons, and its attack is against the whole spirit of the Enlightenment and the subsequent developments in Western society. Modern physics is celebrated because it confounds the certainties of Newtonian physics, and modern technology is espoused because it can offer the surety of advancing technique and the prospect of prodigious use.

At the same time a new duality is offered, underwritten by the religious terminology adopted by the parable – Holy Sepulchre, Infidel, etc. The duality is that of daily mundane life – a product of 'the old sociological order' and exemplified by a 'literature of soporific pleasure and bourgeois delights', as against the liberation brought about by the use of 'the imagination rampant' and by 'projecting ourselves farther and farther into space and time', so that the present is not 'swallowed up in an unusable past'.

The prospectus that is being offered and typified as a crusade is one which, by an unqualified endorsement of all the techno-scientific possibilities inherent in contemporary society, enables the whole of post-Enlightenment history to be discarded in an act of mental surgery, thus

> If the present is detaching itself from the past, this means a rupture, not with all past periods, and not with those that reached maturity, but only with the most recent past, i.e. what we have called 'modern civilization'. This civilization which emerged from the welter of ideas circulating in Western Europe in the eighteenth century; reached its highest development in the nineteenth and spread its benefits throughout the world in the first half of the twentieth, is becoming more and more remote from us.   (p. 26)

The significance of 'not with all past periods, and not with those that reached maturity' must be noted. The prospectus of the crusade is to inherit a future that will be realized by rediscovering an ancient, forgotten past. This is a recurrent leitmotif of occultism in the past 200 years, exemplified by that proto-Nazi Adolf Lanz with 'In our most distant past lies our most modern future', and by Erich von Daniken's *Chariots of the Gods*, the German title of which translates as 'Memories of the Future'.[3] The purpose of this crusade is to make 'manifest everything that binds man to his own greatness, and that greatness to the laws of the Universe'. This is an implicit call for the creation of 'The New Man', the traditional aim of gnostic endeavour and the intention of the Luciferianism central to all occultism and to Blavatsky's programme in particular.

In a sense the remainder of Pauwels and Bergier's text is concerned, in different ways, with making the implicit Luciferianism of the above, explicit. However, the opening chapter of their text has skilfully sketched in some of the major features of Romantic Occultism, but reworked them so that those features depend upon a highly idiosyncratic espousal of contemporary science and technology. That dependency is enforced by an insistent style that is maintained throughout. The derivation of their prospectus is acknowledged only later when Theosophy is introduced and described as 'the name given to the whole vast renaissance in the world of magic that affected many thinkers so profoundly at the beginning of the century' (p. 151). And yet there is an ambivalence concerning the role and nature of Theosophy; the authors are reluctant to identify it as informing their own work, though describing it as a vast renaissance would seem to demand its importance in the world of occult thought. Whereas many central features of Theosophical speculation are to be incorporated into *The Dawn of Magic*, the importance of Blavatsky's system is not as source material, but because it 'added to neo-pagan magic an oriental setting and a Hindu terminology ... providing a link between a certain oriental Satanism and the West' (p. 151).

In the second chapter, entitled 'An Open Conspiracy', the attack upon Enlightenment culture is maintained. The effect of the Enlightenment is of a dead hand of constrictive determinism presenting a visionless science. If, on the other hand, the new horizons being opened up by contemporary science are congruent with the mystical visions of the ancients, then it is possible to present apparatus of the science establishments, research laboratories, international conferences, etc. as being comparable with the working of secret initiatory societies in previous ages. Thus a new science, developed by 'new look' scientists, leads directly to a further motif of occult thinking, the control of society by secret and all-powerful conspiratorial elites.

> The notion of a secret international society composed of men of the highest intelligence, spiritually transformed by the profundity of their knowledge, desirous of protecting their scientific discoveries against officialdom and the curiosity and greed of other men ... such a notion is an extremely ancient and an ultra-modern one ... I would even dare to state that, on a certain level, such a society exists today. (p. 27)

The scientist is now being portrayed in the role of culture hero, as a saviour-magician, dealing in a technology of redemption and developing a science that will force humanity, through the mind of the scientist, into higher planes of consciousness, enabling him to transcend the limitations of his historical self. Therefore there are secret elites who, 'as a group of human beings ... had reached a higher state than the mass of humanity' (p. 25). Such groups are now being formed as a necessity: a necessity imposed by the awesome destructive power of nuclear weapons.

So a point, not of continuity but of connection, has been established. Man's (*sic*) power and knowledge enable him to discard the Enlightenment and its products and to re-establish society along the lines imagined to have existed in the distant past, with mandarin guardians of knowledge and occult power. The example is offered of the Rosicrucians, that much-fabled esoteric society of the seventeenth century that practised an initiation based upon the contemplation of the rose and cross symbols and which has inspired various occult movements ever since. Pauwels and Bergier present the Rosicrucians as a small, select group of scientists of genius who were able to influence the governments and rulers of their day and guide the course of state events.

Techno-Occultism then impresses the forms of Romantic Occultism upon contemporary science and society while rejecting all traditional occult practice and organizations as being mere purveyors of cant.

> Secret and initiatory societies continue to flourish, with their imitative hierarchies and their mumbo-jumbo that imitates the real secret language, *the language of technicians.* (pp. 29–30. Emphasis in original)

This is a significant departure from previous occult practice. Occult speculation, based upon a limited variety of recurrent themes, was always anchored to the claim of derivation from a source of secret knowledge or illuminated experience. Techno-Occultism eschews such knowledge as a primary source of authority, but retains the form or theme of such knowledge as a husk, into which it fits certain aspects of contemporary science and technology. Thus Techno-Occultism does not have the inner vitality of Romantic Occultism and it cannot aspire to those forms of ritual procedure through initiatory activity that had been such a persistent feature of earlier occultism. Techno-Occultism has as its essence a captured activity, namely evocations of certain aspects of science and technology, something that is not its own but which will function as a vehicle for supposition and conjectures that were previously located in an avowedly occult framework.

Contemporary science and technology will thus be the means of revitalizing the myths of Atlantis and Subterranea, of re-presenting discarded cataclysmic theories and of claiming a new Luciferic domain without ever mentioning Lucifer, who cannot be divorced from his Romantic Occult presentations. For the Theosophist a spirit is a spirit: in the code of Techno-Occultism a spirit is an astronaut misinterpreted by ignorant and superstitious primitives.

The remaining sections of the chapter seek to establish further points of contact between science and the secret societies of the past. The importance of nuclear physics and nuclear weapons in forcing the development of an esoteric science is made quite explicit with

> It is true that the existence of the 'ultimate weapon' is an appalling danger for humanity. But the fewer the people who control such weapons, the less likely they are to be used. Human society in the modern world survives only because decisions are taken by only a very small number of men.
>
> Nothing can be done with these 'ultimate weapons' except develop them further. In the realm of avant garde operational research the frontiers between good and evil are continually shrinking. Every discovery at the level of basic structures is AT THE SAME TIME both positive and negative. ... In the end men will hold the key to universal forces in the hollow of their hand. A child will be able to make and handle it. (p. 53. Emphasis in original)

Again the text is rich in meaning and connections. The conflation of science and ethics is made in order to break the polarity of good and evil by association with the physical ambivalence of subatomic states and particles. But the ethical formulation, with its relevance no longer rooted in the realm of human affairs, is the same as that advanced by Theosophy.

> What is evil? Evil is only imperfection, that which is not complete, which is becoming, but has not yet found its end. . . . Evil is not a positive thing; it is the absence of perfection, the state which is ever growing to perfection. (Besant 1912, p. 38)

Further, the Luciferian gnosis of Man becoming a God is proffered through the techno-scientific prospect of prodigious use. The passage continues to construct a political programme that stands aside from concepts of class struggle.

> The so-called 'rulers', the propertied and governing classes, are no longer anything but intermediaries in an epoch which is itself intermediary

and we are told that the wars and struggles for liberation

> resemble nothing so much as a dance of insects interlocking their antennae. (p. 54)

The future, the authors argue, must be in the hands of the technicians, and

> history represents a Messianic movement of the masses. This movement coincides with the concentration of knowledge in the hands of a few. This is the phase we are now going through in our campaign for a growing integration of man into the universe as a whole, and a continuous spiritualisation of the mind . . . we are also returning to the age of the Adepts . . . throughout history, the presentation of techniques has always been one of the objects of secret societies. (p. 54)

It is the neutrality of the technicians, rather than their enlightenment, that will be the only hope for humanity since they inevitably form 'a caste more powerful than governments and political police' (p. 55).[4]

The prospectus is now complete and its validity will be demonstrated through examples. Therefore the following section entitled 'The Example of Alchemy' depicts the practice of alchemy as a genuine science rooted in an ancient tradition dating from civilizations that were much earlier than any known to present-day archaeology; civilizations which, they claim, were probably destroyed by nuclear explosions. Alchemy is an esoteric yet practical discipline. By repeatedly manipulating the chemicals and materials used, the alchemist achieves exceedingly high states of material purity, even of isotopic separation. The alchemist was therefore dealing with atomic energies and reactions. Hence the great secrecy that attached to true alchemy, hence the great devotion required of its practitioners, since the knowledge and experience gained can only be reached by one who has proved himself selfless in the search for true nature wisdom.

Alchemical procedure is viewed from a quasi-Jungian standpoint, inasmuch as the discipline required demands a moral and ascetic life that leads to true enlightenment. For Pauwels and Bergier, however, the alchemical 'Great Work' also yields the Luciferic and Techno-Occultistic goal of experiencing 'a promise or foretaste . . . of what awaits humanity . . . its fusion with the supreme being . . . its junction with other centres of intelligence across the cosmic spaces' (p. 88).

The third and final section of part one is entitled 'The Vanished Civilisations' and opens with a discussion of the life and works of Charles Fort, the American cataloguer of the bizarre. Fort's books, of which *The Book of the Damned* (1919) is the most quoted, are largely a compilation of strange and inexplicable events culled from newspapers and magazines the world over. 'Red rain in Blankenberghe on 2 November 1815—a rain of mud in Tasmania on 14 November 1902—a rain of frogs in Birmingham on 30 June 1892.'

Fort complied over 25,000 such incidents, cataloguing and classifying them and using the apparently anomalous circumstances as a basis for an attack on the establishment and orthodoxy of science. He was not concerned with the substitution of other cosmologies, or the support of theories discarded by orthodox science. Indeed, there is much of genuine mischief-making and frequent humour in Fort's attacks on the accepted beliefs of his day. 'I think we're all bugs and mice, and are only different expressions of an all-inclusive cheese' (quoted on p. 103).

Fort's method was to throw certain suppositions and assertions into the melée of his discourse, thus creating a style that at times comes close to that developed and refined by Pauwels and Bergier. Fort's notions also prefigure Techno-Occultism in their content, as the following passage clearly demonstrates.

> Perhaps we have been visited in the distant past? And supposing the palaeontologists were wrong, and that the great skeletal remains discovered by the exclusionist scientists of the nineteenth century had been arbitrarily assembled? . . . Dark cynicisms arise the moment I come to fossils or old bones that have been found. . . . On one of the floors they have a reconstructed Dodo. It's frankly a fiction. . . . I think we are property. I should say we belong to something; that once upon a time this Earth was no-man's land, that other worlds explored and colonized here. (quoted on p. 102)

The analysis of Fort's work is used to reinforce specific notions introduced on earlier pages.

> Scientific knowledge is not objective. Like civilization it is a conspiracy. . . . We live under an inquisitional regime where the weapon most frequently employed against non-conformist reality is derision. (p. 93)

writes Pauwels, exhibiting in a few sentences the hallmarks of occult diatribe: the outsider possessed of hidden truths, derided by orthodoxy, persecuted for his knowledge. And here we come to the paradoxical treatment of science that is found running throughout Techno-Occultism; certain sciences are designated as being particularly prone to mindless orthodoxy: archaeology, anthropology, palaeontology, since it is such sciences that refute the interpretation of artefacts offered by Techno-Occultism. Nuclear physics, biochemistry and electronics, on the other hand, belong to the initiatory sciences.[5]

Conversely it seems curious that, for instance, nuclear science and technology, which of all activities tends most to the promotion of state control and power (monopolistic development, strict secrecy, vast building schemes, etc.) should be regaled for its ability to break with establishment orthodoxy, and be seen as a liberating activity. But this discrepancy is resolved when it is remembered that it is the theoretical possibilities of such science that are being espoused, and that in any case occult thinking is essentially based on absolutist notions of control over society, whether by initiates, spirits or extraterrestrial astronauts. Thus the inescapably anti-democratic nature of nuclear technology is four-square with a mode of thought that ascribes 'true knowledge' to secret initiatory bodies and regards the Enlightenment and its spirit of free enquiry to be but a temporary deviation in human development. Therefore secretive state technologies are not denounced along with archaeology, etc. On the contrary their requirements serve in a practical way to uncover the secret past.

> Ever since the H bomb the military have been secretly listing the whereabouts of underground caves: an extraordinary subterranean labyrinth in Sweden; caves beneath the soil of Virginia and Czechoslovakia; a hidden lake in the Balearic Islands. . . . Blank spaces in the physical world: blanks on the world of humanity. We do not know everything about man's powers or the resources of his intelligence and psychic make up, and we have invented Islands of Centaurs and Dragon Lands: pre-logical mentality, superstition, folk lore, imitative magic. (pp. 106–7)

The passage also illustrates again how the evocation of vast technologies can be used to conflate modern science and technology with myth. The burgeoning techno-science of the present age is to become the means of understanding forgotten civilizations through an act of imitative magic.

Part two of The Dawn of Magic is compiled by Jacques Bergier and is entitled 'A Few Years in the Absolute Elsewhere'. It consists of an account that shows the 'real' or deeper reality of Nazism and claims to give the true significance of the Third Reich. The 'Few Years' of the title refers to the twelve years, 1933–1945, when Hitler was in power.

The basic thesis is that Nazism was at its core an esoteric, magical and initiatory belief system dedicated to the creation of an utterly different type of society that would destroy humanist morality, put certain of its adherents in touch with 'higher beings' and prepare for a mutational development of the superman.

> It is no longer the question of Germany the immortal or of a National Socialist state, but of a magical preparation for the coming of a Man-God, the New Man whom the powers will establish on the Earth when we have altered the balance of the spiritual powers.   (p. 204)

Bergier argues that having achieved power in 1933, a crucial development was the Roehm Purge, when the social revolutionary SA was replaced by the SS. The SS was to be developed into a proto-state and it was within its ranks, particularly amongst such departments as the Ahnenerbe, which was set up for research into 'German ancestral heritage', that initiatory magic was practised through the 'ceremony of the stifling air', a form of Satanic Mass.

Bergier's claim is that the Third Reich was apolitical within the conventional framework of state polity, but revolutionary in an esoteric sense. The SS had as its physical goal the creation of a new state, based in Burgundy, with the SS overlords living in castles and the ranks in 'Burgs', a sort of medieval barracks, and committed to a programme of mass extermination that would eventually eliminate the whole of the slavic races. It is only in the achievement of the SS state with its vast programmes of extermination that the Nazi experience finally reveals its rationale.

> Creation is not yet completed; the Spirit of the Cosmos is not at rest; so let us be ready to execute its orders which are transmitted by Gods to us here below – we, the dauntless wonder-workers, shaping to our will the blind and bleeding masses! The gas ovens of Auschwitz? Merely ritual.   (p. 206)

An esoteric analysis of Nazism offers immediate advantages over more conventional critiques of the regime in that it creates a rationale for the extermination programmes that is quite consistent, provided the occult premise is accepted. Of course an occult analysis can be amply supported by a selection of the utterances and beliefs known to be held by many prominent Nazis, Himmler's fascination with the occult in particular, being well documented. Certainly the whole of the Nazi movement was imbued with occult theorizing in its early days.[6]

While conventional analyses of the regime accept such connections, they relegate the adoption of occult belief by many of the Nazis to being no more than an illustration of a state of mind given the events of German history in the twentieth century. Bergier's analysis, however, argues that an understanding of occult belief is essential to explaining the growth and development of the Nazi movement. The occult rationale for extermination programmes of ever greater scope and intensity is that death administered on such a scale would bestow upon its perpetrators an occult insight and develop within them powers that would prepare them for the creation of the 'New Man'. Also, and more practically, they would gain an insight into the intentions of their enemies and thus be helped to win the war for Germany.

To argue for the essentially illuminated character of Nazism, Bergier traces the growth and influence of certain initiatory groups prior to Hitler's ascendancy. The analysis begins with a proviso,

> There are innumerable ways of explaining history in terms of mysterious activities on the part of Jews, Freemasons, Jesuits or the International Bank. Such explanations seem to us rudimentary. Moreover, we have always been careful not to confuse what we call fantastic realism with cheap fiction. (p. 132)

The disclaimer is telling, for while it is by no means certain what 'fantastic realism' is, other than speculation about occultism, nuclear physics and mega-technologies, the authors are distancing themselves from traditional conspiracies, just as they distanced the secret society that spoke 'the language of the technicians' from traditional secret societies with particular esoteric programmes. Techno-Occultism is again separating itself from the formulations and methods of Romantic Occultism, and further, through its analysis of Nazism, demonstrating the validity of Luciferianism.

The analysis opens with a brief account of the occult societies that emerged in the 1880s and 1890s, and with a review of the work of the novelist and short story writer Arthur Machen, a member of MacGregor Mather's Golden Dawn. Bergier traces a web of contacts and associations throughout the numerous but often shortlived occult-initiatory societies that formed part of the occult renaissance following the success of Theosophy. In each case it is emphasized that there is a basic conformity in the utterances of the initiate group with the utterances of Hitler, as given by Rauschning. All speak of a contact with higher beings possessed of awful power. 'We leave it to the reader to compare the statement of Mathers, head of a small neo-pagan society at the end of the nineteenth century, and the utterances of a man who . . . was preparing to launch the world into an adventure which caused the death of over 40 million. They belong to the same trend of thought and to the same religion' (p. 150).

Bergier then proceeds to consider the strange cosmologies that resurfaced in Nazi Germany, each finding some adherents within the upper echelons of the Nazi party, though as theories they blatantly contradict each other. The more important of these cosmologies was Hoerbiger's *Welt Eis Lehre*, which became an alternative cosmology and was presented as an extension of Nazi race doctrine. Bergier argues that Hoerbiger

> carried to extremes Hitler's conviction that the German people, in its Messianic mission, was being poisoned by western science. . . . Recent developments,

such as psychoanalysis, serology and relativity, were weapons directed against the spirit of Parsifal. The doctrine of eternal ice would provide the necessary antidote. (p. 155)

Other cosmologies upheld included the notion that the earth was a vast bubble set within an infinite mass of granite, the *Hohl Welt Lehre*. This theory was, naturally, opposed by the Hoerbigerians, but was sufficiently influential for wartime radar stations to have their antennae tuned at an angle of 45 degrees in an attempt to pick up an echo from the other side of the sky. The position being advanced is that because a few of the more influential Nazis were imbued with occult speculation, then we must attach some importance to such speculation because we cannot ignore Nazism in the study of contemporary history.

The section concludes with the consideration of a further group of occultists, the Thule Society, which was responsible for guiding the infant Nazi party in its earliest years. The Thule group believed in the existence of a lost island, Ultima Thule, a sort of Arctic Atlantis, the magic centre of a lost civilization, some of whose secrets survive to be learnt through magic and initiatory rites. Bergier claims that the Thule group were also interested in trying to locate the lost subterranean cities of Schamballah and Agharti, and when he gives 'Names which will be heard again on the lips of those responsible for the Ahnenerbe at the Nuremberg Trial' (p. 197) we see again the process of validating by association.

The central argument is that Nazism was in essence an 'illuminated' movement in which Hitler functioned as a medium. 'It was in this way, beyond any doubt, that Hitler was possessed by forces outside himself – almost demoniacal forces of which the individual named Hitler was only the temporary vehicle' (p. 194). For Hitler as medium there was the controlling magician, Karl Haushofer of the Thule Society. But instead of taking the undeniable dalliance of Nazism with various occult theories as being symptomatic, the connection is reversed. We have to take the Nazis seriously; after all they were the authors of a regime that took the lives of some 40 million people and the destruction of most of Europe to overcome, therefore, since such people took occultism seriously, so should we. It is a line of argument that has as its beginning and ending a mythologizing of history. It is not put forward as a history of the irrational, there is no attempt to place the nexus of often contradictory occult belief within a psychosocial context or to relegate occult acceptance to socio-economic circumstances. Instead Bergier's analysis begins with the *de facto* recognition of occult belief and aspiration, divorced from the cultural milieu that sustained them. Occultism is given a purely hermetic pedigree: eternal truths, guarded by secret societies, remote from the social world in which they originated. The only social connection made is when, on page 136, Bergier, speaking of Weimar Germany, depicts it as a 'rigidly Cartesian' society in which 'an incoherent and partially crazy doctrine was introduced and spread like wildfire'.

Nazism was then an antidote against the same range of values that were decried in the opening section of the book; against a post-Enlightenment society, against the 'historical life'. What is being emphasized is that although the Nazi antidote was 'partially crazy', it was powerful. That it did not succeed cannot be credited to the allies, who did not know 'what the defeated enemy was really like', otherwise 'their conception of the world and of human destiny would have had to have been in proportion to the magnitude of their victory' (p. 134).

In the present world another construction of the 'imagination rampant', the evocative power of science and technology, will serve as an antidote against the poisons of rationalism and democracy.

> It was nevertheless, the 'little men' of the free world, the inhabitants of Moscow, Boston, Limoges and Liège – the little man with his positive and rationalist philosophy, a moralist rather than a religious fanatic, uninterested in metaphysics or the world of fantasy–the type Zarathustra described as an imitation-man, a caricature–it was this little man, a replica of Flaubert's Monsieur Homais, who was to annihilate the Great Army whose mission was to prepare the way for the Superman, the demi-god, who would reign supreme over the elements, and the stars.   (p. 183)

This barbed and ambivalent passage is tinged with distaste for what is seen as the de-mythologizing forces of democracy and rationality, and although Bergier claims (p. 174) that it is not his intention to 'revalorize the philosophy of Nazism', nevertheless the events of the Nazi era 'amplify history . . . and establish it on a level where it ceases to be absurd and becomes worth living, despite the suffering entailed, because it is a spiritual level'. This revealing admission puts the prospectus of Techno-Occultism in a clear context – it is offering a violent irrationality as a means of designating individual meaning in a world where the controlling forces militate against the individual and the life of the imagination. New sources of imagination are offered, new modes of expression are outlined; new perspectives are being drawn, but the function of Techno-Occultism is exactly that of Romantic Occultism, to dissolve the ontological fears of those who feel their purpose and identity threatened by modern civilization.

Bergier's analysis of the Nazi regime is inseparable from its subject matter. The Nazi-occult system is seen as a counterforce to Cartesian rationality and democracy, as also the argument that delineates Nazi occultism. Both the system and its description serve the same end, and we are promised that though the Nazi regime has been destroyed by uncomprehending rationalists, nevertheless the Manichean struggle continues.

> This struggle between gods, which has been going on behind visible events, is not yet over on this planet, but the formidable progress in human knowledge made in the last years is about to give it another form. Now that the gates of knowledge are beginning to open on the infinite, it is important to understand what this struggle is about. (p. 139)

To repeat, the analysis has as its beginning and its end the mythologizing of history.

The third and final section of *The Dawn of Magic*, entitled 'That Infinity Called Man' is written by Louis Pauwels and is concerned with examining various possibilities or circumstances that may indicate the awakening of a new consciousness in humanity. The electromagnetic spectrum is suggested as a model, in which the subconscious corresponds to the infra-red and below, while waking consciousness is confined to the narrow band of visible light; for that part of the spectrum above violet, Pauwels postulates a hyper-consciousness in which knowledge and meaning of a deeper significance is communicated through symbolic representation.

Although dressed in a scientific terminology, the notion derives from traditional occult endeavour, which attempts to make the mind more receptive to a deeper spiritual reality through meditation and mental exercise. There are however many long passages which consider the likelihood of extra-terrestrial intelligence and of this planet having being visited in the past by alien astronauts.

> Have we already been visited by the inhabitants of Elsewhere? It is highly probable that some planets have been visited. . . . Yet it is quite legitimate to imagine that 'Strangers from Beyond' have been to inspect our globe, and have even landed and stayed here for a time. (p. 216)

This is a theme that is to receive attention and popularity a few years later at the hands of von Daniken. Also considered are the possibilities that Sodom and Gomorrah were destroyed by nuclear wars, that Baalbeck in Lebanon with its huge temple-remains was constructed as a launching pad for astronauts and that the now-named 'Tunguska Event' in Siberia in 1908 was the result of the 'disintegration of an inter stellar space ship' (p. 217). The section contains a veritable compendium of themes and material which will be taken up many times and become part of the staple diet of Techno-Occultism.

The above-mentioned and numerous other examples are fitted into the suppositional matrix in which themes such as Atlantis, Subterranea and Cataclysm are revalorized, given a new meaning because they can be interpreted in a techno-scientific connotation. Before nuclear weaponry the methods of destroying Sodom and Gomorrah could only be natural disaster or divine intervention. With nuclear weapons a whole range of options, previously denied, becomes plausible or seemingly plausible. And so too the transmogrification of Lucifer into a visiting astronaut takes place, offering a new validity for the Promethean bringer of technology, a validity endorsed by the plausible extension of rocket technology. Thus many of the central doctrines of occult thinking are revitalized in a techno-scientific guise, while other, and equally important doctrines that do not fit into a techno-scientific exegesis are conveniently forgotten. There is, for instance, no mention of reincarnation or the doctrine of karma. Occult supposition is no longer concerned with demons, angels or spirits, but with astronauts from beyond the earth; Atlantis need no longer be portrayed as a Graeco-Roman temple city but as the original birthplace of nuclear science.

Pauwels claims that it was because the atom bomb, 'came . . . to project us into the Atomic Age' and that 'a moment later, the rockets ushered in the cosmic era', that 'Everything became plausible' (p. 213). He continues to outline the goal for which humanity must strive, the development of a hyper-consciousness which, it is claimed, would be a mutational develop-ment, the emergence of a 'New Man'. 'Did evolution stop at Man? Is the Superman not already being formed? Is he not already among us (p. 220)?' This goal, which it seems is indistinguishable from that of the Nazis in their occult endeavour, is to be realized by control and subjugation.

> Under mass rule the individual dies; but his death is the salvation of the spiritual tradition that man must die in order to be born again. His psycho-logical consciousness is superseded by cosmic consciousness. He is subjected to terrific pressure: he must either die resisting it, or die in yielding to it. Resistance, refusal, means total death. Obedience means death, but only as a stage on the way to total life; for now it is a question of conditioning the masses with a view to creating a universal psychism embracing an awareness of Time and Space and an appetite for Discovery.   (p. 220)

The language, even in its ambiguity, is reminiscent of the pronounce-ments of the Nazi occultists given earlier; even the procedural method, that of 'conditioning the masses with a view to creating a universal psychism' could be read as a synopsis of Nazi propaganda. It is certainly the aim adopted by Techno-Occultism when one considers the totality of texts and the method of argument through supposition, repetition and evocation.

Even in the realization of the mutational man the role of science is crucial, for it is not by esoteric practice or ritual that the new man emerges but rather 'The effects of the radiation generated in the course of the tests', which means that the human race is in danger of being exposed to 'unfavourable mutations' (p. 293). However, humanity, which must expect catastrophe due to nuclear war, must be prepared to welcome the event.

> Finally, it may well be that they think it is a good thing that we should be suffering now the pains of childbirth, and would even welcome some great catastrophe which might hasten a better understanding of the spiritual tragedy represented in its totality by the phenomenon of Man. So that they may act more efficiently and so as to obtain a clearer view of the current that is perhaps sweeping us all to some form of the Ultra-Human to which they have access, it is perhaps necessary for them to remain hidden, and to keep their co-existence with us secret while, despite appearances and thanks, perhaps, to their presence, a new soul is being forged for the new world which we long for with all our heart. (p. 302)

The Dawn of Magic provides a synthesis of occult themes that have been revalorized by being set within a context of specific techno-scientific advances. The prospectus is eventually clearly delineated. Its aim is to create a 'universal psychism' that has as its function the provision of an uncritical acceptance of all technical advances. This conditioning of 'mass society' will ensure that there emerges amongst the ranks of the scientists quasi-esoteric groups who develop a new consciousness. The purpose of this new consciousness will be to re-establish communication with extra-terrestrials of awesome power. In that way a new order of life will be created on the planet. This prospectus is a reassertion of a lost cosmology, one that had been offered by Blavatsky in novel form, but which can now be revalidated due to the events of the Second World War. Nazism was a Luciferian gnosis and praxis, and because we cannot doubt the 'reality' of Nazism, other occult themes from the stables of Romantic Occultism – Atlantis, Ultima Thule, Subterranea – have now to be taken seriously; they too are 'real'.

5

THE VON DANIKEN PHENOMENON

With Ancient Extra-terrestrialism, Techno-Occultism found what was to prove its most popular expression. The term 'Ancient Extra-terrestrialism', is cumbersome but it at least has the merit of being self-explanatory, unlike the genre terms for the belief: 'naphology' or 'nebecism'.[1] Ancient Extra-terrestrialism is the belief that once or severally in the remote past the earth was visited by astronauts from another planet or star system, and that such visits had a decisive influence upon the physical and cultural evolution of humanity. The belief that such visits had been made by *spiritual* entities was of course one of the basic tenets of Theosophy and was fundamental to the contemporary novelty of Blavatsky's cosmology.

> the average Humanity of Venus is near the Adept level, that Adepts from Venus were able to help the work of the Earth Chain at its commencement. . . . These are the 'gods' and 'divine rulers' of the myths of primitive mankind

proclaims *The First Principles of Theosophy* (Jinarajadasa, 1938, p. 226). But that the visits were made by astronauts in spaceships is obviously a belief that takes resonance and reference from contemporary developments in science and technology.

There have been several proponents of the theme; *The Encyclopedia of UFOs* lists some 21 names (Story, 1980, p. 14). Even putting aside the conflation of 'spiritual' and 'astronaut', there are still some 18 proponents who fall within the genre of Techno-Occultism and who argue for a spaceship-borne astronaut arriving from the stars or planets. Some of these proponents achieved a genre popularity within their own right, before Daniken was published: Charroux and Drake, for example (see below). None, however, achieved the popularity of Erich von Daniken, the Swiss 'God Seeker', and Daniken's later texts, due to their style, content and popularity, provided a sudden extension of the range of Techno-Occult explication and debate.

SALES FIGURES FOR THE DANIKEN OEUVRE

The success of the whole of the Daniken oeuvre has been truly remarkable, outdistancing in number and endurance the popular notoriety of Velikovsky's works, or the sales figures of the more prominent saucer advocates, to such an extent that it is no exaggeration to speak of the von Daniken phenomenon. The figures speak for themselves. All the books are still in print, the earlier of them having undergone several reprintings. By 1978 the six books then completed by Daniken had amassed total international sales of over 37,000,000 (Krassa 1978, p. 48), with sales in the United States alone totalling over 13,000,000 (Krassa 1978, p. 40).

Of the first book, *Chariots of the Gods*, published in the summer of 1968 under the title *Erinnerungen an die Zukunft/Memories Of The Future*, the sales figures indicate an unexpected and precipitous increase in demand: 10,000 in June and July, 25,000 in August, and by the end of the year 146,372 copies had been sold in Germany alone (Krassa 1978, p. 80). Even a polemical rebuttal of Daniken's ideas as advanced in *Chariots of the Gods*, and entitled *Erinnerungen an die Wirklichkeit/Memories of Actuality* by Gerhard Gadow, sold 85,000 copies within a few months (Krassa 1978, p. 67). *Gold of the Gods*, published in Germany in 1972, the volume in which Daniken gives details of his discovery of a vast subterranean cave system under Ecuador, sold out a first edition run of 100,000 within eight weeks, for the last six of which it topped *Der Spiegel's* bestseller list. By March 1973 the publisher Econ Verlag of Dusseldorf had recorded total German sales for *Gold of the Gods* of over 300,000.

Such was the popular acclaim of the Daniken oeuvre during the five years after *Chariots of the Gods* that a critical analysis of his ideas appeared in *Encounter* in August 1973, when Daniken's success was at its peak, being titled, 'Anatomy of a World Best Seller'. Of that success, the *Encounter* article argued that it was 'not a product of subtle management – it was more like a natural cataclysm. A flood of readers' letters (17,000 to date) poured into Econ's offices.'

The article continues with:

Nonetheless, the 'fairy-tale book for adults' ... was on the verge of breaking every record in the publishing world. Wehrenalp had notched up total German sales of 1.2 million copies by March 1969 ... The English language sales reached the 3.4 million mark. (pp. 8 et seq.)

The international appeal of Daniken's vision was just as remarkable as the raw sales figures. *Encounter* commented that *Chariots of the Gods* had been translated into 26 languages, and Krassa in his biography of Daniken, *Disciple Of The Gods*, speaks of a three-day conference of the Congress of the Ancient Astronaut Society in Chicago 1974, and of von Daniken being welcomed in India by 'several thousand fanatical devotees in Calcutta' (Krassa 1978, p. 34).

On the other hand, the promulgation of von Daniken's theories has not been confined to published texts. In 1969, in Germany, a film was made by Terra Filmkunst GmbH, based on *Chariots of the Gods*, which was distributed throughout many countries, with CBS televising an abridged version on a coast-to-coast network in January 1973, after which, according to an article in *Der Spiegel* (19 March 1973) 'In Amerika wurden nach einer TV sendung in 24 stunden 350,000 Bucher verkauft.' [350,000 copies were sold in America within 24 hours of the programme being broadcast.] The success of the TV showing led to further TV programmes, one being entitled *In Search of Ancient Mysteries*, and then a further full-length film entitled *The Outer Space Connection*. Finally, to ensure that all should receive the message, the content of his texts has been rendered in a fictional comic narrative and sold throughout Europe and America (see illustration).

Clearly then, with books, films, TV appearances, comics and numerous Ancient Astronaut societies having been formed worldwide, von Daniken constitutes an important phenomenon in the contemporary cultural scene of the 1970s. A detailed scientific appraisal of his ideas has already been carried out and the whole gamut of his works has been subjected to acute and devastating criticism.[2] From such scrutiny it could be thought that no survival was possible, particularly since the critical texts were published in paperback form by well-known publishing houses. The *Der Spiegel* article was headed with 'Der Daniken Schwindel'. However, Daniken continues to write and his sales, although now at a much lesser rate, continue to accrue. His adherents, following their master's example, respond to criticism with arguments somewhat less than objective. As Krassa happily argues in his adulatory biography, 'all over the world the name Daniken has become as common as a trademark ... Today "Daniken" is simply a synonym for "Astronaut Gods"' (Krassa 1978, p. 74). Evidence for such a claim, and a measure of the extent to which Daniken's basic ideas have received a notional acceptance even with the popularizers of orthodox science, is found in the school primer entitled *Space Biology* by C.F. Stoneman, which gives an illustration of a rock drawing in the Sahara desert with the caption 'Does this represent aliens who visited the earth long ago?'.

The task then is to attempt an analysis that will go toward explaining the popularity of the Daniken oeuvre, and to identify those features of his

4   *Daniken's message in comic format for youngsters.*

Techno-Occultism that single it out for worldwide acclaim, an acclaim that is denied to other Ancient Extra-terrestrialists, to anywhere near the same extent.

THE INNOVATION OF ANCIENT EXTRA-TERRESTRIALISM

Before embarking upon an analysis of the Daniken oeuvre it will be necessary to establish the important distinction between flying saucer advocacy – what has been termed Current Extra-terrestrialism – and Ancient Extra-terrestrialism. Although clearly compatible, the two variants maintain a discreet distance from each other, and cross-referencing is surprisingly slight.

The novelty of Current Extra-terrestrialism lay in the explication of unidentified aerial phenomena as technically advanced craft that were currently patrolling the earth's skies. If Velikovsky's Catastrophism functioned as a metaphor at a time when the perceived threat was of a pre-emptive Russian attack with atom bombs, then flying saucer advocacy became more pertinent and popular at a time when the threat was due to the far more powerful thermonuclear weapons which had the potential for global destruction.

It was at this time, in the late 1950s, that the flying saucer came to be portrayed as a redemptive symbol offering the promise of a future beyond the earth, amongst the 'brotherhood of the stars'. The flying saucer thus began to achieve the status of an orthodoxy. Flying saucers became ubiquitous symbols – in books, advertisements, cartoons, jokes, films, toys, comics, even to be found in jewellery and decorating powder compacts. The meaning of the flying saucer symbol could be universally though imprecisely understood. Whether as the subject of ridicule or serious advocacy, the flying saucer came to stand for the promise of a material solution for a technical society whose future must seem to be always conditioned by the nuclear threat.

Nuclear proliferation had in effect frozen the future: whatever prospectus was offered for the future, the threat of nuclear annihilation would always be present. The flying saucer came to represent a means of neutralizing that threat – by promising the prospect of an extra-terrestrial future in an advanced technical society. Crucially this promise would only be realized by humanity if it made further technical advances.

After the Cuban Missile crisis, with international tensions easing, with détente on the agenda and the developing 'space race',[3] flying saucer advocacy lost some of its appeal and a more varied range of UFO interpretation was offered. It was at that stage that Pauwels and Bergier's synthesis became significant in that it extended the range of Techno-Occult supposition beyond the narrow possibilities offered by confusing saucer encounters.

The emergence of Ancient Extra-terrestrialism post-dates these develop-ments, and it never addressed itself to those anxieties grounded in nuclear weaponry. The idea of the God-astronaut never became the metaphor for annihilatory fears.

Indeed, rather than being a solution to the problems posed by contemporary technology, Ancient Extra-terrestrialism is a celebration of contemporary technology. Its innovation, taking the cue from Pauwels and Bergier, is that it promoted its own contemporary technology, that of the late 1960s, to being the most decisive human activity and the sole arbiter of evolution. Not God, not Darwinian Natural Selection but the technology of the 1960s and early 1970s, the very source of concern for human survival, is presented as the reason for human origins and the means of achieving a future earth-free existence.

This celebration of contemporary technology, which was to be so astonishingly popular in the late 1960s and early 1970s, in all industrial societies, clearly relates to different conceptions and preoccupations than those which saucer advocacy and Velikovskian Catastrophism fed upon. It will be the later purpose of this chapter to attempt to identify the nature of and reason for the switch in the role of contemporary technology as a promoter of occult expression.

ANALYSIS OF THE DANIKEN TEXTS

(page references from Corgi paperback editions)

It is now necessary to consider in detail the works of von Daniken and the development of his particular brand of Ancient Extra-terrestrialism, which rapidly became the cynosure for all adherents to the theme. The curious point however is that although it is a commonplace that Daniken writes books on the 'God was an astronaut' thesis, to progress much beyond that basic starting point is rather unexpectedly difficult. The reason is that although his complete thesis is quite detailed and compre-hensive, it changes in essential points from text to text, with the result that it is not always possible to say exactly what his theory asserts.

Originally his thesis may be summarized as follows. Astronauts from beyond the planets visit the earth. Their destination is elsewhere, but the earth has been chosen as a stopping-off place because it has supplies of *fissionable* material which can be used to replenish the astronauts' depleted stocks. The visitors are observed by the indigenous primitives with awe and they bring gifts to pay homage. Hence,

> Our astronauts would try to teach the natives the simplest forms of civilisation and some moral concepts in order to make the development of social order possible. A few specially selected women would be fertilised by the astronauts. Thus a new race would arise that skipped a stage in natural evolution. (von Daniken 1971, p. 25)

Thus to begin with, 'natural evolution' is still the prime mover, it is just that the process has been hurried along somewhat by some form of 'fraternization' with the natives. Already crude racist assumptions as to the nature of evolutionary progress are beginning to emerge.

In his second book, *Return to the Stars*, there arises some confusion. Again native women are selected for fertilization, which is described as 'artificial mutation', an uncertain process that yet entails direct sexual coupling, for a few sentences later we are given 'Who implanted the feeling of shame in connection with the sexual act?' (1972, p. 27).

With the third title, *The Gold of the Gods*, Daniken's thesis undergoes further modification. By this time Erich von Daniken has become a household name and the centre of stormy controversies concerning the astronaut-god thesis. It was in *The Gold of the Gods* that Daniken moved on from a simple identification of the God of the Old Testament as a visiting astronaut to a complete cosmology derived from occult belief of the nineteenth century. There are still many points of confusion and even contradictory details, but his cosmology is now almost fully developed.

The complete cosmology is set out in a sixteen-point programme. Because this all means much amendment and modification of the argument advanced in the earlier texts, Daniken feels it necessary to offer some proof to justify these more detailed claims. The proof is introduced immediately, the opening sentence of chapter one reads: 'To me this is the most incredible, fantastic story of the century' (1974, p. 1), and he launches into a description of a 'gigantic system of tunnels, thousands of miles in length and built by unknown constructors at some unknown date'. These tunnels, which surface in Ecuador, contain, it is claimed, fantastic remains that offer conclusive proof of the astronaut theory – cosmology he is about to present. No matter that these caves have not been shown to other researchers and that even as he went to print with *The Gold of the Gods* counter-claims and refutations were made. He argues that the existence of this vast cave network with its huge subterranean halls containing museums, models of animals and saurians and, most important, a 'library of metal plaques . . . created to outlast the ages' to tell of truths that 'might turn our neat but dubious world picture completely upside down' (1974, p. 10) provides positive proof for all his claims and theories.

The sixteen-point programme is given below in full; it reads as follows:

1. In the unknown past a battle took place in the depths of the galaxy between intelligences similar to human beings.

2. The losers in this battle escaped in a spaceship.

3. As they knew the mentality of the victors they set a 'trap', in that they did not land on the planet that was 'ideal' for their existence.

4. The losers chose the planet Earth which was just acceptable in comparison with their home planet, but certainly did not offer ideal conditions. For many years the losers continued to wear gas masks in the new atmosphere in order to get used to the terrestrial mixture (hence the helmets, trunks, breathing apparatus, etc., in cave drawings).

5. They burrowed deep into the earth and made the tunnel systems out of fear of their pursuers who were equipped with every kind of technical aid.

6. In order to deceive their opponents completely they set up on the fifth planet of our solar system (i.e. not the Earth) technical stations and transmitters which emitted coded reports.

7. The victors fell into the trap and believed the bluff. They brutally annihilated the fifth planet. It was destroyed by a gigantic explosion; parts of its substance shot through the planetoid belt.

8. The victors thought that the losers were destroyed. They withdrew their spaceship to their home planet.

9. Owing to the destruction of the fifth planet the gravitational balance in our solar system was temporarily thrown into confusion. The earth's axis moved a few degrees out of position. This resulted in tremendous inundations.

10. The losers emerged from their magnificently built catacombs and began to create intelligence on earth. Using their knowledge of the molecular biology, the losers created man *in their image* from already existing monkeys.

11. The former losers, now absolute rulers and therefore *gods*, found that the progress and evolution of the human race was too slow. They knew perfectly well that the beings created by them were 'like gods', but they wanted more rapid progress (Genesis 1. 6). . . . The gods were often hot-tempered in their impatience; they were quick to punish and wipe out the malcontents and those who did not follow the biological laws laid down, 'pour encourager les autres'. The gods had no 'moral' feelings about such radical cleaning-up operations, for they felt that they were responsible, as creators of men, for their future development.

12. But men were afraid of the gods and their punitive expeditions, especially once the gods were no longer first-generation gods . . .

13. Then whole groups of men began to dig themselves underground hideouts out of fear of divine judgement. Perhaps these groups of men still had tools available that they had made under the gods' guidance – tools with

which they could perhaps work stone more easily than architects can imagine today.

14. It is a fact that today more and more gigantic underground dwellings that are *not* identical to the tunnel systems in Ecuador and Peru are being discovered annually all over our globe. The subterranean cities which are constantly being discovered are obviously the work of many hands, they were not made with sophisticated technical equipment such as the thermal drill.

15. If men, namely our ancestors, built safety bunkers underground by hand, with the expenditure of tremendous effort, they did not do so for pleasure, nor for protection against wild animals, nor to the glory of their religious ideals. Nor did they do so out of fear of some alien conquerors, who would have had no difficulty in forcing these crazy defenders to surrender. They had only to sit down outside the cave entrances and starve the inmates to death.

16. I say that there was only one reason for the underground caves built by human hands and that was fear of attack from the air! But who could assail men from the air? Only those whom they knew by tradition, those gods who had once visited them long ago.   (1974, pp. 212–15)

Clearly what is now being offered is far more than the elementary 'god was an astronaut' thesis, tied to the notion that the astronauts happened upon the earth merely to replenish stocks of fissionable material and then decided, out of passing interest, to experiment with the proto-human species. Instead, the complete range of Blavatskian cosmology regarding the emergence of the Fifth Round, the creation of humanity and the 'War in Heaven' is now subsumed within his cosmology. Daniken quotes from the Book of Dzyan, which he describes as 'a secret doctrine ... preserved for millennia in Tibetan crypts. The original text, of which nothing is known, not even whether it still exists, was copied from generation to generation and added to by initiates' (1974, p. 57), without informing his reader that the Book of Dzyan was the authority claimed by Blavatsky for her Secret Doctrine, and was unknown to the world prior to her invention of the manuscript that could only be read by the 'inner light'.

It might be expected that by now Daniken has completed his cosmology – far from it; his next title, *In Search of Ancient Gods*, offers further detailed explanation. For instance, the reason for the astronauts making the journey to the earth (point 4 of the 16-point programme) is now because their own sun is approaching its explosive end and so, since

the more developed an intelligence is, the more carefully it would register all the changes in its mother sun. It would not want to die. It would try to prevent the knowledge amassed over thousands of generations from being wiped out at one stroke. This intelligence would strive to preserve its continuity   (1976, p. 202) the alien astronauts had embarked upon a journey of great significance, during which they happened upon the planet earth, on which,

> hundreds of thousands of species of animals abounded on land and sea and one species was humanoid, like the strangers. These humanoids lived in caves, in groups. They had long shaggy hair and roamed from one feeding ground to another. They possessed simple tools, but the race was dumb, stupid and grunted like animals. (Daniken 1976, p. 202)

However, for reasons not made clear, the captain of the spaceship decided that he would give the primitives some 'technical assistance' and so, selecting their finest specimens he 'mutated their cells by artificial manipulation'. The specimen primitives were then preserved for mating, their children brought up on segregated and protected reserves. Inevitably, it is claimed, the children of the artificially manipulated parents were of much greater intelligence than their parents. At this point Daniken's account becomes a techno-literal rendition of the Genesis account, for the captain tells these more intelligent children, 'You, my friends, are now the most intelligent creatures on this planet! You can rule over plants and animals. You can subdue the planet to your power. Only this commandment do I impose on you: Never shall you mate with your former people who did not grow up in this paradise' (Daniken 1976, p. 203).

Thus *Homo sapiens* are created by intelligent manipulation of the evolutionary process, the implication, not as yet realized, being that such an action by the visiting astronauts is to serve a specific purpose. The time of the astronauts' visit is given as being anything between 30,000 and 450,000 years ago. Daniken is uncertain of the date and claims it is irrelevant.

It is now becoming clear why, after establishing a complete scientific account of Blavatsky's myth of the 'War in Heaven' and the creation of humanity by Lucifer, he needs in this fourth text to give further information. The purpose now is to provide the other half of the occult vision by reducing the significance of the Bible and reworking the Genesis accounts. Hence all of the Genesis stories must be rendered in terms of his techno-exegesis. If the visiting astronauts account for the emergence of humanity from crude apelike species, they must also account for the near-destruction of humanity in the Flood of the Genesis account.

Daniken therefore provides a return visit, with the same astronauts returning centuries later, not having greatly aged themselves since, given the possibility of Einsteinian time dilation, 'No eternity had passed for the "gods" since their first visit to earth' (1976, p. 206). The developments that have taken place on earth during their absence of thousands of years dismay the astronauts.

The captain's horror is understandable. His creations had not kept the commandment he laid down. Instead of meeting an intelligent, technologically advanced race after thousands of years the spaceship crew found hybrid beings of all kinds, contaminated, depraved, a terrifying mixture of intelligence and beast . . .

and the result was that

The captain decided to wipe out this wretched brood, with very few exceptions. What means were employed? It could have been done with fire, water or chemicals. The legends of mankind give many clues, such as the Flood or the destruction of cities from heaven (Sodom and Gomorrah), not to mention the overthrow of whole peoples by 'divine dust'.   (Daniken 1976, p. 204)

At this point Daniken immediately begins a reworking of what he has already given, adding further and not necessarily corroborative details to extend his exegesis. 'I speculate', he writes

that before he departed the captain left behind a groundcrew for other operations. . . . Then the worst happened! Perhaps the crew experimented of their own accord, perhaps the captain came back later than they had foreseen. At any rate the crew assumed that they had to spend the rest of their lives on earth. They mated with the daughters of earth. The prophet Enoch knew all about it. . . . He says quite bluntly what he is talking about . . . slept with women, defiled yourselves with the daughters of men, taken wives unto yourselves and done like the children of earth and begat sons like giants . . .
    The captain certainly did not unleash a deadly ray that would destroy mankind. Perhaps he dared not or could not take such a radical step, as children of his guardians were already in existence. Legends also tell us that the heavenly ones took many men into their spaceship before they flew away.   (Daniken 1976, p. 205)

And not being satisfied with the conflicting accounts of the captain's behaviour, he then offers the possibility that

did the captain, as the myths relate, return after a losing 'battle in the universe' to seek safety amongst his own kind? If my version of mating between alien cosmonauts and the children of earth is accepted, the phenomenal puzzle of the dual nature of man is solved. As a product of this planet he is earthbound, as a co-product of extraterrestrial beings he is simultaneously 'son of the gods'.   (Daniken 1976, p. 206)

These varied and often conflicting accounts serve a greater purpose if seen as a unity; they enable Daniken to demote Biblical accounts on the one hand, and invest the Blavatsky cosmology with heightened meaning on the other, and the device for accomplishing both ends is the same, a detailed techno-exegesis of both texts. A considerable achievement and one that struck an obvious chord if the sales figures provide any guide. Daniken had revitalized a nineteenth-century occult cosmology by giving it a technological meaning, the same meaning that refuted Biblical and other myth systems.

From this point on it is worthwhile noting other points of connection between Daniken's techno-vision and Blavatsky's occult cosmology, since they serve to develop the moral ground upon which Techno-Occultism stands.

Blavatsky offered in Stanza 8, verses 31–2 of The Book of Dzyan:

THEY (the animals) BEGAN TO BREED. THE TWOFOLD MAN (then) SEPARATED ALSO. HE (man), SAID 'LET US AS THEY; LET US UNITE AND MAKE CREATURES'. THEY DID . . .

AND THOSE WHICH HAD NO SPARK (the narrow brained) TOOK HUGE SHE? ANIMALS UNTO THEM (a). THEY BEGAT UPON THEM THE DUMB RACES. DUMB THEY WERE (the narrow brained) THEMSELVES. BUT THEIR TONGUES UNTIED. (b) THE TONGUES OF THEIR PROGENY REMAINED STILL. MONSTERS THEY BRED. A RACE OF CROOKED, RED HAIR-COVERED MONSTERS GOING ON ALL FOURS. A DUMB RACE TO KEEP THE SHAME UNTOLD. (Blavatsky 1888, vol. 2, p. 184)

Thus for Blavatsky, miscegenation, men copulating with female animals, was the real meaning of the Fall, which Daniken has matched with his spaceship crew finding 'hybrid beings of all kinds . . . a terrifying mixture of intelligence and beast' (1976, p. 204). For Blavatsky's 'War in Heaven', the strife between the 'Sons of God' and the 'Sons of the Shadow', Daniken offers his battle in the depth of the galaxy at some time in the unknown past, and his losers in the battle are those whom Blavatsky identifies as 'transformed subsequently into evil Spirits and lower gods', but who are in occult reality 'the gods of the Secret Wisdom' (Blavatsky 1888, vol. 2, p. 500) and later to be identified as the 'Fallen Angels' of the Christian church, which have been 'degraded in Space and Time into opposing powers or demons'. But the 'real character' of the fallen angels is given with the information that they were 'the "host" of the planet Venus . . . Lucifer, the genius of the morning star, or the army of Satan . . . the Titans, the demons and giants . . . the progeny of the "Sons of God" and the "Daughters of Men", and the Nagas (serpents or Seraphs), the semi-divine with a human face and the tail of a Dragon . . . the Initiate hermits . . . living in caves' (Blavatsky 1888, vol. 2, p. 501).[4]

So Daniken's account becomes identifiable as a techno-rendition of Blavatsky, with losers in spaceships for the fallen host of Lucifer, the Titans and the Serpents who lived in caves. Miscegenation is the reason for the Fall, a punishment imposed by the Lucifer-Captain of the spaceship. Even the argument in Daniken's thirteenth point that 'they could perhaps work stone more easily than archaeologists can imagine today' is a recurring notion in Romantic Occultism; Steiner in his *Cosmic Memory* (1959, p. 84), for instance, gives, 'For in the Lemurian and even in the Atlantean period, stones and metals were much softer than later'.

This is a significant development, other Techno-Occult writers – Leslie,

Charroux, Pauwels and Bergier – had all referred to Blavatsky, even subjecting certain aspects of her cosmology to a techno-rendition, but Daniken with his far more detailed, programmatic account, brings the events of the occult past up to the present when he asks if

> our creators observe us from time to time? Are they annoyed at our arrogance and blindness? Are they furious because we reject the midwifery they supplied at our 'birth'? Could our creators break off 'Experiment Earth' one day?   (Daniken 1978, p. 271)

Rejecting the 'midwifery' they supplied can only refer to what is conceived of as a particular form of contemporary miscegenation, namely racial interbreeding. Furthermore, the prognosis of 'our creators breaking off the experiment' can only be avoided by an uncritical adoption of all the possibilities inherent in modern technology. Indeed, taking his cue from Pauwels and Bergier, the eager adoption of all technical and scientific possibilities becomes a positive imperative, the ruling moral dictate in Daniken's universe. 'So it would be like committing hara-kiri', he writes, 'to turn our ancient mission upside down: to calumniate the advance of technology' (Daniken 1981, p. 250).

There is obviously no equivocation here; any force that deters or delays technical progress is clearly bad, and those who stand in the way of such progress are damned. 'If the technology of space travel manages to achieve speeds close to the speed of light in fifty years – and it will, provided the Black Order of Pessimists does not succeed in wrecking our future' (Daniken 1981, p. 175). That future and the 'ancient mission' referred to is that of humanity being reunited with its Luciferic creators in the 'Brotherhood of the Stars'.

Consequent upon this techno-imperative is a revaluation of the Christian-humanist moral value systems, and by gathering the various references throughout the texts a new moral order is indicated with: 'The gods had no "moral" feelings about such radical cleaning up operations' (1974, p. 214), in relation to the Flood or the destruction of Sodom and Gomorrah, and that: 'Seen in this light the Flood becomes a preconceived project . . . with the intention of exterminating the human race except for a few noble exceptions' (1971, p. 61).

Picking up the clues offered by 'noble exceptions' we find that there is a selective list of men of genius who, we are told, have not created their works out of their own understanding, but simply because 'information was programmed on the punched cards of our life by unknown intelligences' (1972, p. 69). Further, 'since we men are programmed by the "gods", we shall soon be master of the same technological miracles' (1972, p. 104). The miracles are the secrets of travel using space-time dilation, etc.

The exegesis has revealed a complete Techno-gnosis which yields a completely deterministic development of humanity, with all history implanted in a eugenically selected 'genesis'. From the base of this certainty the future is to be realized by men of genius who are able to read the punched cards of knowledge that have been implanted in them. His view of the future is of a megalomaniac technology as may have been dreamt up by a Himmler and pressed into realization by a Stalin. He offers 'an army of deep frozen soldiers who will be thawed out as necessary in case of war' (1971, p. 105) and

> Shall we live to see hyper intelligent dolphins, programmed in underwater research, go to 'diving stations'? Shall we see apes whose brains have been 'programmed' to handle road-making machines working in the streets? (1972, p. 62)

and

> Pictures and writing will be projected into space for a thousand kilometers. On the side of the new moon ... flickering letters will read: Coca-Cola-Coca-Cola. At full moon religious communities will warn us with black laser beams: the Last Judgement is at hand. (1981, p. 157)

A particularly telling fusion of capitalism, Christianity and desecrating technology.[5]

In Daniken's universe the only good lies in the application of technology, and in that good lies the meaning of human existence. Technological achievement is the end and the means and there must be no scruples. This is clearly shown when he discusses the possibility of using a detached human brain to control complex spacecraft, and he has no hesitation in suggesting the use of the brain of an unborn child, as that would be most suitable for programming.

It therefore goes without saying that any concern for the environment, or the effect of these technologies upon human society, must be resolutely set aside. Indeed, any problems caused by the depletion of earth's resources to feed rapacious technology will be simply solved by the recourse to market forces at their most extreme. Thus we are offered the answer

> to replace dwindling raw materials by others. The sum is simple. Rare raw materials are dear, and the rarer they are, the dearer they become, until one day they are priced out of the market. At this moment at the latest, intelligent man remembers that he can achieve the same effect with another material. Man will always find the way. (1981, p. 250)

In the meantime, with an exclusively male crew of astronauts, with humanity's future depicted as being totally male-dominated and with women being relegated to being merely the vessels for sexual experimentation, Daniken is still fretting about the sexual act, still offering alternative versions of the development of the species. We are told that

It is quite possible that woman was created from man, but Eve can hardly have blossomed forth in her naked beauty from the narrow rib of the male thorax by a conjuring trick – after a surgical intervention? Eve must have been produced in a retort. . . . Could foreign intelligences with a highly developed science and knowing about the immune biological reactions of bones have used Adam's marrow as a cell culture and brought the sperm to development in it? (1972, p. 40)

Daniken's supposition represents a complete fusion of the essential cosmology that lay at the core of Romantic Occultism with the evocational perspectives inherent in contemporary science and technology. The fusion is of equal parts, for the techno-scientific input is not just as dressing for nineteenth-century occultism; it functions to revalorize the old beliefs by fixing them within the plausible horizon of an extrapolative future determined by the mid-century consensus as to the advances that would be made in science and technology. The techno-scientism in Pauwels and Bergier had played the same crucial role, although with Daniken it is more specific and detailed.

This is exemplified by a further example of Daniken's supposition that is unmistakably derived from Blavatsky. With the genesis role of God now handed over to the captain of the spaceship, a Lucifer in all but name, Daniken argues that the supreme being, the original deity that created the universe, is no more than a relegated god who can only await the growth of consciousness to awaken his own creation. He states:

The original prodigious force which existed before the beginning of all was a neutrum. IT existed before the big bang. IT unleashed the great destruction. IT caused all the worlds in the universe to originate from the explosion. IT, incorporeal primordial force . . . became matter and IT knew the result of the great explosion. IT wanted to reach the stage of lived experience. I suggest that one should imagine a computer that works with 100 billion thought units . . . If this computer exploded its 'personal consciousness' would be destroyed, had not the intelligent computer magnetized all its billions of bits before the explosion. . . . The originally centralized computer consciousness no longer exists, but the clever self-destroyer had programmed the future after the explosion. All the magnetic bits with their separate information will meet again some time at the centre of the explosion. (1974, p. 229)

The passage is highly compact in terms of occult ideology. The depiction of the ultimate deity as being a 'neutrum' who plays no active role in the created universe is derived from Blavatsky.

An Omnipotent, Eternal, Boundless and Immutable Principle which is beyond the range and reach of human thought . . . it is of course, devoid of all attributes, and is essentially without any relation to manifested, finite Being. (Hillard 1907, p. 11)

So also its 'function' or mode of operation, with the clearly depicted cycle of explosion–implosion which derives from Blavatsky's 'Eternal Infinite All, the Omnipresent Unity ... becoming through periodical manifestation a manifold universe' (1888 vol. 1, p. 8). The difference is that Blavatsky speaks of the undulatory nature of the ultimate being whereas, characteristically for his time, Daniken uses the metaphor of explosion–implosion. As with Blavatsky, Daniken's supreme being is morally neutral.

> With the assumption that we are all parts of the mighty IT God no longer has to be simultaneously good and bad in some inconceivable way; He is no longer responsible for sorrow and happiness. ... We ourselves have the positive and negative powers within us, because we come from the IT that always was. (1974, p. 232)

Clearly Daniken's presentation of God as an assemblage–disassemblage of billions of computer bits gets its validity as a piece of supposition from the circumstance that it derives also from the plausibilities of extrapolated advances in computer science, it being a commonplace that one day artificial computer intelligence will be realized.

There are, however, formidable problems to be faced by the complete exegete, and Daniken's techno-scientific occult vision is no exception. Since his technical parables are wedded to the Blavatskian conception of the literal truth of all myths, he must be able to incorporate all myths into his techno-gnosis, and so it necessarily follows that any myth that speaks of gods from the stars, of cosmic messengers, of divine intercession in human affairs, must be an account of contact with ancient astronauts. This necessity leads to considerable tangles and preposterously detailed assumptions, though all made with characteristic aplomb, to produce an exegesis. For example, his literal transcription of mythic detail means that he has to deal with the certainty that at least some of the astronaut gods were giants. This is inescapable due to Genesis vi.4: 'And there were giants in the earth in those days.'

There are further problems with the miscegenation that was the cause of the Fall, and he offers: 'Were the bodies of pregnant women dragged down by the abnormal weight of the foetus? Could these poor creatures only waddle along a few weeks before birth?' (1981, p. 127). He suggests that stone age fertility figurines such as the Willendorf Venus with their gross breasts and buttocks are exact anatomical models.

To this grimly humorous interpretation must be added a number of other bizarre instances, all necessary given the premiss that myths are eye-witness accounts. Therefore we have the following from *Return to the Stars*:

> Old books say that even in historical times these hybrid beings lived in hordes, tribes and even in large units like peoples. They tell of specially bred hybrids, who spent their existence as 'temple animals' and seem to have been the spoilt darlings of the populace. (1972, p. 155)

The problem is that nothing in myth or fable can be omitted from the exegesis. So Jacob's vision (Gen xxviii.12) of a ladder reaching from earth to heaven becomes 'Had Jacob surprised the "servants of god" loading goods into a spaceship?' (1972, p. 173). And the Ark of the Covenant becomes 'a marvellous machine. It stored up water from the night dew, then mixed it with a microscopic type of green algae and produced as much food as was needed' (1981, p. 20). Elsewhere even 'Open Sesame' and Aladdin's lamp resulted from direct experience of technological phenomena.

The next problem is somewhat more formidable in its implications for his techno-exegesis; it lies in the universality of myth. Wherever myths and legends occur relating to messengers from the skies, the ancient astronauts must have interceded and brought their technical skills into play. The universality of myth means the near-omnipresence of the astronauts. Daniken admits to the difficulty that this leads to when the well-known and perplexing statues of remote Easter Island have to be explained, and so he is led into a detailed and preposterous hypothesis to overcome the problem. He assumes that: 'A small group of intelligent beings was stranded on Easter Island owing to a "technical hitch".' It is noted that in spite of their advanced technology, the 'hitch' led to several months passing before the astronauts were discovered by their own kind, they having lost all communication as well as power to their vehicles.

The problem is of course that there are literally thousands of such islands in the Pacific Ocean and they could not all have been the scene of visitations by astronauts in their spacecraft, faulty or otherwise. Daniken acknowledges this when dealing with the citadel and temple remains found in the Caroline Islands. Of these remains he writes: 'Help by alien astronauts does not satisfy me as an explanation either. Why did they seek out this miserable little islet?' (1976, p. 140).

A more basic problem for the techno-scientific exegete is what may be termed the 'Graeco-Roman lacuna'. Myth and artefact from far and wide are subjected to a techno-scientific exegesis. It seems that there is no society or culture that does not reinforce his interpretation of myth and fable as visitations by extraterrestrials at some point in the past. There is however one notable area of exception: the myths and artefacts of the Graeco-Roman world, the world of classical antiquity and nascent Christianity. With, for instance, the little-understood civilizations of pre-Columbian America or in the scant remains of an even remoter antiquity, he is safe in assuming that his readership is unlikely to have sufficient background knowledge to challenge his assertions. However, the myths of classical antiquity and the story of the development of Christianity are different; he can no longer assume that the ignorance of his readership will protect him from absurdity.

Of course the Graeco-Roman myths and the Jesus story are packed with images and detail that are as capable of sustaining a techno-scientific exegesis as the myths of other, less familiar civilizations. The myth of Prometheus, the account of Jesus' resurrection, or the star of Bethlehem, would all prove grist to the mill of techno-gnosticism.[6] But with Daniken it is not so, and with the exception of his *Miracles of the Gods* there are barely more than half a dozen references to classical antiquity in his works. The immediate reason is of course quite obvious; far too much is known about the world of classical antiquity. Not only the variant details of the capricious cosmologies of Greece and Rome, but also their evolution and reception in the then contemporary mind. Equally the Graeco-Roman mastery of the plastic arts denies the remotest possibility of a technical explication. These gods are human, they wear or carry the artefacts of the Classical Age. The religions of that age were subject to dissemination and development due to factors and forces that are clearly understood in an imperial civilization: thus the importation of Mithraism and the dispersal of Christianity.

The same difficulties pertain when we come to consider the teachings of Jesus and the various New Testament accounts of his life. Although wrapped in moral parables, the words of Jesus are too numerous to admit of the possibility that he was an astronaut. The world of classical antiquity is simply too well known and understood, debates about crucial issues notwithstanding, for it to be rendered up to techno-scientific exegesis. A technical exegesis of classical myths would not even bear a passing scrutiny. It also means that the centuries following in which the Christian church was established throughout Europe and became the belief system out of which Western civilization was to emerge, are forbidden territory for the techno-scientific exegete. It would clearly be ludicrous to suppose, for instance, that medieval artists painted gold haloes in the belief that the apostles were astronauts, or that an infant Jesus painted by Duccio is really a depiction of an implanted mutation, its swaddling clothes being a metal cocoon, rich in amniotic fluids.

There is therefore a major breakdown, a lacuna in the exegetical method, as the very paucity of references to classical antiquity all too clearly illustrates. It is partly because he is aware of this problem that Daniken wrote his fifth title, *Miracles of the Gods*, which, subtitled 'A hard look at the Supernatural' is largely an analysis of the Jesus Christ myth together with selected aspects of classical antiquity offering parallels with Christian account and experience [page references to Miracles refer to Souvenir hardback 1977 edition].

In all of his other texts a techno-scientific exegesis has been the method of building up a complete techno-gnosticism that claims the scope of universal vision. Yet in *Miracles of the Gods* there is not a word of techno-scientific exegesis. The myths dealt with are no longer eye-witness accounts, and an interpretation is reached by placing them in their contemporary milieu. Thus Jesus becomes a mere preacher, well-intentioned but deluded, a product of a resistance movement. 'Jesus was a teachable pupil in the desert: he learnt the methods of mass psychology from the preacher John' (1977, p. 74); and 'Jesus was a devout man, but not "God's only begotten son", a political activist, but not a redeemer' (1977, p. 78); while Pauline Christianity is merely a derivation from older cults. We are told therefore that 'Practically everything that forms present-day Pauline Christianity is to be found in the cults of Attis, Dionysus, Mithras and Isis' (1977, p. 90).

In other chapters he deals with the obviously problematical area of Christian visionary experience, particularly that which relates to the Virgin Mary, not an image that can easily be incorporated into an essentially masculine techno-gnosticism. Hence, sidestepping the issue, he launches into a social criticism of the commercialism of Lourdes and reduces the visionary experiences associated with such centres to a materialistic interpretation. 'Physical laws lie at the root of the unknown causes of visions', and adds 'But it is always the devout, the undisputed faithful, who insinuate themselves into the mass suggestion of "Holy events"' (1977, p. 182). It will be noted that these explanations are not proffered for the more ancient or distant visions which were subjected to techno-scientific exegesis.

Furthermore, he compares and contrasts the healing centres such as Lourdes with those of classical antiquity, particularly the healing centre at Epidaurus, where the 'able members of the Asclepian priesthood became experienced observers of human nature who knew exactly how to exercise psychic influence on the sick' (1977, p. 129). Again, it is noted that alone among the priesthoods of the pre-Christian world, those of Greece and Rome were trained observers and psychotherapists. No astronauts giving a hand with advanced technologies here.

The implication is unavoidable. Two of the greater epochs in Western history, the flowering of classical antiquity and that of Western European civilization, were both achieved without the aid of extra-terrestrials. For the rest, however, from Egypt to the Caroline Islands, from the American Indian to the Dogon tribes of Africa, aid from ancient astronauts was indispensable; indeed it was the central cultural event of those societies. With *Miracles of the Gods* Daniken aims at demoting and dismissing the Christian and Graeco-Roman heritage in order to obscure the fundamental lacuna in his thesis.

There is of course another aspect of the lacuna, which is that it serves to further the Luciferianism of his argument. Daniken's concept of Jesus, as an historical figure, a teacher, a product of the Essenes who became the victim of his own messianic delusion is, of course, four-square with Blavatsky's treatment of Jesus. However, she did assert that Jesus, while not the Christ, since such a concept had no esoteric meaning other than as a teaching, was nevertheless a 'great initiate' who spoke in parables for the masses. Christ Jesus's teaching, as understood by his contemporaries versed in esoteric knowledge, was that of revealing the doctrines of the Logos, 'who is WISDOM but who as the opponent of ignorance, is Satan or Lucifer at the same time' (Blavatsky 1888, vol. 2, p. 230). But, having stripped his Luciferianism of its Romantic Occult trappings of spirit and mystery, Daniken's concept of Jesus cannot even fulfil an esoterically validating role, and so he becomes but a humble, mistaken preacher; human, all too human.

Consideration of the Daniken oeuvre thus reveals a cumulative and sometimes contradictory building up of a complete thesis that reaches back in its essential aspects to Madame Blavatsky's Theosophy and even further in its intuitive stance to the gnostic heresies of the early centuries after Christ.[7]

THE STYLE OF THE DANIKEN OEUVRE

The task that confronts the analyst of Daniken's oeuvre is to identify those features of his Techno-Occultism that single it out for worldwide acclaim, an acclaim that is denied to other proponents of Ancient Extra-terrestrialism to anywhere near the same extent, and which was just as extensive in countries beyond that of initial publication.

One important pointer towards explaining his enormous popularity is the style adopted for all of the texts, other than *Miracles of the Gods*. It has been remarked in earlier chapters how a characteristic style that is well adapted to the suppositional nature of the texts runs throughout the genre; in the chapter on *The Dawn of Magic* particular attention was drawn to the highly refined style, which well suited the mixture of supposition and evocation that dominated the entire narrative. With Daniken the style is again of great importance. Clearly of the type of the genre, it is yet highly developed as a particular variant, one that differs from that of Pauwels and Bergier in a number of aspects.

The blend of assertion and supposition that characterizes the general style of Techno-Occultism can be seen to have derived from the style adopted by Blavatsky in her *Isis Unveiled* and *The Secret Doctrine*, a style that in her hands contributed in no small measure to the complexity of those lengthy tomes, which at times become well-nigh incomprehensible. Hence the compact *A Primer of Theosophy* and kindred works that were to present the occult cosmology in a more accessible format, texts that were to be so necessary once Theosophy had been set upon its proselytizing course in the late 1880s.

It was, however, claimed that Madame Blavatsky wrote under the influence of an occult trance, her message dictated directly to her by hidden masters, and it is an interesting comparison with Daniken that he, alone amongst the advocates of Techno-Occultism, claimed to have written his works out of a state of extra-sensory perception. Indeed, Daniken believes that it is this talent that will enable him to refute his critics and prove, for instance, the existence of the vast subterranean cave system that he was shown in Ecuador. Krassa, his uncritical biographer, states:

> So Daniken's name is still on everyone's lips. As a result hopes are high that his activities, his search for evidence, will end successfully. Will he satisfy those expectations? EvD is sure of it, and bases his conviction on a guardedly intimated extra sensory talent of his which he calls *espern*. (Krassa 1978, p. 124)

In the *Der Spiegel* interview Daniken claimed that he had his first *espern* experience when he was at a Catholic boarding school, and that his experience convinced him that astronauts from other stars and galaxies had visited the earth. To the question, 'Then E.S.P. is an essential source of your cognition?', he replied, 'A source which brought me to the certain conclusion that extra-terrestrial astronauts visited the earth. I know it. And I know that an event will happen in the near future to prove I am right' (19 March 1973).

If Daniken does write out of extra-sensory perception, creating his works out of a witnessed *phantasie*, then it may help to account for his particular refinement of the style of Techno-Occultism. Unlike Pauwels and Bergier, whose style permitted a text that was rich in half-glimpsed meaning, their Luciferianism having to be teased out of a thicket of ambiguous phrases, unexpected associations and constant exhortation, Daniken adopts a style that is repetitive certainly, but also brutal and simple in the presentation of its message. At times the narrative structure breaks down completely, as with passages like

> Who can imagine that human hands and human endeavour excavated, transported and dressed this block?
>
> What power overturned it?
>
> What titanic forces were at work here?
>
> And to what end? (1971, p. 38)

A further exai ₁ple from *Return to the Stars* runs

> What race did they represent?
>
> Were they lone wolves?
>
> Were they wrongly programmed products of mutations?
>
> Were they direct descendants of gigantic cosmonauts from another world?

> Were they especially intelligent beings with advanced technical knowhow
> who had originated according to the genetic code? (1972, p. 47)

Here question becomes argument, since each question is also an assertion
or supposition. Inevitably coupled with such batteries of questions is the
evocation of what are claimed to be inexplicable artefacts. Whereas there
are few writers in the genre who do not mention examples such as the
rustproof iron column at Delhi, the mammoths of Siberia, Dean Swift's
knowledge of the satellites of Mars, the Piri Re'is maps, Daniken uses all
of them and many more, blatantly purveying them as a challenge to
science that cannot be taken up and therefore 'proof' of his astronaut
thesis. Corroborative detail is never given. 'At Delhi there is an ancient
iron column that contains no phosphorus or sulphur and so cannot be
destroyed by the effects of weathering' (1974, p. 197) and 'The print of a
shoe was found in a coal seam in Fisher Canyon Nevada' (1974, p. 199).

This aggressive and repetitive style is unashamedly challenging. 'It
took courage to write this book and it will take courage to read',
commences the introduction to *Chariots of the Gods*, so that from the outset
he places himself as arguing from a position of strength, and the intention
is that his texts are seen as being revelatory in nature; their intention is
never to convince by patient argument, rather to create for the reader a
mental state that corresponds to the *phantasie* out of which the work was
created. The style is more crude, the nature and use of the supposition is
far more blatant than is found in Pauwels and Bergier; the message,
though programmatically complex as the techno-exegesis is developed
from text to text, is hammered home to the extent that the basic premiss
has become a commonplace, while the essential Luciferianism – which at
some level precedes the techno-explication – remains buried within the
thesis. Inevitably a vein of iconoclasm runs throughout the texts and on
subsequent pages of *Chariots of the Gods* we have

> Let us get used to the idea that the world of ideas which has grown up over the
> millennia is going to collapse. A few years of accurate research has already
> brought down the mental edifice in which we had made ourselves at home.
> (1971, p. 12)

The position is the same as that advanced by Pauwels and Bergier, but
without preamble, attempt to convince, or historical definition.

But alongside such brutalism there is also a strangely childlike quality
to the writing. Often Daniken writes not just with enthusiasm but with a
naïve excitement and simplicity. *The Gold of the Gods* opens with 'To me
this is the most incredible, fantastic story of the century'. And later in the
same text he gives, 'Once again not even the cleverest man on earth
knows who painted the paintings on the walls' (1974, p. 158). In *In Search
of Ancient Gods* he suggests that we should look at the work of comic-strip
artists and illustrators. 'It is worth while looking at these imaginary

drawings, for we should remember that technically minded boys are becoming familiar with phenomena that they may yet experience in reality and will come as no surprise to them' (1976, p. 128). This is an argument that makes sense only when one recalls Daniken's claim to have written out of an imagined reality which creates a true picture of his beliefs. This method of imaginative portrayal is based upon the potency of the visual analogue for the child, and indeed the very essence of Daniken's evidence is derived from visual analogue, a striking throwback to an earlier age when, as Foucault argues, 'resemblance played a constructive role in the knowledge of Western culture' (1973, p. 17).[8] Marks on cave walls 'look like' retorts, or helmets worn by astronauts, channels carved in Inca stones 'look like' channels for power cables in modern factories. In each case there is given a visual correlation, a sudden leap from style or artefact of the past to the fashion of contemporary technology is being made. A lengthy section in *Return to the Stars* describes his journey from Zurich to New York 'As it might have been told by one of our remote ancestors if he had flown . . . in a modern jet aircraft' (1972, p. 136) and demonstrates the importance of the visual analogue not only for evidence and argument but also for the written style. It is the very act of working out of his imaginative *phantasie* that creates the text, not the exercise of critical or analytical faculties, with the result that long passages read with the obscure facility of a surreal film.

Consider the following example from *Return to the Stars*:

What was the special thing about Aladdin's lamp? The fact that it could materialize supernatural beings whenever young Aladdin rubbed it. Is it possible that he set a materialization machine going when he rubbed it?

In the light of present-day knowledge there is a possible explanation of the magic lamp. We know that atomic technology turns mass into energy and that physics turns energy into mass. A television picture is split up into hundreds of thousands of lines that are radiated over relay stations after they have been transformed into waves of energy.

Let us take a leap into the fantastic. A table – including the one I am sitting at now – consists of a countless number of juxtaposed atoms. If it were possible to split the table up into its atomic components, send it out in energy waves and reconstruct it in its original form at a given place, the transport of matter would be solved. Sheer fantasy? I admit that it is today, but in the future . . .

Perhaps the memory of the men of antiquity was still haunted by the remembrance of materialisations that had been seen in very remote times. Today steel is dipped in liquid nitrogen to harden it. To us a natural process that was discovered in modern times. But probably owing to a primitive memory this hardening process was already a reality in antiquity. At all events it was practised with very crude methods. For case hardening, the men of old plunged red hot swords into the bodies of live prisoners! Yet how did they know that the human body is pumped full of organic nitrogen? How did they know the chemical effect? Simply by experience?

> How, I ask, did our ancestors get their advanced technology and their modern medicinal knowledge if not from unknown intelligences? (1972, p. 65)

In comparison with most other writers in the genre Daniken uses the salient features of Techno-Occultism's distinctive style in extreme measure and welds them into a coherent whole by reading his text out of the state of mind that he has characterized as *espern*. The result is that method and meaning become indistinguishable, although the text has none of the dense thicket of Pauwels and Bergier's supposition and is more available to the reader. In this way he has created a number of texts that are both potent and powerful at a certain uncritical level of perception, and they have won an unprecedented readership within a few years.

There are two corollaries to the above analysis of Daniken's style that are particularly interesting in that each of them would seem to give scope to detractors, though in fact neither of them does so. The first corollary is that one feature of Daniken's presentation is that it is, as was mentioned earlier, time-fixed. That is to say that by using the visual analogue as argument and evidence, he can compare the artefacts held up for consideration with the artefacts of contemporary technology. This leads to an inevitable illogicality.

Though the technology of the visiting astronauts must, of necessity, have been far in advance of that of the mid-twentieth century, nevertheless it is the technological artefacts of our present age that the primitive statues and artefacts imitate. So the interpretation of cave paintings as being of men in spacesuits with UHF aerials in the helmets, as would have been conceived by a science as accomplished as that of the 1960s. So too with the interpretation of the 'earphones' on the Toltec statues, or with the argument of channels for power cables cut into the Inca rocks, and of course, with the hypothesis that the astronauts alighted on the earth to renew their supplies of 'fissionable' material.

The weakness of the method is highlighted if one compares a wireless set of the 1920s with a Sony Walkman (remember that the moon astronauts would have been amazed if presented with a pocket-sized calculator) or looks at the techno-scientific presentations of the future that were made in the 1930s when electronics was based upon valves, and plastics had made no serious inroad into metal usage. Techno-scientific presentations of the future are time-fixed, their validity based solely upon a narrow extrapolation of technical and social factors that are rooted in the present of those predictions. But it would be absurd to assume that a technology that could achieve intergalactic space travel and that had mastered the 'time warp' would still be reliant upon fission processes to power its spacecraft and would fashion its artefacts in a style consonant with the technological capability of a bygone age.

The second corollary is that there is an undeniable suggestion of satire in Daniken's writing. The opening sentence of *Chariots of the Gods*, 'It took courage to write this book and it will take courage to read it', or the section in *Return to the Stars* describing modern flight as it would appear to a primitive, contain a strong suspicion of being a 'send-up'.

This quality in Daniken's writing was observed from the outset. Theo Bos, a Daniken disciple, argues that 'Erich differs from other writers in that his books do not forget humour. . . . In the end Erich's popularity is based on just this deliberate provocation' (Krassa 1978, p. 85). Professor Hans Wunderlich, the author of several works on popular science, is quoted in *Encounter* as claiming that Daniken is 'the most important and brilliant satirist in German literature for at least a century' (August 1973). Daniken's retort, given in an interview in *Playboy*, was 'The answer is yes and no. We have a wonderful word for it in German – *Jein*. In many respects I am absolutely no satirist; I earnestly mean what I say. On the other hand I like to make people laugh' (Krassa 1978, p. 85).[9]

The ambiguities in Daniken's attitude to his own work have clearly not hindered the sales of his texts. Possibly many of his readers were not aware of the suggestion of humour or mockery, probably most of his rapidly growing band of adherents were too convinced of the truth of Ancient Extra-terrestrialism to care. On the other hand, the undeniable humour and occasional grossness that surfaces in what a fellow author in the genre, Josef Blumrich, has termed a 'frantic and unacceptable . . . street style' (Krassa 1978, p. 82), may well speak of a genuinely subliminal creative process, one that goes beyond the expected concerns for style, clarity and veracity, and goes towards supporting a widespread adoption of the Ancient Astronaut thesis at a non-critical level by so many earnest adherents.

OTHER ANCIENT EXTRA-TERRESTRIALISTS

The argument that individual style is partly the reason for his popularity is supported by comparison with other Ancient Extra-terrestrialists. Pauwels and Bergier have already been mentioned, but they did not specifically advance the thesis and so comparison with them is not particularly relevant. Instead, it is other writers who maintained a solely Ancient Astronaut thesis who make an interesting and valid comparison with Daniken; writers such as W. Raymond Drake in England and Robert Charroux in France.

Drake is credited, in *The Encyclopedia of UFOs*, as having provided in his Gods and Spacemen series of books texts that are 'the most thorough to be written on the extra-terrestrial interpretation of unsolved mysteries of the past' (1980, p. 104). In all, Drake has written some eight books on the Ancient Extra-terrestrialist thesis. His first, *Gods or Spacemen?* appeared in 1964; his second, the most widely received of the series, *Gods and Spacemen in the Ancient East*, was published in 1968. Drake therefore narrowly predates Daniken, certainly in the English-speaking world, but the margin is not wide enough to deny Drake the particular mixture of socio-political and technological circumstances which, it will later be argued, favoured the reception of the Daniken texts. Thus predating Daniken by such a narrow margin, particularly in the much larger English-speaking world, should have offered Drake, who was maintaining substantially the same thesis, every market advantage. That in fact Drake's books never remotely approached the success of the Daniken works, and indeed were possibly pulled along by slipstreaming behind Daniken's popularity, would indicate that the reasons for the relative failure of the Drake texts to make a comparable impact are most likely to do with presentation and focus. Drake wrote eight books to Daniken's seven (up to 1982) over a fifteen-year period, and yet he never became more than a cult author, his sales largely confined to Britain and America. Consideration of Drake's texts, however, shows that his theme is presented in a style redolent of nineteenth-century Romantic Occultism.

> In the glorious days when our earth was young ... Celestials winged down from the stars to teach the arts of civilisation to unsophisticated Man, creating that Golden Age sung by all the poets of Antiquity.   (Drake 1973, p. 9)

So reads the opening sentence of *Gods and Spacemen in the Ancient East*. The chapter continues with passages such as

> Man evolves through suffering. As light requires the dark to realize illumination, so divine law decrees that good should be tempered by evil ... mystics suspect that God though perfect needs deeper perfection, so is dreaming into existence an endless sequence of universes.   (p. 9)

What is interesting is that even in the short passage given, many of the key themes of occult supposition are quickly touched upon: the passive relegation of God, the ambiguity between good and evil, the Promethean Lucifer as the teacher of humanity. There is certainly economy and concision here, though the style, which is maintained throughout, with its archly romantic phraseology, its specific mention of spirits, its mystical and, in later sections, joyous contemplation of God and the universe, is all thoroughly nineteenth-century. The result is that Drake's works, by their very manner, distance themselves from the technological essence of his thesis and they carry all too clearly their romantic imprimatur ... 'occultism is the science of Divine Unfoldment' (1973, p. 13). Drake fronts his texts with an occultism that is still dressed in a romantic vocabulary and still conceptually dependent upon Theosophy even for its exegesis.

By contrast Daniken never mentions occultism or spirits. He uses his techno-scientific exegesis not only to promote the central role of technology to his creed but also to distance his theses from their origins in Blavatsky and Romantic Occultism. So, whereas the Daniken oeuvre has a stylistic unity such that the whole universe can be subsumed from contemporary technology and a complete techno-gnosis offered, Drake, with his more leisurely style, never achieves this separation, and his style drags twentieth-century technology into a nineteenth-century perspective, stifling the potential of the Ancient Astronaut thesis.

This is nowhere more clear than when comparison is made of Drake's deity, as given above, with Daniken's dissembled computer, which he calls IT. Drake places humanity's experience of suffering as being central to his evolutionary plan, whereas Daniken's conception, more closely attuned to a consumerist society and values of utility, trumpets the triumphs of technology as the force that will enable 'man' to reach his intergalactic destiny.

Like Drake, the French author Robert Charroux narrowly pre-dates Daniken as an Ancient Extra-terrestrialist. Indeed Gilbert Bourquin, editor of the Swiss magazine *Blick*, and Sergius Golowin collaborated to write *The Daniken Story*, in which they accused their compatriot of misappropriating the substance of Charroux's ideas (Krassa 1978, p. 67) and Gadow's *Erinnerungen an die Wirklichkeit*, mentioned above, also charged Daniken with extracting his ideas from Charroux (Krassa 1978, p. 68). Whether it be plagiarism or parallelism that accounts for the rash of Ancient Extra-terrestrialist texts appearing in the late sixties, the point is that Charroux's earlier work, *Legacy of the Gods* (1963), 'only sold a paltry 58,000 copies' (Krassa 1978, p. 68) in its German edition – circumstances that would again suggest that Daniken's supremacy lies in the unity and style of his thesis. Almost all of the essential elements of Daniken's techno-gnosis are to be found in Charroux: rejection of Darwin; insemination of indigenous females by visiting astronauts; a techno-literal rendering of myths, marginalizing of a historic Jesus and the promotion of the Promethean Lucifer. Nonetheless, the Charroux texts never achieve Daniken's thematic unity; they seem curiously static in comparison, and have frequent references to Blavatsky and Theosophical doctrines that are nonsensical given the astronomical knowledge of the 1960s. So, for instance, in *Masters of the World* (1979, p. 166) Charroux, maintaining the occultist's fascination with Venus, offers

Lucifer is the name of Venus, the morning star. Lucifer is an 'angel' who came

from the bright planet to give life, knowledge and love to mankind ...
According to Theosophists the four Masters of the World, who are Venusians,
live in Chamballah (the Gobi Desert) in the Jade Palace.

This is neo-Theosophy: its nineteenth-century origination is all too
apparent. Daniken is much too sure-footed to cite Venus as the origin for
his astronauts, he avoids the talismanic appeal that the second planet has
for occult speculation. Thus both Drake and Charroux fail to realize the
potential of their thesis to present a uniquely twentieth-century technological cosmology that is as thrusting and assertive in its own way as
was Blavatsky's Theosophy in its day. Honour for that achievement
goes unequivocally to Daniken, whose thoroughgoing Techno-Occultism
hides its roots and, laced with wit, satire, absurdity and abrasive
certainty, focuses entirely on the potential of an unfettered technology in
the contemporary age for a unique addition to the variants of occult
speculation and the presentations of the Hero-Lucifer.

THE POLITICO-SOCIAL CONTEXT

Other factors, divorced from textual analysis, need also to be carefully
considered, particularly in America, for such a popularity as was achieved
by Daniken cannot be explained by purely internal and comparative
considerations of text. Clearly Daniken's works must have both tripped
off and responded to powerful resonances in Western society at large,
and in American society – with its 13,000,000 sales – in particular. It is in
considering some of the major social and cultural features of America in
the late sixties that we find not only clues as to Daniken's popularity, but
also to the all-important switch from a pessimistic to an optimistic
perception of technology as discussed above. This switch from pessimism
to optimism is an important feature in distinguishing Daniken's works
from the inspiration for the majority of Techno-Occultistic texts.

It was argued in Chapter Three that the developing space race, with the
achievement of the American moon-rocket programme, had the effect of
endorsing certain variants of flying saucer advocacy, producing a dual
reaction within the cult; promoting on the one hand an extra-galactic
interpretation of flying saucers that involved exo-biology and an appropriation of flying saucers by the scientific establishment; and on the other
hand a strong reaction against such an appropriation and the intrusion of
such Romantic-Occult concepts as Keel's Mothman.

With Daniken, however, the relation of his works to the moon
programme is quite different and not at all complex; the NASA programme and its successful realization is enthusiastically endorsed, since

that programme promoted his exegesis. Both projects, that of NASA and of Daniken, were reciprocally supportive. 'Danikenitis', such as swept America in the late sixties and early seventies, undoubtedly helped NASA in its budgetary claims upon the American taxpayer, and it is no exaggeration to say that Daniken and NASA enjoyed a symbiotic relationship, certainly for the six years or so after 1968.

Before the significance of this symbiosis can be appreciated it is necessary to chart the radical change in the public perception of rocket technology between the first Sputnik in 1957 and the confident assumption of success in the race to the moon, by about 1967. During that decade the American public's perception of rocket technology switched from one grounded in traumatic pessimism to one grounded in unguarded optimism.

At various points in the history of modern society a particular technology and its achievements becomes separated out from the presentation of technology as a complex manifold with diverse and intermingling values. Such a separated technology carries with it an aura of presented connotations, as relating to humanity, society, the future, and other politically useful generalizations, to such an extent that one may speak of it as having a hegemony over the media-promulgated perceptions of the significant present and the meaningful future. The achievement of atomic weaponry, for instance, led to that technology becoming separated from technology in general and being extolled as the defining technology of the time. The atomic age – not 'nuclear physics' but 'atomic science' and 'atomic scientists', were the agencies for determining the future, be it through the destructive features of the bomb which would 'stir history to its deepest depths' in the language of the *New York Herald Tribune* for 7 August 1945, or in the plausibly constructive aim of 'harnessing the atom for peace', to produce electricity for the national grid. Nevertheless, in spite of the nuclear power programmes, atomic science carried an essentially pessimistic aura of connotations. This was due in part to media manipulation which, paradoxically, at the same time as it underplayed many of the dangers of an atomic explosion, radiation in particular, and by popularizing the notorious 'duck and cover' exercises as a practical rough-and-ready personal defence, yet played up to America's vulnerability to a sudden atomic strike. Thus the American media helped to fashion the pessimistic perceptions of atomic science whose threat was both universal and individual, 'No one is safe but some can be saved'.

With the new and inescapable evidence of the successful launch and orbit of the first artificial satellite in October 1957 by the USSR, a new technology becomes separated out, gradually displacing atomic science and the 'atomic age' from its hegemonic position. Newspaper headlines that carried the news of the Sputnik indicate the trauma of the event to American self-esteem, and also the totally pessimistic perceptions which attached to rocket science from the outset. 'The work of self preservation is at hand' and 'America's technological Pearl Harbor', proclaimed *The Evening Star*, equating the Russian success with an act of aggression, a tone also found in the *Chicago Daily News's* sub-headline, 'How Russ "Moon" will affect us', and 'Scientists cite loss of face'; while the *Boston Daily Globe* trumpeted, 'Red Moon flies at 18,000 miles per hour'.

In his account of the history of the moon programme, *The Right Stuff*, Tom Wolfe argues that

> It would be hard to realize that Sputnik ... would strike terror in the heart of the west.
>
> After two weeks, however, the situation was obvious: a colossal panic was underway with congressmen and newspaper men leading a huge pack.
>
> From a purely strategic standpoint, the fact that the Soviets had the rocket power to launch Sputnik 1 meant that they now also had the capacity to deliver the bomb on an intercontinental ballistic missile. The panic reached far beyond the relatively sane concern for tactical weaponry.
>
> Nothing less than control of the heavens was at stake. It was Armageddon, the final and decisive battle of the forces of good and evil. Lyndon Johnson, who was the Senate majority leader, said that whoever controls 'the high ground' of space would control the world. (Tom Wolfe 1981, p. 57)

adding

> The *New York Times*, in an editorial, said the United States was now in a 'race for survival'. The panic became more and more apocalyptic. Nothing short of doom awaited the loser, now the battle had begun. When the Soviets shot a Sputnik called Mechta into a heliocentric orbit, the House Select Committee on Astronautics ... said that the United States faced the prospect of 'national extinction' if it did not catch up with the Soviet space program. 'It cannot be over emphasised that the survival of the free world – indeed, all the world – is caught up in the stakes'. (Tom Wolfe 1981, p. 58)

Missile technology, now become rocket or space technology, is the vehicle system for the nuclear weapon and therefore inevitably partakes of the aura of destructive, threatening and pessimistic connotations that have centred on the popular and public perceptions of atomic science.

Within a decade all was to change. The 'atomic age', for all its monumental significance in the official scheme of things, gave way to the 'space age', and the technology of rockets and satellites was to reign as the hegemonic technology, giving the language its own value-heightened vocabulary: 'lift-off', 'mission control', 'module', and carryng its own quite different aura of connotations. Instead of Einstein's 'general annihilation beckons', it was now 'everything is A-Okay' as the bland neutrality of space provided a magnificent backcloth for the achievements of American technology. The optimistic connotations of rocket science were given specific sanction with Kennedy's speech made after Shepherd's Mercury flight, just three weeks after Gagarin's more spectacular first.

Referring to Shepherd's brief space flight, Kennedy proclaimed, 'We have shown by the fact of Astronaut Shepherd's flight . . . that space is open to us now', and added, in terms suggestive of Star Trek, 'We go into space because whatever mankind undertakes, free men must fully share'.

Thus by 1961, with the presidential seal of approval, space had become politicized, and success in space had become a significant theme in American policy. Rocket science had become the hegemonic technology and so long as the NASA programme was being successfully realized, everything was 'A-Okay'. The aura of connotation is optimistic: the challenge is taken up, the plan will be achieved.

The impact of achieving hegemonic status upon a technology may have a deleterious effect upon the inner dynamics of that technology. American engineers and pilots had been developing and testing ever more sophisticated versions of manned rocket planes, achieving speeds and heights that made man-controlled space flight a distinct possibility: yet within a few months of the Russian Sputnik successes, and with Kennedy's avowed aim of realizing a moon-rocket programme, the complex, advanced technology of the Bell series of rocket planes was relegated in the race to provide a relatively crude vehicle that was not controlled by humans. The astronauts were preceded by dogs and chimpanzees. The astronauts were simply 'riding the can' and they played a relatively passive role compared to the test pilots of the rocket-plane project. Such developments and changes of emphasis illustrate that the promotion of a technology to hegemonic status is a real condition. The result is that internal and technical decisions can become immediately subservient to considerations arising out of the aura of connotation and perception attached to a hegemonic technology and which leads to policy change at the most fundamental level.

Ironically, in the age of the micro-chip, with the monumental space age having proved as brief in duration as the atomic age, America has returned to the development of piloted re-entry vehicles that it abandoned back in the sixties, though it now matters not, rocket science is no longer a hegemonic technology. At the time of writing computer science holds that honour and it is Silicon Valley, not Cape Canaveral that grabs the headlines.

The switch of rocket science from a pessimistic to an optimistic aura of connotations did not go unaided; contemporary political developments greatly facilitated the switch. During the summer of 1963 Kennedy had announced on television that a nuclear test ban agreement with the Russians had been reached. Andrei Gromyko, the Soviet Foreign Minister, had proposed a ban on placing nuclear weapons in satellites in earth orbit. Then on 30 August the 'hotline', the telephone link between the White House and the Kremlin, was established. Such developments and the progressive détente of the following years not only reduced the perceived nuclear threat but helped to demote atomic science and at the same time promote the new rocket science in its increasingly optimistic aura. As Wolfe comments, 'When Kennedy was assassinated on 22 November by a man with Russian and Cuban ties, there was no anti-Soviet or anti-Cuban clamour in the Congress or in the press. The Cold War, as anyone could plainly see, was over' (1981, p. 366).

But crucial to an understanding of the popularity of Daniken's works is the realization that rocket science achieved its hegemonic status and its optimistic aura at a time when public doubt, uncertainty and division in American society became ever more marked. Indeed, the very apogee of rocket science, the successful moon landings, occurred at the very time when it appeared that American society was on the verge of breakdown, such that commentators have spoken of 'times in 1968 when it looked as though social tensions and conflicts of the 1960s had reached a pitch of such intensity that the very fabric of American society was threatened' (Snowman 1980, p. 178).

The crucial years 1968 and 1969, rather than appearing as a climacteric to a decade of dissent and agitation in the 'Great Society', appeared to provide a decisive step towards anarchy and complete social breakdown, at least to many commentators of the time. At the end of March 1968, Lyndon Johnson concluded a television address to the nation on the Vietnam War with the announcement that he did not intend to seek re-election as president in the following November. Snowman comments that 'The America whose presidency L.B.J. was so relieved to hand on to another was torn by severe social and political cleavages and by outbreaks of individual and communal violence unparalleled for a century' (1980, p. 177).

Reading the back numbers of popular photo-journals such as *Life* and *Look* reveals the degree to which social unrest and violence could be balanced by the progressive and aseptic certainties of NASA's moon programme. In issue after issue the polarity of social confusion and pessimism with technical optimism is presented to the reader. *Life* for 29 April 1968, the issue covering the assassination of Martin Luther King, records how 'In city after city: Washington, Baltimore, Chicago, Pittsburgh, Cincinnati, Kansas City, the violence that followed the shooting of Martin Luther King brought huge damage . . . 39 people died'. The same issue quotes Episcopal Bishop C. Kilmer Myers as saying of the assassination, 'I am ashamed . . . henceforth let us not speak about the black problem, let us speak about the white problem', and the selfsame issue carried an extensive photo-feature of Kubrick's new film, *2001*.

Already by April 1968, Jane Fonda in *Barbarella* could be said to have established a space chic, though that film fostered the mixture of science fantasy and sado-masochistic eroticism that derives from the covers, rather than the contents, of earlier science fiction magazines. Kubrick's

2001 however was to be taken more seriously, 'A mind boggling new movie', proclaimed *Life*. Discussing the famed monoliths that feature in the film, the article continues with, 'They have Godlike powers. They are forces for evolution. They are cosmic calling cards of some superior intelligence'. The article continues with, 'one kind of non-biological being may be an advanced computer, a non-stop thinking machine'.

Such notions are consonant with central elements in Daniken's Techno-Occultism, a circumstance that in itself helped to promote his first texts, since Kubrick's involuted fable was itself enormously popular in Europe and America. The *Life* article pointed out that 'Kubrick wanted the story to take place within the lifetime of most of today's moviegoers', hence the title, *2001*, a circumstance that indicates the progressive and confident assumptions being made as to the American moon programme.

Continuing with the survey of 1968 numbers of *Life*, the issue of 10 June spoke of 'A new American tragedy: The death of Robert Kennedy'. The issue for 19 August carried a feature article on Governor Wallace which quotes him as saying 'Bam Bam Bam. Shoot 'em dead on the spot . . . I'd drag 'em by the hair of their heads, college students raising money for the Vietcong and I'd throw them under (*sic*) a jail'. The article continues, arguing that Wallace 'appeals to people of various economic levels who are fearful of "what's happening to this country" and who are apprehensive of their own ability to "do something about it"'.

The final number for 1968 carried a feature entitled 'America in 1968: The Bright And Dark Perception'. Its author, Max Ways, speaks of 'the US . . . drifting amidst external and internal dangers, or worse . . . controlled by morally destructive forces'. Ways claims that in a 'consensus of anxiety . . . a great many Americans are prepared to believe the worst about the basic character and trend of US society', adding that the 'Dark Perception . . . contains all the elements for a scenario of revolution'.

Against such a background the NASA programme stood in stark contrast. The issue for 20 January 1969 shows colour pictures from the Apollo VIII mission. The feature is entitled 'Man at the Moon', and following issues featured several such articles on the moon programme in which the white (racially and literally in terms of colour) technology of the NASA space apparatus is set against a velvety black space, inspiring a new brand of kitsch in captions such as 'The moon voyagers and the earthly beauty that beckons them back'. So intoned the issue for 17 March, which in earlier pages had spoken in its editorial of 'Liberating the campus from the liberators'. Throughout the whole of 1969 the prominent themes that get repeated coverage are alternatively social upheaval, 'Student dissent and racial tension have now enveloped one of the most cherished of all US institutions – the public school system', as given in the 26 May issue; or the space programme, 'The great adventure of Apollo X

... 80 million earthlings watched their world shrink', as given in the 9 June issue.

Inevitably the apotheosis of July 1969 brought a special issue 'Off To The Moon', with the anodyne poetry of James Dickey and family 'pics' of the astronaut crew. The public images of the astronauts and their families as average, folksy, homespun Americans conveniently avoided urban humanity and the upheavals of the cities.

So it was that by 1968–9, not only had NASA's space technology become the hegemonic technology, but its aura contained positive, progressive, heroic and optimistic perceptions. Further, the glossy-paged illustrations carried a potent sub-text, with the white penetrative rocketry, modules and probes being set, defined and precise against the amorphous, anonymous blackness of space. The polarities of black and white (with no shades and little other colour), of positive and negative, of defined aim and boundlessness, reaffirmed a male white domination, in an area beyond reach or doubt – it was on television for all to see. What a contrast with the appalling dangers of identity-loss, of loss of knowledge, in either the black emptiness of space or social collapse.

Atomic science had produced villains such as the 'Judas Fuchs'; rocket technology produced homespun American heroes, all too ready to voice American virtues to a fascinated public. Yet there were alternative readings to the space programme, and as with atomic science in the fifties, rocket science in the sixties came to be presented within its own mythology. But whereas the bomb came to be presented in 'A consensus language ... in terms of religious awe and invoking simultaneously the forces of life and death' (Chilton 1982, p. 98), the space technology of the late sixties was to find its mythologue in Norman Mailer.

His semi-official account of the moon programme, *A Fire on the Moon*, written for serialization in *Life* and published in book form in 1970, mythologized the NASA programme. For, in what he describes as 'the most soul destroying and apocalyptic of centuries', man was setting out from a world, 'half convinced of the future death of our species, yet half aroused by the apocalyptic notion that an exceptional future still lay with us' to 'Look for God ... or to destroy him'.

It is Wernher von Braun, the 'deus ex machina of the big boosters', the 'real engineer, the spiritual leader ... the inventor, the force, the philosopher, the genius of America's Space Program' (p. 63), who has created 'Saturn 5 ... Lucifer or the Archangel ... a furnace, a chariot of fire' (p. 63). Von Braun is later cited as claiming for the moon programme, 'I think it is equal in importance to that moment in evolution when aquatic life came crawling up on the land' (p. 70); a statement that could have come straight from the pages of Daniken.

Throughout *A Fire on the Moon* Mailer sustains a religious and apoca-lyptic imagery. 'Two mighty torches of flame', he writes, describing the rocket launch, and gives 'white as the white of Melville's Moby Dick, white as the shrine of the Madonna in half the churches of the world, this slim, angelic, mysterious ship of stages' (p. 94), and the week after the launch, when the module is speeding towards the moon, is described as 'the greatest week since Christ was born' (p. 105).

Given the above circumstances and such a depiction of space science, the symbiotic relationship between the NASA programme and the Daniken oeuvre becomes quite clear. Daniken's depiction of the future is for man (sic) to succeed to the 'brotherhood of the stars' through an unfettered technological advance. The NASA moon programme is to be but the first step towards securing that future. Daniken's programme is active and optimistic, at a time when Western societies were being confronted with profound contradictions, radical change and the loss of unquestioned assumptions. Daniken's programme means that man (sic) is not passively at the mercy of sudden global catastrophe, qua Velikovsky; neither is he the passive object of scrutiny by alien spacecraft – significantly there is barely a mention of flying saucers in Daniken's works, though the natural fusion of Ancient and Current Extra-terrestrialism would seem to be an obvious ploy. The NASA programme is also confident and optimistic, turning its back on the troubled world, literally and metaphorically. It is a programme that is loaded with positive perceptions of control, conquest and domination at a time when society is subjected to upheaval and self-doubt. Even the physical act of techno-logical man escaping the conflicting uncertainties, the turmoil of the real world into the enduring, albeit harsh, certainties of space, as an emancipatory act, has its analogue in Daniken's total rejection of past scholarship in order to inhabit the future offered by his own techno-gnosis.

In the foregoing account of the extra-textual reasons for the popularity of Daniken's works the analysis has focused upon the American market. Clearly the perception of social collapse does not apply when considering the extra-textual appeal in the European market. On the other hand, the NASA propaganda was bruited throughout the world and the European audiences for the space spectaculars were numbered in millions. The appeal of the space-rocket technology as a hegemonic system and its close, often conscious, association with the Daniken theory meant that its appeal was not limited to national boundaries, and in Europe as in America the 'race to the moon' engendered interest in the Daniken oeuvre.

6

READERSHIP AND CONTINUITY OF APPEAL

The previous chapters have concentrated upon giving a text-based analysis of the key variants of Techno-Occultism, indicating some of the cultural presentations and appropriations such texts offer. That analysis has demonstrated that, in spite of thematic differences, Techno-Occultism constitutes a definite genre of popular literature whose success has been sustained for almost half a century. The problem that has not yet been addressed is that of identifyng the readership of the genre.

In the case of Theosophy, in Chapter One, the identification of readership presents relatively few problems. Memoirs, commentaries and some, albeit limited, statistics enable the historian to make a reasonable deduction as to the support that Theosophy won, as a belief system or as a functioning society. With Techno-Occultism the situation is clearly more complex.

The success of Techno-Occultism throughout Europe and America since the mid-forties encompasses enormous social and cultural change, and clearly the readership of the 1950s, if it could be socially identified, may not correspond with the readership of the 1980s. In any case it would be simplistic in the extreme, given the volume of sales figures accrued by numerous texts, to assume that a neat identification of the 'average reader' would be possible. Nevertheless, the question of readership cannot be ignored, if only because of its constantly pertinent complexity. It is important to ask who reads the texts when they are not producing bestseller sales figures. What is the appeal of Velikovsky's texts when they are reissued in paperback in the 1970s, when the original, external factors that had supported their sale in the 1950s no longer applied? What is the readership that takes von Daniken off the library shelves with such frequency when the 'space race' is no longer prominent in media presentations?

The question of readership is therefore the question of residual readership. The problem of the appeal of the genre is the problem of the continuity of appeal.

The analysis offered in this chapter will fall into two parts. To consider the reader appeal of the genre at the time of its first emergence in America in the 1950s; and then to look at those factors which provide a continuity of appeal up to the present time.

POST-WAR AMERICA AND THE LOGISTICS OF VICTORY

Post-war America provides us with its own starting point, for it was among the social commentators of those years that a certain perception gained a general-acknowledgement. It was that the nature of American society had undergone a fundamental change and that the change was itself rooted in America's experience of the war years.

There is clear and well-documented evidence that the Second World War produced perceived changes in class stratification and problems of class identity. The ending of hostilities in 1945 and the subsequent demobilization of American forces presented unique and enormous problems for the American economy. Jack Stokes Ballard in *The Shock of Peace, Military and Economic Demobilization after World War Two* has detailed the attendant problems of demobilization. He writes that

> Early in World War II there was serious concern for the post war years . . . It seemed obvious to the astute economic observer and the general public alike that a severe dislocation of America's industrial system could take place. What would happen . . . when millions of discharged servicemen flooded the labour market just at the same time that millions of war workers were displaced from factories with cancelled war contracts? (J.S. Ballard 1983, p. 15).

Ballard gives various war-period estimates for post-war unemployed, with figures reaching as high as 19 million. Demobilization when it came, at a rate of 17,000 per day, brought the situation that by 1946 well over 8 million men and women had been discharged from the armed services (pp. 16, 17 and 18).

Conversely the manufacturing industry had enormously expanded as a result of the war effort and the attendant demand for war material. Ballard describes how the aircraft, shipbuilding and munitions industries that collectively employed only 0.7 million in 1939 had, by the wartime peak, employed some 5.6 million, and how the aircraft industry alone had expanded some twenty-fold in its labour force between January 1940 and December 1943 (p. 124). The index of manufacturing production reveals the enormity of the change. With the index for 1947 being 100, the figure for 1938 stands at a mere 46!

John Brookes, in *The Great Leap: 25 Years Of Change: The U.S.A. And Ourselves. 1940–1965*, a title that in itself is illustrative of the perception of radical social change wrought by the war and its aftermath, comments that

> Gross national product more than doubled between 1940 and 1945, while the cost of government and government enterprises was more than quadrupling. But what would happen to the economy when the war ended, removing the need for war production and thus taking the props from under the artificial boom? Industrial managers and academic economists were, for once in agreement: both groups expected a collapse. (J. Brookes 1967, p. 47)

Such global figures mask particular social factors in employment growth, factors that added a further note of dissonance to the immediate post-war problems. The growth of both manufacturing industry and the armed forces had seen the incorporation of previously excluded racial minorities into what had been once exclusively white enclaves.[1]

The situation then was that the end to hostilities required enormous readjustment of the American economy – its manufacturing industry in particular – and of the individual worker or demobilized soldier, and Ballard concludes that

> The vast preparation and planning for the post World War II period, the frenzied discharging of over 8 million servicemen and the large scale readjustment made all previous demobilizations look minute in comparison. The sheer magnitude of all aspects of the war to peace transition seriously challenged the nation. (Ballard 1983, p. 193)

The circumstances of such a transition bear closer examination. The Second World War had, more than any previous war, been decided by the quantity and/or quality of technological means; not just in armaments but also in the supply of essential back-up services merely to transport the vast quantities of men and material to and from the widely dispersed battlefronts. To be always 'The firstest with the mostest', was seen as the key to victory. Hence, as a general position, it can be said that both discharged industrial workers and soldiers were techno-literate. They could use the tools of production, transportation and battle, while their skill and number in producing and using such means had decided the eventual outcome of the war. It was the often but recently acquired techno-literate qualities of the American industrial worker and member of the armed forces that had proved the final arbiter in the Second World War.

The American forces had a higher rate of support troops to combat troops than any other of the combatant armies. The American forces also had logistical problems that dwarfed those of all the other belligerents.

Hence, perhaps inevitably, the American soldier, sailor and airman, as also the civilian, became bureaucratized. Neil Wynn, in an essay 'World War II And The Afro-Americans' speaks of 'the proliferation of government agencies that occurred during the 1940s', citing such examples as: The War Manpower Commission, Office of War Mobilization, Office of War Information, Office of Scientific Research and Development, Office of Defense Transportation, Office of Censorship, Office of Civilian Defense. Wynn concludes that 'practically every aspect of life in America was subject to government intervention' (p. 48). Ballard also draws broadly similar conclusions; when talking about manufacturing industries as a whole, he states that 'All this expansion of production facilities and employment was accompanied by an extensive government control structure' (Ballard 1983, p. 124).

The situation then is that in 1945 there were in America millions of men, most of whom can be described as being techno-literate and familiar with new forms of bureaucratic organization or dispensation, with their lives and/or those of their families being to some extent controlled or regulated by the new bureaucratic bodies. These men faced the manifest uncertainties of peace, having only recently experienced the stability, achievement-goals and hierarchies of war and wartime production, in which their every effort had been extolled throughout the media as being virtuous and leading to victory.

The problems posed by the ending of hostilities, great as they were, were solved in the long term by switching from production of war material to production of new consumer goods. As Brookes put it:

> The wartime props were summarily removed all right – from the wartime peak of almost $1000 billion in 1944 and 1945, government expenditures dropped off to only $33 billion in 1948 – but so great was the public's appetite for automobiles and other items of consumer goods of which it had been deprived all through the war that the total output of the economy hardly dropped at all. (Brookes 1967, p. 47)

Ballard instances that General Motors planned for a total annual production of 2.8–3.4 million units, and how this represented a 25–50 per cent increase over the record number of 2,260,000 units in 1941 (Ballard 1983, p. 19).

But the growth of the 'car-owning democracy', which was achieved by proliferation and expansion of the consumer industries, was facilitated by those industries adopting the goals and aims of the war industries, and also by adapting the administrative and managerial constructs of the war years, to sustain the newly techno-literate workforce and to reach the demand schedules imposed by an expanding consumer economy. During the war years workers experienced 'a degree of conformism and individual anonymity ... the factory worker submerged his personal ambitions and made his first priority winning the war' (D. Snowman 1980, p. 114), and during the post-war years workers witnessed the complete assumption of wartime slogans of 'getting on with the job', of 'winning the war', within the bland absorption of techno-bureaucratic values imposed by management, only now to produce 'soft' consumer goods and services instead of 'hard' war material, as they laboured to meet urgent production demands.

The impact of such developments upon a society can to a certain extent be measured in statistics: of gross output of specified industries, of graphs of employees in government service, in charts of capital investment per annum, but the present interest is to view the way such developments participated in changing the perceptions of society, to changing 'the structure of feeling'.

THE STRUCTURE OF FEELING

In chapter 2 of *The Long Revolution* Raymond Williams introduced the concept of 'the structure of feeling', of which he wrote, 'In one sense this structure of feeling is the culture of a period: it is the particular living result of all elements in the general organization . . . it is a very deep and very wide possession in all actual communities precisely because it is on it that communication depends'.

The opening section of this chapter has argued that war production and modes and bureaucratic structures were carried over into the post-war years, and that thereby fundamental changes took place within, initially American, and latterly European societies; socio-economic changes, so fundamental as to affect the life style, work and expectation patterns of the majority of those populations. As a consequence of such large-scale social change there will emerge within, for instance, post-war American society, a new structure of feeling: 'For here most distinctly, the changing organization is enacted within the organism' (R. Williams 1984, p. 65).

The structure of feeling will be represented in any cultural expression of the period, 'it operates in the most delicate and least tangible parts of our activity' (p. 65), but certain cultural expressions will more easily yield the main configurations of the new structure of feeling. For instance if we have, as we do, a new genre of literature that functions as a popular culture and that presents, as its conceptual objects, entities that have no historical dimension, for example flying saucers, then that genre could be expected to more readily yield the structure of feeling than, for instance, a traditional genre of popular literature, such as romantic or historical fiction. Techno-Occultism should therefore readily reveal something of the structure of feeling, and if we concentrate on the generation of 1950–70, the texts published within these years in America – the Velikovsky books, the majority of saucer titles and the early Daniken titles – should, if considered as a totality, delineate an American structure of feeling with ample connections and responses between the domain of the texts and the popular perceptions of the period.

But there is another genre that will also readily reveal the structure of feeling – the works of contemporary American sociology. It is to some of the popular and indeed seminal texts of American social science, one of the 'more tangible parts of our activity' that we can turn to discover the structure of feeling of those years in clear and sharp detail.

Contemporary texts of indigenous American social commentary, though differing in their methods and analysis, accept in the main a common premiss – that their contemporary society was novel and made a fundamental break with the past, as represented by traditional belief, perception and social activity. 'In what period have so many men been so totally exposed at so fast a pace to such earthquakes of change?' demanded C. Wright Mills in his opening chapter to *The Sociological Imagination* (1959, p. 4). He continued in the following paragraph with 'Even when they do not panic, men often sense that older ways of feeling and thinking have collapsed and that newer beginnings are ambiguous to the point of moral stasis. Is it any wonder that ordinary men feel that they cannot cope with the larger worlds with which they are so suddenly confronted?' (p. 4). Clearly the change is so profound that even feeling, the most basic of human activity, is changed. Further, the emphasis on **men** (rather than men and women) is significant, and so too the category 'ordinary men', as distinct from average men. The connotations are quite different.

John Brookes, in a text already cited, *The Great Leap; 25 Years of Change*, opens with a socio-economic description of America in 1939 and then comments that, 'If the country thus described now seems rather bleak, frugal, sparse, quaint and faraway, it may seem even stranger when one knows that the year was 1939' (p. 10), and continues to offer evidence for the thesis of a social saltus.

> But sober historians and scholars have joined enthusiastic journalists in making the point. 'The gulf separating 1965 from 1943 is as deep as the gulf that separated the builders of cities from Stone Age men', writes cultural anthropologist Margaret Mead. 'The date that divides human history into two equal parts is well within living memory', writes Kenneth Boulding. . . . And in 1962 the members of the American Historical Association listened to a paper delivered by their president Carl Bridenhaugh, in which he called into question the very relevance of past history to contemporary events, so drastic did he consider what he called 'the great mutation' of this century. (Brookes 1967, p. 14)

_____

171

The novelty of this new society lay largely in the perceived role of tecnological innovation, how it was applied to the economy, changing work and life patterns. Social thinkers concurred that technological advancement and the attendant socio-economic changes were a conditioning factor that determined their present and their prognosis of future society. Not surprisingly, they appropriated the organizational prestige of technology as they adopted a quasi-technological jargon to identify those elements in the new society that set it in contradistinction to previous societies. Thus Victor Ferkiss in *Technological Man: The Myth and the Reality*, summarizing the work of earlier sociologists, offered

> Some of the sociological prophets have devised their own names for the new society. Ellul calls it 'technological society'. For Marshall McLuhan the 'mechanized' evironment of the industrial age has been replaced by the 'totally new environment' of the 'electronic age'. Bertam Gross talks of the 'mobiletic revolution'. Brzezinski writes of the 'technetronic era'. . . . Others eschew such neat or provocative labels and simply speak of . . . vast changes that will take place in 'the next generation', 'tomorrow' or by the 'year 2000'.   (Ferkiss 1969, p. 78)

Such a list does not exhaust variants or proponents.

A further tendency of social thought was to present the new society as if it were a simple unitary structure, subject to social dynamics *in toto*. 'Where does this society stand in human history? What are the mechanics by which it is changing? What is its place within and its meaning for the development of humanity as a whole?' asks C. Wright Mills (1959, p. 6). Society is presented as a uniform entity; there are no interstices and it is a technical metaphor that is summoned to account for its change. Again it is a society that, via the first question, stands in contrast to all previous societies. This tendency is found in the sociologists of culture whose prevailing pessimism was founded upon the nation of 'mass society' and where great emphasis is given to the manipulative functions of the mass media, and of radio and television in particular. Thus in compilatory texts such as *Culture for the Millions? Mass Media in Modern Society* (1961) the persistent emphasis is upon a homogeneous view of society, functioning as a passive unity, consuming (*sic*) the 'mass culture' offered by the electronic media.

Clearly such a depicted society must be, to a large extent, class-amorhpic, and sociologists of the period acknowledged such a feature as they argued for new groupings and class shifts within the new society. Thus William H. Whyte opens his classic social text of the period, *The Organisation Man*, with: 'This book is about the organisation man. If the term is vague, it is because I can think of no other way to describe the people I am talking about. They are not workers, nor are they white collar workers in the usual, clerk sense of the word. These people not only work

for The Organisation. The ones I am talking about *belong* to it as wll.'
Packard, also writing in the late fifties, viewing the continuing expansion
of consumer industries, wrote of technological progress that it had

> opened up many opportunities at the white-collar and technical level. The
> demand for technicians to manage complex machines and the professionals
> had risen more sensationally than that of any other type of personnel. There
> had been a tremendous expansion in the industries that service products such
> as TV repair and auto repair. (V. Packard 1963, p. 256)

Contemporary social commentators were aware that the new society as
presented was class-amorphic, and so they struggled to define new
heirarchies. Vance Packard again, in *The Status Seekers*, speaks of a
division between 'The Diploma Elite' and 'The Supporting Classes', the
highest strata of the latter being rather tellingly labelled as 'The Limited
Success Classes', of whom he writes that

> Its members place great store in demonstrating that they are respectable,
> proper cultured and socially above the working masses ... To pursue the
> military parallel, they are the non-commissioned officers of our new society.
>
> Virtually all its members have high school diplomas ... training in technical
> schools, two-year colleges or secretarial schools.
>
> In offices, they are clerks ... on main street they are the clerks in the quality
> store, or the small shopkeepers or the smaller contractors. In industry they are
> the foremen, technical aides – a spectacularly expanding group – and skilled
> craftsmen.
>
> In short they include the lower ranks of the genuinely white collar world and
> the upper ranks of the blue collar world ... Both groups are success minded.
> (V. Packard 1963, p. 44)[2]

Depicted as being success-minded, seeking upward mobility, with limited
training, usually in technology-based trades, this new social category
troubled social commentators. We have already seen Whyte's admission
'If the term is vague, it is because I can think of no other way to describe
the people I am talking about'. The problem lay in the circumstance that
the new society with its 'ad-mass' was portrayed as representing such a
break with the past, and as being to a certain extent class-amorphic that
the new hierarchies did not appear to have a meaningful class history.
The bitter labour disputes of the inter-war years were not perceived as
contributing to the aims and attitudes of Packard's 'Limited Success
Class', whose essence was its newness, whose future was seen to be more
determining than its past.

David Riesman writing in 1950, whose book, *The Lonely Crowd*, was at
once a work of sociological scholarship and a bestseller, had as its central
thesis the argument that a new character type had emerged, the 'other-
directed' man, whose main characteristics were an easy-going, likeable
personality, someone who took his cues from his immediate social group

and from the celebrities of the mass media. He changed his values as others changed theirs, his only deep compulsion being to give 'close attention to the signals from others' (D. Riesman 1950, p. 21). Here is an archetype for the 'ad-mass', a relative existence, denied tradition, the vestigial remnants of class culture or ritual having no meaning. Life is only made real by spending, and the prominent social dynamic for such a person is to claim the future delineated by his consumer potential.

Such consumer-workers were to be driven by the rhetoric and style of wartime production, to achieve production-consumption levels that would maintain the regimented uniformity of urban life and guarantee the success of the new way of life. The civilian worker was perceived as having being militarized to fight the surrogate war of increasing consumer demand that now underpinned the American economy.

C. Wright Mills in *White Collar* (1951, p. 235) observed that

> The overall formula of advice that the new ideology of 'human relations in business' contains runs to this effect: to make the workers happy, efficient and co-operative, you must make the managers intelligent, rational, knowledge-able. It is the perspective of a managerial elite, disguised in the pseudo-objective language of engineers.

Against the class-amorphism of, 'In every major area of life, the loss of a sense of structure and the submergence into a powerless milieu is the cardinal fact' (1981, p. 321), C. Wright Mills portrayed the loss of self-identity as being traded for the security of consumer conformity as designated by advertisers' iconography of materialism. Mills offered a critique of the destructive impact of consumerism upon the individual self with 'The media tell the man in the mass who he is – they give him identity' and 'They tell him what he wants to be – they give him aspirations and he continues, giving a four-part litany of how the media shape the very nature of individual existence' (1981, p. 314).

To summarize, then, a review of the more popular works of indigenous American social commentary of the fifties and sixties yields an aggregated perspective that must partake of the structure of feeling. It is of a 'new' society, one that will expand to become a global society, one that can be rendered explicable by technological metaphor. Within this society, old class structures are said to have become so diffuse as to be meaningless, the 'new' society is presented as class-amorphic, thus the traditions and divisions of the past have little value. On the other hand there emerges a different type of 'man', and the masculine gender is curiously stressed even by the standards of the time (after all the media and advertising addressed much of their output specifically at women). The new man is techno-literate, bureaucracy-dependent and seeking upward mobility. His (*sic*) life values are seen to be relative, his (*sic*) culture is passively received through the electronic media and his (*sic*) future is made more real than his past, the future being clearly delineated by the perceived technological innovations of progressive consumerism.

There are clearly several areas of consonance here with what Techno-Occultism yields. That genre too offers the prospect of a decisive saltus, brought about by atomic and missile technology (Adamski, Keyhoe). Its products, cataclysm or flying saucer or ancient astronaut, speak to a global society. That is not to say to all humanity but rather to a techno-literate male humanity, living and working in a consumer society – a humanity that is agnostic in its religious views. It too deals in technical artefacts and offers in the flying saucer the technical artefact that is always just beyond the horizon of the technically realizable but within the future of the technically feasible. Here too we find the technical metaphors and terms that were so necessary and prevalent to the social commentators.[3] Here again we find the depiction of the 'limited success class' as the witnesses of saucer events. Examples from the Keyhoe texts have already been cited, but a further and later depiction is offered by John Keel in *Visitors from Space*, when he writes that 'The neat modern homes of the valley boasted more than their share of colour television sets and late model cars. The people are not hillbillies but, for the most part, are skilled technicians employed in the many factories; well educated, well paid Americans leading quiet, average lives' (J. Keel 1976, p. 76), a description that could be a footnote for Whyte's, Mills's or Packard's analyses.

It is such a strong consonance of shared or adjacent perceptions that will serve to indicate the generalized areas of readership for the new genre.

READERSHIP

If it is Packard's 'limited success class' that provides the mass readership of Techno-Occultism, a group that has always been depicted as class-amorphic and having its domain defined by techno-bureaucratic organizations, the question remains as to what values this readership derived from the new genre. What connections were made?

Here we must step beyond the confident assumptions made by the social commentators of the fifties and sixties as to the homogeneous nature of the 'ad-mass' and the monodirectional nature of its culture. Barbara Ehrenreich has already amply demonstrated that within the bland neutrality of the male 'ad-mass' there were severe sexual-social pressures upon the individual. Her *The Hearts of Men* demonstrates how there were severe pressures that demanded total conformity to a sexual norm largely dictated by consumerist expectations. She writes that 'Marriage – and with that, the breadwinner role – was the only normal state for the adult male. Outside lay a range of diagnoses, all unflattering' (1983, p. 15). According to Ehrenreich, any man who rejected such a role was simply labelled immature, and she comments that

> In the scheme of male pathology developed by the mid-century psychologists, immaturity shaded into infantilism, which was in turn a manifestation of unnatural fixation on the mother; and the entire complex of symptomatology reached its clinical climax in the diagnosis of homosexuality. (Ehrenreich 1983, p. 20)

These sexual-social pressures are found mirrored in the 'stag' magazines of America of the fifties and sixties. Magazines such as *Man's Adventure* and *Wildcat Adventure*, which offered a mélange of bathing beauties and stories that almost invariably featured Nazi or 'Red' brutes, jack-booted and wielding whips, upon chained young ladies in conveniently ripped dresses, while the lean American hero is forced to watch. Conversely it is the American who is being tortured while a pouting beauty mocks his silent agony. The inevitable theme that runs through hundreds of such magazine editions is one of sado-masochism, in which the American was either recipient or forced observer, and such cameos invariably provided the cover picture (see illustration). And yet, significantly, and quite different from the glossy-paged 'girlie' magazines of today, the advertisements that sandwiched stories and photo-features offered upward social mobility through correspondence courses and training kits: How to speak and write like a college graduate; You can become an expert accountant, auditor or CPA; Earn big money – learn electric appliance repairing in your own house; Learn radio-television electronics in your spare time; How to build a big-pay future in the air conditioning and refrigeration industry with CTI home training kits. These are the offers being made to Packard's 'limited success' class, the above examples all being found in but two numbers of such magazines, and they nowhere near exhaust the list. Between the lash and scream stories, answering to the fraught repressive fantasies of the 'ad-mass' male, are enticements to designated achievement through techno-literacy and the promise of greater consumer availability. For the depicted ever-smiling consumer worker, so beloved by the advertising industry: 'How close to divorce did you come? Free, 30 days supply of High-Potency capsules'. Socio-sexual 'normalcy' can also be marketed.

Techno-Occultism offered to its readership the imaginary resolution of such pressures and anxieties in terms and symbols it could readily read. Personal fears and self-doubts over sexual potency or a propagated canon of normalcy could be subsumed within the greater American male anxiety over the new weaponry, with its inescapable connotations of male virility.

5   *Man's Adventure – lash and scream stories with adverts for self improvement by technical correspondence courses and sexual normalcy by doctor's prescription.*

The symbolism of cities being 'naked and defenceless' under a 'sneak Red attack' has already been noted. The variants of Techno-Occultism provided universal solutions through the tantalizing symbol of the flying saucer, technically perfect, denoting a higher male technocracy, offering a simple absolutism to be set against the complexities of the real world and life as it must be led, away from the exhortations of advertising and the media.

But absolutism brings a further value that the genre offered its readership – hierarchy. It was noted in the chapter on flying saucers that the leading writers on the subject frequently assumed bureaucratic forms of organization and address, giving themselves an office and a role within such an organization, using a terminology that echoed the large corporation. Appendix 4 gives a list of thirteen such organizations and brief details of their activity, all taken from *The Encyclopedia of UFOs*. A similar trait was noted in the discussion on Romantic Occultism, but then it was the *ancien régime* significations of priestly or aristocratic role that were adopted: the self-ennoblement of Adolf Lanz, Guido List and MacGregor Mathers, to give three prominent examples. With Techno-Occultism we have the style and language of the 'Organization Man'. The president, the head of an acronymed organization to dispense the official version of UFO intention and, most tellingly, to file and catalogue the records of thousands of encounters.

Though the new society may be presented as being to a certain degree class-amorphic, the 'limited expectation' class clearly demanded a hierarchy, and one that related to the social and economic constructs of a consumer society. Hence, Techo-Occultism provided a hierarchy within its own structure which was presented in terms that made sense to its own time, to the 'limited success class' and the 'diploma elite' that provided its readership.

A further indicative feature of the genre is that, apropos of the designation of a hierarchy in acceptable contemporary terms, it also served to sanctify the parental generations in a new authority. It served to reaffirm status for those whose values, mores and fashions were not just rejected by the young, but openly ridiculed. A growing teenage population in the mid-fifties onwards was a legacy of the post-war years, and the teenage break with the fashions and attitudes of their parents was inevitable. However, in the mass consumer society it was quickly discovered that the teenage market was of considerable value, and corporations and media rushed to support the phenomenon of a youth culture having economic power, dismissive of old ideas and values, asserting its own market-modified norms. Consumer capitalism quickly learned that youth fashions in clothes and music, even cars and motorbikes, meant a vast and sustainable market, and it quickly underwrote the prominent features of youthful rebellion to produce marketable stereotypes whose values were consumer-fixed. Youth rebelled with the weapons of afflu-ence and won the goal of market autonomy. Brookes wrote that 'In 1939 they (jeans) were worn chiefly by cowboys, laborers and children at play; in 1965 150 million pairs of them were sold in the United States ... and titles of fifty American songs began with the words blue jeans' (1966, p. 144). Even the term 'teenager' was an invention of the early fifties.

The continuity of youth's rejection of parental status is best exemplified by comparing two popular films: *Rebel Without a Cause* and Spielberg's recent *Back to the Future*. Thirty years apart, they yet exhibit a remarkable continuity of attitude. In both films the parents are represented as being weak, vacillating and even ridiculous. In *Rebel Without a Cause* the youngsters even form their own pretend family to replace the absent parents and the familial values they have been denied. Parents are unable to intervene in the fights and disputes of the teenagers, even though such disputes lead to death. The teenage culture is partly defined by the automobile, and all the teenagers have ready access to cars. In Spielberg's essay on the generation gap the teenage hero, courting oedipal disaster, is spirited back by auto-magic to the years of his parents' teenagerhood, where he solves his quest by persuading his proto-father to redeem himself and win the love of his wife to be, by the predictable stratagem of urging him to stand up to the local bully and hit him fair and square on the jaw. The result is that the present from which he has travelled is redeemed and on his return his parents, who have previously been weak and unable to cope, were now archetypes of an American ideal. In both films there is just one adult figure that was acceptable to the teenage hero: in the Dean film a concerned police detective, in the later film a loony scientist, both well-established Hollywood icons.

But Techno-Occultism, with its pseudo-science, its developed vocabu-lary, its corporate mimicry, has the ability to claim for the parental generation a type of authority once fixed in religion. The 'ufologists' spoke of an absolute authority – they interpreted the mysterious lights in the sky, they told of a technology that lay in the future of the youth of the day, thereby offering a techno-scientific reality that could not be mocked by youth, and which, at the same time, spoke of a past that was remote, beyond even the reach of biblical fable. And crucially, unlike religion, there was no emphasis on self-denial or prayer. The new genre offered an effortless belief – patience and vigilance were all that were required. It was an essentially passive doctrine that made no demands on personal behaviour. Here was an authority that the parental generation could claim for itself and sell to the young. Here was a belief system that would appeal to those described by C. Wright Mills as 'Men ... who often sense that the older ways of feeling and thinking have collapsed and that newer beginnings are ambiguous to the point of moral stasis'.

Clearly, in the values outlined above as being what the general readership of the genre derived from the texts and advocacy of Techno-Occultism, the emphasis is again on masculine concerns and needs. It is no surprise then to find that the genre is overwhelmingly male-dominated. The extensive booklist that makes up Bibliography 1 contains only three female authors: Joan Whritenour, Sally Landsberg and Jenny Randles.

Text analysis also reveals a depth of sterotype, with women playing a passive role. Consider Daniken's exegesis, in which the ancient astronauts mated with earthly primitive women – an act of racial miscegenation. In the texts dealing with flying saucers women rarely feature, since they are not airline pilots, meteorologists, air traffic controllers or sheriffs. When women are introduced as witnesses they are usually presented as housewives and their feminine aspects constantly stressed. Hence John Keel in his *Visitors from Space* introduces his female subjects of UFO encounter with a whimsical stereotypicality that is strongly reminiscent of the style of the *Penthouse* letter. He gives 'In March 1966, a shapely housewife . . . was waiting in her car for her children (p. 43), and 'What is it? Mary Mallette, a strikingly attractive brunette, cried from the back seat' (p. 60) or 'Mabel McDaniel came to the door, an attractive woman' (p. 76).

These values: authority, heirarchy, gender enforcement and the absolution of male insecurity, relate to the historical needs for reinforcement in a class or group that faces class-amorphism in what was seen to be a decisive break with the past. Techno-Occultism offers a perennial restructuring garbed in a strictly contemporary vision.

CONTINUITY OF APPEAL

The sustained interest that the major texts continue to exert over the years is largely explicable by the feature that the main themes of Techno-Occultism increasingly approximate to the popular presentations of science. Or, put the other way round, from the mid-seventies the presentations of science began to inhabit the same domain of catastrophe and global problems that features so strongly throughout Techno-Occultism. This process is best illustrated by the example of the popular presentation of nuclear science. In the following the sources used to illustrate this approximation will be popular magazines or texts dealing with science at a general level.

We can begin in 1953, with an article in the *Saturday Evening Post* of 5 December entitled 'Life History Of An A Bomb'. Its subtitle read . . .

Eight years ago, one big bomb could have wiped out our entire atomic weapons production line. Today that line that winds through 43 states, ends up in secret caverns underground. Here is the ore to stockpile story of the most expensive and complex industrial operation the world has ever known.

In the ensuing description of the atom bomb production line, the 'prodigious expansion' of which 'dates from that time ... Four months after Russia exploded her nuclear device', general details are given of how

> Non-nuclear components of the bomb, broken down into sub-assemblies ... are manufactured in hundreds of plants ... scattered through 43 states. Where all these myriad parts are brought together for assembly, and where the ready weapons are finally stored, is known to few. The whole production line at this point vanishes in mystery, into secret caverns underground.

Also within the article, Atomic Energy Commissioner Thomas E. Murray is quoted with 'For years the splitting atom, packaged in weapons, has been our main shield against the Barbarians'.

In the tone and rhetoric of the above is found a striking similarity with that of Techno-Occultism. The scale of the operation with 'hundreds of plants', the complexity of the whole scheme, with 'myriad parts' which are brought together to be stored in 'secret caverns', knowledge of which is 'known to few'. And yet this is not the scenario devised by a science fiction author or film maker, and the rhetoric of the article is intended to convince the American public of the necessity and efficacy of such endeavours to guarantee their survival against the 'Barbarians'. Atomic science is no longer the property of eccentric boffins in laboratories, now that its secret has been betrayed by the 'Judas Fuchs' and the whole project of nuclear arms production has become industrialized, with armies of workers labouring at components whose ultimate destiny is unknown to them. No more will the American public hear of 'the father of the A bomb', personalities will not emerge from the presentation of the project, specific endeavours such as the Manhattan Project will not be identified, even after the event; now the mask is seamless.

But it is a familiar mask. State and science are fused in intention and endeavour, in a project that will guarantee the survival of the American nation; and yet to guarantee the authenticity of such a project, its depiction is supported, not with facts and figures as to the precise number of factories, the size of the workforce, the depth of the caverns, etc., but instead with elements from a fictive scenario. It is not that generalized factors as to scale and size would betray the project, but that such details would counter the fictive scenario. It is important that 'the whole production line ... vanishes in a mystery'. Thus Americans can feel secure, and forget about the whole troublesome issue of nuclear weapons, their production and deployment. For, as Snowman comments

> By 1953 Americans had been living with some sort of crisis for nearly a quarter of a century. There was nothing that most yearned for so much as national and

international peace and quiet and the opportunity to get on with their own individual lives in as comfortable and uninterrupted a way as possible. (Snowman 1980, p. 131)

Thus even in the early 1950s we have a recognizable point of thematic equivalence between the future scripts of Techno-Occultism and the public construct of state-defence science. But in the mid-fifties the public's mind was being turned away from the literal and metaphorical strivings of a state-hired Nibelungen: public attention was now to be turned to embrace the possibilities offered by the peaceful use of the atom. The same *Saturday Evening Post* article of 5 December 1953 states, referring to the use of atomic science, 'it is to become a God-given instrument to do the construction work of mankind ... We should all feel that justifiable satisfaction which comes with carrying out the creator's plan'. The inference is clear. All hope and optimism for the technological future of humanity is based upon the development of the peaceful potential of the atom.

In the same week as the article appeared Eisenhower announced the 'Atoms For Peace Programme'. The atoms for death programme is henceforth to go unnoticed as optimistic schemes for atomic science to realize its promised potential proliferate. 'Carrying out the creator's plan' is to include schemes for nuclear-powered aeroplanes and the use of atom bombs to blast a channel for a new Panama Canal. Nor was the optimism confined to America; in Britain the *Eagle* comic in August 1952 featured a cut-away drawing of an 'atomic' locomotive. *Illustrated*, a photo-journal magazine, in August 1958 carried a series of articles entitled 'Your Friend The Atom', with cosy pictures comparing members of a family to different isotopes.

These were halcyon days, if propagated expectation be the yardstick. As mentioned earlier, Kenneth Heur's *The End of the World* (1953) with eight chapters, has but one giving an end brought about by man's agency – that through an atomic war. Heur's conclusion is simple: 'If the nations of the earth succeed in establishing international control of the weapons of war ... a golden age would open upon the earth. This age is within the grasp of man' (Heur 1953, p. 121).

Another contemporary work of popular science, *The Drama of the Atom* by Werner Braunbeck speaks of 'a glittering promise and diabolical terror will reach out to the very ends of the earth' (1958, p. 2). Clearly drawn opposites of light and shade, but the bright promise is in nuclear power stations, the medical use of radio-isotopes, and it is enthusiastically promulgated. *Atomic Energy: A Layman's Guide*, by Egon Larsen (1958) concentrates on the multiple practical uses that atomic science can yield, and photographs of designs for giant nuclear-powered oil tankers and the use of radio-isotopes in farming are but two examples that are dealt with in the text. *The Boon of the Atom* by George Bankoff (1949) concludes with 'A generation hence man will laugh at our talk of the curse of atomic knowledge. Instead they will regard it as the boon it is' (p. 158).

The optimism of these years, the early to late fifties, was not to last. These were the 'Bilko Years', probably the only time in post-war America that the army could be safely depicted as comprising the goofs and gambling-mad rookies of the Fort Baxter motor pool, with Commander Hall, abetted by stone-faced symbols of authority, forever being out-witted by Ernie Bilko, who would never be in a position to fire a shot in anger. Lacking a foreign adventure after Korea and with the defence of the nation ensconced in nuclear dungeons, the army suffered temporarily from role relegation.

But an unqualified optimism over the peaceful deployment of atomic technology was gradually to prove unfounded, and books of popular science began to voice doubts concerning the safety, or even the wisdom, of the peaceful use of atomic energy. Within a decade the popular perception of atomic science was being totally reversed. Thus *The Perils of the Peaceful Atom* (1970), subtitled 'The Myth of Safe Nuclear Power Plants', gives details of earlier accidents at nuclear power plants and concludes a chapter on the effects of radiation, entitled 'The Thresholds of Agony' with

> henceforth man must live in constant dread of a major nuclear accident which will wreak death and harm on a level potentially surpassing Hiroshima and Nagasaki. . . . But we must realise that even if such accidents are averted, the slow, silent saturation of our environment with radioactive poisons will be raising the odds that you or your heirs will fall victim to any one of the horrors depicted here, and possibly to some unexperienced in human history. (Curtis and Hogan 1970, p. 44)

The optimism of a decade earlier is now completely absent. Yet by the 1980s the prospects raised by *Perils of the Peaceful Atom* are taken as established fact. *The Nuclear Barons* by Pringle and Spiegelman contains, as a cover blurb, 'The inside story of how they created our nuclear nightmare', while the back cover carries the claim, '*The Nuclear Barons* is a damning indictment of the folly and greed of a race for power which has brought the world to the edge of destruction'. In concluding their text Pringle and Spiegelman assert that the instinctive fear of radioactivity is not irrational, as the nuclear advocates assert; it is also universal and so enduring that it is a political fact of life' (1982, p. 446).

The situation that has developed is that not only has civil nuclear science undergone a change from positive to negative presentations, but that fictive elements have also now been incorporated within the negative presentation 'they created our nuclear nightmare', which proclaims the nuclear nightmare as an established fact and hints at a conspiracy with the telling use of 'they'. Fictive elements are also introduced by Curtis and Hogan with their 'and possibly to some unexperienced in human history'. Therefore with fictive and conspiratorial elements featuring in a negative and pessimistic presentation of nuclear science, points of equivalence are being established with certain areas of Techno-Occult supposition.

Such points of equivalence are by no means limited to features and possibilities inherent within nuclear science. Though Heur's 1953 text concentrates on stellar events in an unforeseeable future, later texts on the same topic find more immediate agencies for world destruction being brought about by human activity. Gordon Rattray Taylor's *The Doomsday Book* (1970) focuses almost exclusively on human activity as being the agency of world destruction, whether as a result of pollution, over-population or climatic change induced by unfettered industrialization. In each circumstance it is human activity that is crucial, and the end is depicted in the foreseeable future, rather than at some remote point in time. The contrast between Heur's and Taylor's texts is enormous, and reveals the radical transformation in the popular presentation of science that had taken place by the beginning of the seventies. At this time Techno-Occultism and the popular presentations of science share a common ground and are often based upon similar axioms, hence the reissue of Velikovsky in paperback edition.

Universal catastrophe was now officially plausible, even possible, at some point in the near future. The self-imposed destruction of humanity, the planet, all living creation, is analogous to the proclaimed destruction of Atlantis, itself supposed to have been an advanced scientific civilization. And the decade sees a number of Techno-Occult texts dealing with the Atlantis theme being published: Brad Steiger's *Atlantis Rising* (1973) and Robert Scrutton with *The Other Atlantis* (1977) being two typical examples. The immediate prospect of global catastrophe as depicted by Taylor is paralleled, for instance, by Charles Berlitz in *Doomsday 1999*, which, subtitled, 'Countdown to the New Apocalypse', is a work of Techno-Occultism that has passages that could be inter-changed with the dire prognosis offered by Taylor in *The Doomsday Book*. Thus:

> As nation after nation develops its own nuclear warfare capabilities in a sort of international contest of self-esteem it is evident that within the next fifteen to twenty years all industrial or developed countries which are striving and being helped to become developed ... will doubtless have their own nuclear weapons. And with the testing of such weapons the poisoning of the planet will be hastened even if war does not come. (Berlitz 1982, p. 10)

Although the succeeding paragraph immediately betrays the Techno-Occult imprimatur with talk of 'an increasing possibility that the earth, as it approaches the second millennium of our era, may experience a wandering of its magnetic poles . . . and reversal of the magnetic fields of the earth with catastrophic consequences' (Berlitz 1982, p. 10).

A further text, *Doomsday, the Science of Catastrophe*, by Fred Warshofsky (1979), takes a Velikovskian line on catastrophe, elevating it to 'an essential force in nature, not aberrational but inevitable' (p. x). Warshofsky's *Doomsday* is a work of popular scientific presentation that inhabits almost completely the same ground as Techno-Occultism. His conclusion that 'The knowledge crisis is one that every cultural species on every inhabitable planet in the universe must surmount at a point in its evolution, or become extinct' (p. 243), shows the influence of exo-biology and also the shared premiss of extra-terrestrialism.

In the above-quoted works that are concerned with popular presentations of scientific ideas or material, it is axiomatic that our present age is set apart from previous historical experience by the nature of the problems it faces. They assert that humanity is facing a 'make or break' situation. 'These questions lead one, forgivably, to wonder whether human nature itself is not at last confronted with the imperative to change', argue Curtis and Hogan in *Perils of the Peaceful Atom*. 'Man has reached a turning point in his history . . . it is quite on the cards that he may mismanage his powers so badly that he causes, in some degree, a disaster. It is the future of the human race we are talking about', concludes Gordon Rattray Taylor's *The Doomsday Book*, and both conclusions are consonant with Pauwels and Bergier when they give 'these are the forces at work in science and technology which will demolish the old sociological order' (1971, p. 22).

So, from the 1970s onwards several variants of Techno-Occult supposition gain plausibility and an associative credibility, by comparison with the popular presentations of science which are seen to dwell on similar premisses of catastrophe, evolutionary saltus and extra-terrestrial intelligence. Indeed, the distinction between Techno-Occultism and popular science becomes quite blurred with, for instance, the addition to the *Observer Colour Supplement* of February 1986, issued by the Earthlife Foundation, which promised that

> In the minute it will take you to read this page, one hundred acres of tropical rainforest will be destroyed. . . . Half of the species alive on earth depend on these forests, and will vanish with them. . . . The biological holocaust is burning great holes in the web of life that sustains us all. . . . The effects of the death of the rainforests could be as severe as those of nuclear war. In many ways the threat is greater. Until the first weapon is launched the final war may be averted – but the ecological Armageddon is already well advanced.

The notion that Armageddon is already with us, the scale of the damage, the rate of destruction – all presented in the tone that it might already be too late – could well have come straight from a Techno-Occult text of any time during the previous thirty years. The flying saucer texts carried the same sense of urgency, the same warnings of an unknown future dominated by quite different concerns from those that operate in the present.

A further important factor that goes some way to explain the sustained appeal of Techno-Occultism is its racist sub-text. This has already been discussed in connection with the appeal of the Daniken oeuvre, but consideration of the other variants of the genre reveal an aggregated sub-text that runs throughout. For science and technology can be read white, western society; contact with extra-terrestrials can be read as signifying the supremacy of that science and of the white Aryan type, *qua* Adamski's Venusian. The Brotherhood of the Stars both beckons to and indicates the absolute power of the racially pure Aryanic god-man and, by inference, the relegation of all other races, left behind on an earth vacated by the white technologists – Daniken's 'army of deep frozen soldiers who will be thawed out as necessary in case of war' or his apes programmed to mend roads.

This racist subtext runs throughout the genre, only occasionally being clearly articulated when, for instance, Daniken argues that perhaps the 'black race' was 'a failure' and that the extra-terrestrials changed 'the genetic code by gene surgery and then programmed a white or yellow race' (1981, p. 70). Or again, when he speaks of the extra-terrestrials being 'furious because we reject the "midwifery" they supplied at our "birth"? Could our creators break off "Experiment Earth" one day?' (1978, p. 271). Here is clear warning against racial interbreeding; the astronaut gods may forsake us yet, deny the white, male, techno-supremacists their rightful heritage amongst the 'Brotherhood of the Stars' if they do not desist from racial miscegenation.[4]

With Techno-Occultism prescriptive racism is again on the agenda, not as a conscious formula, but sublimated within and endorsed by the greatest contemporary force for social change-white technology.

It was a major, determining feature of Romantic Occultism that it denied the industrial-urban state and sought to establish an 'Elsewhere' safe from change and pluralism. It was to the secret palaeo-history that the texts of Romantic Occultism inclined, where an absolutist, priestly state exemplified the authority and certainty that was felt to be lost with the growth of industrial society. With Techno-Occultism the situation is the reverse, for its appeal is derived from the constructs of its contemporary society: certain features of scientific theory, the potential, or appearance even, of various aspects of technology, serve to provide material for its own version of 'Elsewhere'.

Techno-Occultism offers the adamantine certainties of Romantic Occultism's palaeo-society in its own rendition of Atlantis and in the technological absolutism of the flying saucer. The metonymy of the flying saucer – a seamless, gravity- and inertia-defying artefact, maufactured by processes conceivable but not attainable, place it always beyond the limit of contemporary technology but within the horizon of the extrapolated future. Its origin is proclaimed as being within a society that can delegate god-like powers to its 'ufonauts'.

The real horizon that has been crossed by the 'ufonaut' society is not the physical one of having freed itself from a planetoid existence, but the social horizon of having escaped from the contradictions and problems in mass urban and democratic society. The extra-planetary nature of the 'ufonaut' society therefore provides an imaginative liberation from the tensions such problems arouse.

REFRESHING AMBIGUITY

The introduction to this work opened with the claim that there is a refreshing ambiguity inherent in the term 'popular culture'. The study of Techno-Occultism serves to restate this claim with a genre that is enduring and prolific and which arises independently of those mass media whose hegemony is assumed to be near total. At times Techno-Occultism set itself against the prevailing orthodoxy of its day, insisting that the greatest fears for humanity were not concerned with the politics of Cold War polarities or even, latterly, with environmental issues, but that the hope for humankind was by technological man inheriting his destiny through unbridled technical achievement. Indeed many of the texts were mildly subversive, insisting on a joint conspiracy of science and government to keep the essential facts from the intelligent and observant citizen.

On the other hand, when the symbols and scenarios of the genre served as metaphors for Cold War anxieties, Techno-Occultism functioned as a palliative, serving to deter any real challenge to a state machinery that insisted on the manufacture of global weapons of destruction as a necessary defence of freedom.

Techno-Occultism may be depicted as being an expression of intuitive revulsion against individual uncertainty or anonymity, against the accepted perception of class amorphism in a consumer society. In this it fulfils the historic role of occult speculation. Its complex of ideas derives directly from the occult cosmology of Madame Blavatsky, itself a compendium of reworked ideas, some of which are to be found in the gnostic beliefs of the early Christian era, some from the Hindu pantheons of the East. That such ideas can be set within a context of an extension of twentieth-century technology and form the thematic seedbed for a popular culture says much for the fecundity of such notions and the ambiguity inherent in all popular cultures.

It would seem that the more successful variants of Techno-Occultism now have little more than a residual appeal and that it is the texts of Romantic, Gothic and ritual occultism that are now beginning to fill the bookshop shelves in reprint or reinterpretation. At the moment, in Britain at least, when the taste is for appliqué Tudor and post-modern eclecticism, the formulations, metaphors and symbols of Techno-Occultism suddenly seem curiously dated by their very modernism, rather like the chrome-fronted modernity of cars some twenty-odd years ago. Now the interest is held by photographic albums of crop circles or by the accounts of Whitley Strieber, whose 'Number One Bestseller', *Communion* is being made into a film. The popular is becoming popularized: the market smells money and the individual quest has always been the most marketable parable. Conversely Daniken, Velikovsky and the traditional 'ufologists' now retain little more than a minor, genre appeal; hardly surprising when the anniversary histories of spaceflight offer little more than a whiff of nostalgia and a future marred by uncertainty. One prediction that can be made with certainty, however, is that the genre will not rest in its present quiescent state; the anxieties engendered by modern civilization will demand a new soteriology that the prescriptions of occultism will doubtless supply.

NOTES

INTRODUCTION (pages 7–9)

1. In stark contrast Science Fiction presents a far more complex case when it comes to attempting a definition. Patrick Parrinder in *Science Fiction: Its Criticism and Teaching* admits from the outset that 'Science fiction, though in many ways a highly conventional kind of writing, is one that cannot be defined uncontroversially. At first glance it might appear to invite self-evident definition, as detective fiction is fiction about detectives and the art of solving crimes. Yet this is not the case, as is proved by the innumerable attempts that have been made to define it. On close inspection science fiction turns out to be a highly self-conscious genre: that is, the way it has been defined has an unusually close and symbiotic relationship with the way it has been written. For this reason, the question "What is science fiction?" will be initially answered by looking at the critical history of the term itself and of its antecedents. Definitions of science fiction are not so much a series of logical approximations to an elusive ideal, as a small, parasitic sub-genre in themselves' (pp. 1–2).

The problem does not arise with Techno-Occultism: there appears to be no self-conscious genre, no attempt, even by practitioners, to indicate a genre, and thus no symbiosis (or parasitism) between definition and some of the less frequent variants. But this is slight and relatively uncontroversial given the powerful homogeneity of base theme and style that runs throughout.

CHAPTER 1 (pages 10–43)

1. The word Theosophy (literally the knowledge or wisdom of God, or divine knowledge) had been in use by theologians for several centuries before Blavatsky and her fellow co-founders used it to describe their occult quest. Used generally it signifies any mystical knowledge or practice that has as its object the knowledge of God. When used with a capital letter it refers

to that brand of occult knowledge and belief manufactured by Madame Blavatsky and her society.

2. Beer continues with 'And "educated reader" here must imply not a simple level of literacy but a level of shared cultural assumptions and shared cultural controversy' (p. 46). But these shared values reached a wider audience than attended the Oxford debate, hence for instance 'The controversial hue and cry set up upon appearance of the *Vestiges* reached a far wider audience than the one which had followed the relatively temperate discussion of uniformitarianism. For several decades all the respectable leaders of scientific opinion, of whatever school, had been actively engaged upon the project of popularising natural philosophy amongst mechanics and disseminating science to untutored multitudes' (C. G. Gillespie 1959, p. 150). Thus the shared cultural assumptions, both scientific and religious, reached a wide audience (see also n. 4).

3. Gillespie offers '*Vestiges* struck a note which, besides being erroneous, was "dangerous" – a word which creeps into all the reviews and into all the correspondence and reflects a state of mind transcending scientific disapproval'.

   'Whatever the explanation, *Vestiges* was enormously read. It went through four editions between October 1844 and April 1845 and eleven editions by 1860. There was, thought Chambers, a great demand for his book among working men, and the fifth, sixth and seventh editions were priced to satisfy it' (p. 163).

4. Lynd argued that the 'older theory of natural law had been an attempt to defend moral values on logical grounds. The newer theory abandoned the false logic involved in this attempt in favor of "scientific fact"; in so doing it abandoned the moral values as well.' The crucial difference between the two moral theories, she held, was that the 'emphasis had shifted from human nature to physical nature, from the validity of human rights to the unalterable character of natural forces. This carried with it a belief in the helplessness rather than the rights of man, and in the necessity of man's submitting to the supposed laws of society' (Lynd 1945, p. 69).

   Here we see a further instance of the fusion of metaphor, underwriting Beer's observation that 'evolutionary ideas are even more influential when they become assumptions embedded in the culture than while they are the subject of controversy' (p. 4) and that 'Who had read what does not fix limits' (p. 6).

5. Young argues that 'the reinterpretation of man's place in nature was not primarily due to the work of Darwin but involved a more general debate', and that 'the impact on conventional belief did not involve anything which had not been said many times before' (p. 9). Young's essay is concerned with demonstrating that the shock of Darwin's thought to mid-nineteenth-century opinion has been simplified and greatly overstated. The essay is convincing, although it has a self-proclaimed limitation in that Young gives 'I want to argue that the period from 1820 to 1875 was one in which science made it clear to *enlightened theological opinion* that a third interpretation of the relationship

between science and theology was necessary' (p. 10, my italics). The argument advanced in this text is the response to Darwinism beyond the confines of enlightened theological opinion.

6. Between 1841 and 1881, the nation's population rose by 60 per cent, whereas the seventeen main professional occupations increased their numbers by 150 per cent' (M.J. Wiener 1981, p. 15).

   Up to around 1885, despite the relative mobility of English society, the peerage remained well protected against the intrusion of parvenus, and the barriers separating the world of titles from the world of business continued to function efficiently. Between 1886 and 1914 about 200 peers were created, and one can now talk about the arrival of industrial England in the House of Lords' (F. Bedarida 1976, p. 129).

   'The widest definition of the middle class . . . was that of keeping domestic servants. Their numbers . . . increased very substantially from 900,000 in 1851 to 1.4 million in 1871' (Hobsbawm 1968, p. 131).

7. R.D. Knoepflmacher, 'The Novel Between City And Country', a thoughtful essay on the presentation of the Victorian city in English novels of the nineteenth century, in *The Victorian City: Image And Reality*, vol. 2, edited by Dyos and Wolff. The same volume also has P.J. Keating, 'Fact and Fiction in the East End'. Keating observes that, 'The London of the mid-Victorians (the London of Dickens in effect) was a mixture of all classes; the slum backed on to the mansion, so that there was always the chance that the rich individual would step round the corner and save a poor individual. By the eighties one crucial aspect of this kind of paternalism had gone' (p. 593).

8. It is not being suggested that the problems of the city were new to the 1880s. Cf. Asa Briggs, *Victorian Cities* (1963). The argument is that in the 1820–1840 period the problems posed by cities were seen as being a consequence of the industrialization process, whereas in London in the 1880s the problem was closer to the seats of power, more acute, more complex. The importance of the proximity of the squalor of the East End to the wealth of the City is found in many utterances on the problem, General Booth and Jack London being but two of the more celebrated examples.

9. Of course there was nothing new in the use of this metaphor. Asa Briggs in *Victorian Cities* (1963) gives 'The "dark city" and the "dark continent" were alike mysterious, and it is remarkable how often the exploration of the unknown city was compared with the exploration of Africa and Asia. Richard Oastler set the fashion early in the century when he compared conditions in the worsted mills of Bradford with those in "hellish" colonial plantations' (p. 60).

   But again the comment is made that the problem of the East End of London was felt to be of a different nature, scale and proximity to the earlier problems of the Northern cities. Keating, op. cit. offers 'For the late Victorians "Outcast London" epitomized the class conflicts they most feared. A similar situation had existed in the 1840s, when the threat of class warfare had focused attention on the industrial worker. A being distant and strange, the industrial worker, considered in the mass, had carried with him connotations of strength and power. He represented muscle, the furnace, the engine. .... The image of Manchester that obsessed the early Victorians was a mixture of power and suffering. The image of East London created in the eighties was entirely different, a mixture of passivity and suffering' (p. 593).

10. Clarence Rook's *Hooligan Nights*, named after one eponymous Patrick Hooligan, a street-king of Lambeth, published in 1899, told of the exploits of Alf, a streetwise youngster whose determination to live off his wits and his fists portrayed a quite different morality to the passive helplessness and hopelessness that was the keynote of the East End. A street Tory, entrepreneurial primarily and criminal secondary, Alf's exploits revealed a quality of roguery that must be set apart from East End life. Eschewing alcohol, smoking cigars, Alf and his streetmates did not starve, neither did they accept employment, but lived a precarious hand-to-mouth existence, taking what they could, whatever the consequences, for themselves or their victims. *Hooligan Nights*, with its catalogue of beatings, petty forgery and burglary, must have been even more shocking to some of the middle class, bearing in mind that it was youngsters of Alf's class that would be taken into their homes as domestic servants. Their response would probably have been less altruistic than Toynbee's 'We will dedicate our lives to your service'. Rook's *Hooligan Nights* and Somerset Maugham's first novel, *Liza of Lambeth*, recorded different strata of poverty and alienation that indicated that social and moral concern could not be confined to the blatant enormity of 'the Nether World'.

11. Podmore, also a keen member of the Progressive Association, is described by James Webb (1971, p. 228) as being, 'not only a member of the Society for Psychical Research, but is said to have been a Theosophist; and more certainly was instrumental in the founding of the Fabian Society . . . itself a centre of the Progressive Underground'. Webb adds the rather surprising example of members of the Fabians; Herbert Burrows, who also was to become a Theosophist and co-author with Besant of *A Short Glossary Of Theosophical Terms*, and E. Nesbit, who were also members of the initiatory and ritualistic magical order of the Stella Matutina; The Star of the Morning, an offshoot of The Golden Dawn. Surprising in that the very essence of ritual occultism consists of absolute submission to a posited hierarchy of psycho-spritual forces; hardly a convincing background for an advocate of English gradualism. Other mystically inclined Fabians included the homosexual poet Edward Carpenter, and the famous spirit medium Eileen Garrett. Concluding his analysis of the fusion of mysticism and political creeds, Webb remarked that, 'Such beliefs naturally allied themselves with rejected political aspirations, in the same way that politics, Art and occultism had joined forces in Bohemia' (p. 228).

12. Logie Barrow in *Independent Spirits – Spiritualism and English Plebeians 1850–1910* has shown that in England there was a tradition of spiritual doctrine and practice that differed from the American practice of spiritualism. The English authoritarian tradition was however supplanted by the imported American mode, which had no space for prophets and dogma.

13. Spritualism is not mentioned in the two volumes of *The Secret Doctrine*, while spiritualists get but three mentions, vol. 1, p. 235 and vol. 2, pp. 86 and 229. Each of these is but a passing reference.

14. Nethercott (1961, p. 313) gives the following account:
'The *Sun* and *Star* sent their society reporters to the grand opening of Mrs Isabel Cooper-Oakley's first restaurant for West End working girls. As they saw the affair, it was a sensational success, with social luminaries, especially ladies everywhere . . . And in the midst of them all were the two lionesses of the hour, Mme Blavatsky, smoking cigarettes as usual . . . and her newest acquisition, Mrs Annie Besant. In fact most of the ladies were smoking cigarettes, and a crowd gathered outside, pressing their noses against the window, to see the shocking sight and get a glimpse of the latest goings-on in high society'.

CHAPTER 2 (pages 44–75)

1. Carl Sagan in *Broca's Brain* has a chapter entitled, 'Venus and Dr Velikovsky', which subjects the Velikovsky thesis to a scientific analysis, with particular reference to the thermo-kinetic consequences of the cometary hypothesis. Sagan deals specificially with the predictions as to the temperature and constitution of the Venusian atmosphere and demonstrates that these predictions are 'neither original nor correct'. Nonetheless Velikovsky's claims in 'Additional Examples of Correct Prognosis' (in Grazia *The Velikovsky Affair*) offer sufficient material to keep the issue alive.

CHAPTER 3 (pages 76–109)

1. The flying saucer carries the connotation of absolute values, it originates from a society that is able to proffer both parable and warning to contemporary society, fulfilling the same function as the tales of 'Elsewhere' of the late nineteenth century, with the added significance of urgency – flying saucers intrude with their message into contemporary society.

2. This same quality of style will be noted with but small variations in *The Dawn of Magic* and the works of von Daniken. The following section from Blavatsky's *Isis Unveiled* (vol. 1, p. 573) is offered for comparison.
'What explanation can the archaeologists, philologists – in short, the chosen host of Academicians – give us? None whatever. At best they have but hypotheses, every one of which is likely to be pulled down by its successor – a pseudo-truth, perhaps, like the first. The keys to the biblical miracles of old, and to the phenomena of modern days; the problems of psychology, physiology, and the many "missing links" which have so perplexed scientists of late, are all in the hands of secret fraternities' (*et seq.*).

3. Consider for instance the following example:
'Experiments with sensitive apparatus have proved what the Sanskrit and sensar writers always knew: that the human brain emits electric currents; that

thought is, or causes, an electrical impulse. They seem to think that this brain current is very, very powerful. If not the actual current emitted by the brain, the current it can induce is powerful enough to raise huge rocks in the air. The button that starts a great machine is weak enough in its thrust (one finger power to be precise), but look what it can do. The mighty bridges that open, the liners that cross the ocean, the high-speed lifts of a skyscraper are all started by one little finger pushing one little button' (Leslie, p. 73).

This is a far cry from the talk of etheric forces and materializations that characterized Romantic Occultism, now the analogies are all with contemporary technology. (See also von Daniken, *Return to the Stars*, p. 65.)

4. For a detailed analysis of feelings induced by the threat of thermonuclear war, or even the mere existence of the hydrogen bomb, see Lifton and Falk, *Indefensible Weapons: The Political and Psychological Case Against Nuclearism* (1982).

5. See for example *There Are Giants In The Earth*, by Michael Grumley (1976).

CHAPTER 4 (pages 110–130)

1. In 1960 Editions Gallimard of Paris published *The Morning Of The Magicians*, jointly authored by Louis Pauwels and Jacques Bergier. The text was translated into English and published in 1963 by Anthony Gibbs and Phillips Ltd under the title, *The Dawn Of Magic*; under this title it went into paperback edition by Panther in 1963. The book was popular both on the continent and in the English-speaking world, it being claimed on the cover of the 1971 edition that over a million copies had been sold under various imprints. The work has been reissued in paperback, published by Granada, in 1971 with reprints in 1972 and 1973. Somewhat confusingly the Granada republication was under the original title of *The Morning Of The Magicians*. In this chapter the page references are from the 1973 Granada imprint of *The Morning Of The Magicians*, although the text will be referred to in the original English title of *The Dawn Of Magic*.

2. The rapidly growing corpus of texts dealing with the 'New Physics' threatens to become a genre in itself. Interesting connections and cross-references are made with certain aspects of Techno-Occultism. For instance, Paul Davies in *God And The New Physics* (1984) begins with a claim that could have come straight from *The Dawn of Magic*, when he offers 'More relevant to the decline of religion is the fact that science through technology, has altered our lives so radically that the traditional religions may appear to lack the immediacy necessary to provide any real assistance in coping with contemporary social and personal problems' (p. 2).

The claim for a scientific elitism is found with 'The vast majority of people do not understand the scientific principles, nor are they interested. Science remains a sort of witchcraft' (p. 3). Against the conflicting and often socially repressive claims of religion is offered and upheld the superior mystery and explication of science, with the promise that its revelations will be far beyond the grasp of the non-scientist. 'Failure of the human imagination to grasp certain crucial features of reality is a warning that we cannot expect to base great religious truths (such as the nature of creation) on simple-minded ideas of space, time and matter gleaned from daily experience.'

3. Manfred Nagl, *SF, Occult Sciences, and Nazi Myths*. Nagl observes that 'The epitome of all counter-revolutionary slogans, Lanz's "In our most distant past lies our most modern future", was the socio-political motto of fascism. In SF – German and US – this concept is still constantly utilized and reanimated (as for von Daniken's bestselling title *Memories Of The Future* – the German title of *Chariots of the Gods*, one could almost start a copyright-suit against him).'

4. The depiction of the class of 'technicians' leads to the Ehrenreichs essay, 'The Professional-Managerial Class' in *Between Labour and Capital (Marxist Theory and Contemporary Capitalism)* (1979). They state 'We define the Professional-Managerial Class as consisting of salaried mental workers who do not own the means of production and whose major function in the social division of labor may be described broadly as the reproduction of capitalist culture and capitalist class relations' (p. 12). Pauwels and Bergier's 'technicians' would thus seem to be a call for a class consciousness, a summoning of that class to a realization of its power. Thus there is scope to claim that there are both class and gender fantasies deeply ingrained in Pauwels and Bergier's depiction of the future controlled by 'technicians'.

5. A similar typology exists with the popular presentations of science; the 'new physics', microbiology and other 'threshold' sciences are invested with exciting connotations, whereas archaeology, botany and anthropology, for instance, receive scant attention from the popularizers.

6. Nicholas Goodrick-Clarke's *The Occult Roots of Nazism* offers the definitive account of how the Nazi movement was imbued with occult speculation in its early days. Clarke has charted how the volkish philosophy and Theosophy were fused to create a racist gnosis, and how National Socialism first emerged from the 'netherworld of fantasy' in the years after the First World War.

CHAPTER 5 (pages 131–165)

1. Briazack and Mennick's *The UFO Guidebook* (1978) offers:

Naphology. A branch of science or a field of study which deals with and examines all manner of phenomena and events which are reported to exist or to have happened, but for which there exists no scientific explanation (*et seq.*).

Nebecism. A naphological theory which argues that there are other advanced beings in the universe, that these beings landed on Earth in the remote past, and that during their stay on Earth they influenced the course of man's evolution (*et seq.*).

2. See for example Ronald Story, *The Space Gods Revealed* and *Guardians Of The Universe*.

3. Alan Wolfe in *The Rise and Fall of the Soviet Threat: Domestic Sources of Cold War Consensus*, The Institute For Policy Studies (1979), argues for periodic swings in American perception of the Soviet threat and claims that by the early sixties there was a 'second valley' that 'Started fitfully in 1963 with Kennedy's American University speech and continuing into the Nixon Administration' (p. 9). See also the quote from Tom Wolfe given on page 329 below.

4. See for instance *The Secret Doctrine*, vol. 2, book 2, part 2, XVIII, 'The Many Meanings Of The "War In Heaven"', pp. 492 *et seq.*

5. The term techno-gnosis is here used to indicate that Daniken has progressed from a techno-exegesis to a defined corpus of knowledge that is presented within a totally realized technical-capitalistic framework. Daniken's programme has moved beyond the evocation and claim of Pauwels and Bergier to a practical programme in which the message of a gnostic teaching is put into effect.

6. For example, *The Star Of Bethlehem Mystery* by David Hughes offers a purely scientific account of the mysterious star.

7. The account of the teachings of Mani given by Hans Jonas in *The Gnostic Religion* (1963), is particularly interesting in that it is possible to see elements of a later techno-gnosis such as advanced by Daniken, implicit in the wording of Mani's teaching, for example, 'The five elements of Light which the Primal Man puts on as an armour', p. 218, or 'The escaping Light is received by the angels of Light, purified, and loaded onto the "ships" to be transported to its native realm', p. 226. Although Jonas applies a symbolic interpretation to such elements, it is impossible after reading Daniken not to see the basis of a crass literal interpretation and a crude techno-gnosis.

8. Daniken's thinking is a remarkable example of what, according to Foucault, was the form of thinking that 'guided exegesis and the interpretation of texts', prior to the end of the sixteenth century. For Daniken relies upon what Foucault has termed The Third Form of Similitude: Analogy, a quite different concept from that designated by the same term today. In the earlier form of analogy, the connection was reversible and polyvalent, which meant that analogy was endowed with a 'universal field of application' (p. 22). It is this reversible polyvalency which enables Daniken to construe by analogy the various forms of modern technology within the ancient world and present current technology as a magical process as observed by a primitive.

9. Of course Daniken's personal attitude towards his theories does not make any difference to their reception, just as it was pointed out that the personal circumstances of Velikovsky and Donnelly at the time of developing their theories made no difference to the success of those theories. Daniken's ambivalent attitude to his own work provides yet another parallel with Madame Blavatsky, who also exhibited, at times, a dismissive attitude towards her Theosophical system. Webb and Brandon have commented upon the circumstance that, at times, Blavatsky dismissed Theosophy as being little more than a joke while Webb claims that impenetrable style of The Secret Doctrine was in part due to a deliberate attempt to confuse and dismay.

CHAPTER 6 (pages 166–188)

1. For example, Neill Wynn in 'World War II And The Afro-Americans' in the Open University *War & Society*, unit 28, gives the instance that in 1944 there were some 17,000 Mexican workers in the shipyards of Los Angeles when there had been none in 1941. Such an influx of foreign workers indicated a growth of shipyard employment, rather than replacement of indigenous American employment by American workers, none the less such a growth of an industrial skilled and semi-skilled workforce due to war needs would undoubtedly bring uncertainty and insecurity to the shipyards at the end of the war. Wynn further discusses the implications of black and white troops serving in the same combat units, a situation that marked a radical departure from existing military practice in 1944. Daniel Snowman in *America Since 1920* (1980) offers the view that 'On the industrial world the war years had both a liberating and a repressive effect. To the extent that they stimulated massive and unprecedented productivity, they clearly did wonders for the management side of industry. But in so far as labour was virtually forced to subordinate its interests to the exigencies of the prolonged national emergency, the war – as became clear immediately after its termination – had an effect not dissimilar to that of temporarily plugging a volcano (p. 123). Snowman's observation thus serves to remind us that the pressures and determination to retain full employment in an expanded industrial complex were not entirely economic.

2. Packard's *The Status Seekers* is subtitled 'An Exploration Of Class Behaviour In America', and he opens by asking 'What happens to class distinctions among people when most of them are enjoying a long period of material abundance?' Packard's thesis is that the twenty years of the forties and fifties in America have been marked by a consumer prosperity the effect of which is to present the appearance of a classless society. This is a delusion according to Packard, although it is true, he argues, that the traditional presentations of class no longer hold. There have been changes in class structure 'We shall see that the people of the United States have and are refining, a national class structure with a fascinating variety of status systems within it' (p. 13). Packard argues that it is the Second World War that initiated the social upheaval he is to describe, and that the post-war reorganization of the economy to maintain the increased manufacturing potential furthered these changes and class redirections, and he offers the following new class structure.

THE DIPLOMA ELITE.
    (1) Real Upper Class.
    (2) The Semi-Upper Class.

THE SUPPORTING CLASSES
    (3) The Limited-Success Class.
    (4) The Working Class.
    (5) The Real Lower Class.

Of the Semi-Upper Class, he writes that they are 'most confident, energetic, ambitious people who went away to college, then began a career somewhere away from their home town or neighbourhood. Most of them are with fairly large organizations where they are decision makers serving as managers, technologists or persuaders. The remainder are professional men or successful local businessmen' (p. 41).

It is also interesting to compare Packard's Semi-Upper Class with the 'ufologists' listed in Appendix 5, and his 'Limited-Success Class' definition with the contactees listed in Appendix 5.

3. In this context it is worth mentioning L. Ron Hubbard and *Dianetics: The Modern Science Of Mental Health*. Hubbard founded the tellingly named Church of Scientology, which practised his system of Dianetics, a quasi-occult system of developing occult (mental) perceptions by training the mind to focus back on recalling pre-birth experiences in order to undergo an individual liberation. Hubbard's methodology is explained by the adoption of a wide range of technical metaphors, thus: 'there are no real demons in dianetics. ... A dianetic demon is a parasitic circuit' (p. 86). Hubbard's therapy, carried out by an 'auditor', deals with a subject, termed as a 'pre-clear' and is accomplished by the use of 'engrams'. Thus typical traditional occult axioms as to mind functions and potential are rendered in a new vocabulary that can only be described as being bureau-technocratic in nature and appropriation. Thus, speaking of memory and its controlled recall, Hubbard offers ...

The index system of the standard bank is a wonderful thing to behold. Everything is there, filed by subject, filed by time and filed by conclusions. All perceptions are present.

With the time file system we have what is called in dianetics a *time track*. Going back along this track with part of 'I' is *returning*. It is definitely present for both conscious and 'unconscious' data. The *time track* is of vast and interesting concern to the auditor.

The mind is a well built computer and it has various services. Auditors backing off from Latin and complexity, call the source of one of these services the *file clerk*. This is not a very dignified name and it is certainly anthropomorphic. ... The *file clerk* is the bank monitor. 'He' monitors for both the reactive engram and the standard banks. (pp. 197/8).

4. It is interesting to note how often the extra-terrestrials described by the contactees who claimed personal meetings with the visitors manage to conform to a recognizable stereotype. Thus Adamski described his Venusian in *Flying Saucers Have Landed* as being 'smooth-skinned, beardless and well-dressed. He had shoulder-length blond hair, was about five feet six inches tall, and wore what looked like a ski suit with a broad belt around the waist' (R. Story 1980, p. 3).

Angelucci's extra-terrestrials were described as 'a suprahumanly splendid man and woman bathed in light' (R. Story 1980, p. 21).

Menger's contacts with extra-terrestrials revealed them to be of a similar appearance; he describes one as being 'a beautiful, golden-haired woman ... the most exquisite woman my young eyes had ever beheld! The warm sunlight caught the highlights of her long, golden hair as it cascaded around her face and shoulders. The curves of her lovely body were delicately contoured – revealed through the translucent material of her clothing' (R. Story 1980, p. 229).

The gist of most of the personal contactees' accounts is that the extra-terrestrials live an idyllic life free of the concerns and anxieties that are the norm of earthly existence; their bearing, dress and appearance could well have come from the illustrations in the racist journals of Adolf Lanz.

APPENDICES

APPENDIX 1

A List of Titles of Atom Bomb, or Atom Bomb-related Articles appearing in *Time* between March and December 1950

6 March, p. 83   Physicists Disagree on Destructiveness of 'A' Bomb

13 March, p. 71   Lilienthal Plays Down World Doom Prophets

10 April, p. 24   Russian 'A' Bomb Cuts West's Advantage

22 May, p. 69   US Possesses Small Bombs ('A' Bombs)

29 May, p. 41   Suggestion That All US Be Dog-Tagged For Blood Types, Preparation For Atomic Disaster

11 Sept., p. 22   Major-General Orvil Anderson Advocates Launching 'A' Bomb Attack On Russia; Disciplined

18 Sept., p. 30   US Superiority Over Russia Argument for Preventive War

2 Oct., p. 12   US Mobilizes Civilian Defenses. Hypothetical Raid On N.Y. City

6 Nov., p. 8   Booklet: You And The Atom Bomb

11 Dec., p. 24   Bombing Russia Or Red China Among Alternatives

APPENDIX 2

A List of Anti-Soviet Articles appearing in the *Saturday Evening Post* Between April 1949 and April 1950

2 May   I Learned About Communism The Hard Way

4 June   Now The Russians Are Fleeing Russia

11 June   They Guard Our Coasts From Aliens

2 July   Hungarian Fugitives' Account: I Saw Russia Preparing For War

9 July   Hungarian Fugitives' Account: How Moscow Sabotages Its Own Satellites

16 July   Hungarian Fugitives' Account: Doomsday In Moscow

23 July   Moscow's Phoney Peace Campaign

6 Aug.   Is Japanese Youth Going Communist?

13 Aug.   Should We Grab Formosa?

1 Oct.   I Saw The Russians Snooping (1)

9 Oct.   I Saw The Russians Snooping (2)

22 Oct.   The Commies Don't Even Say Thankyou

5 Nov.   Russia's Triple Crisis

12 Nov.   My 3 Years In Moscow: What Kind Of Man Is Stalin?

19 Nov.   My 3 Years In Moscow: Housekeeping Headaches In A Public State

26 Nov.   My 3 Years In Moscow: Why The Russian People Don't Rebel. Red Rape Of Albania

3 Dec.   Falsehood: Russia's Sharpest Weapon

10 Dec.   God Won't Stay Underground In Russia

17 Dec.   What Really Happened At The Moscow Conference

31 Dec.   Do The Soviet Leaders Want War?

7 Jan.   Why We Lost China (1)

14 Jan.   Why We Lost China: We Opened The Door For The Commies.

21 Jan.   Why We Lost China: The Foredoomed Mission Of General Arthur

28 Jan.   The Highest Paid Spy In History

4 Feb.   The Reds Are Rapping At Our Arctic Door

11 Feb.   How Our Commies Defame America Abroad

18 Feb.   The Students Strike Back At Stalin

25 Feb.   How Finland Baulks Her Communists

11 Mar.   We Are Losing Asia Fast

18 Mar.   How Are We Fixed For Uranium?

1 April   Communism's Child Hostages.

APPENDIX 3

Examples of Hermetic Nature of Typical Flying Saucer Contact or Sighting Account

Examples taken from The New UFO Breakthrough by Brad Steiger and Joan Whritenour (London: Tandem, 1975, pp. 47, 48 and 49. (**Bold type** indicates italics in original)

On 20 May, Steve Michalak was not considering the method by which he had been burned by a UFO – he only knew that he had been left with a seared chest, the remnants of an undershirt with a geometrically shaped burn in it, a hat with a hole burned through it, and a smell 'coming from **inside** me – and I can't get rid of it'.

Michalak had been looking out at land just north of Falcon Lake, Manitoba when he was alerted by the cackling of geese. Looking up, he saw two objects coming from a south-southwesterly direction. The objects were 'glaring red. I can't describe how fast they were going. You just can't put it in time. One was cruising about ten feet above the ground, and one landed.'

Michalak was not about to rush forward with his hands raised in the **Homo sapiens** traditional salute of peace. He watched the grounded UFO for half an hour before he approached it.

'It gave off rainbow reflections', Michalak said. 'When a door finally opened, all I could see was a brilliant violet color. It seemed to be making a sort of whistling noise, like it was sucking in air or something.'

Michalak described the object as being about thirty-five feet long, eight feet high, with a three-foot protusion on top. It seemed to be constructed of stainless steel, and the Canadian was awed by 'the most perfect joints I've ever seen. I can't understand how it was done. There was no welding, no rivets, no bolting, and when the door closed I could see nothing.'

As Michalak approached the object, he could hear voices coming from within the shiny shell. Being multilingual, Michalak addressed the UFO in English, Russian, German, Italian and Polish. At the sound of his voice, the door in the side closed and the object began to move in a counterclockwise direction. Before the UFO took off into space, jets of heat came from a pattern of holes in the side of the object. These seared Michalak and burned his clothing.

Michalak's wife told the press that her husband had not been able to retain food since his frightening experience, and she also complained of the strange odor he described.

On 13 June, a man from Eastern Henrico County, Virginia, was burned on the arm and face by what appeared to be a deliberate act of hostility on the part of a flying saucer. Charles W. Fletcher, sixty-nine, was sitting in his yard reading a newspaper when a bright light swooped down from the skies, hovered above him and ejected a purplish substance which dropped onto his left arm near his elbow. While Fletcher was wiping the strange liquid off his arm with a newspaper, the UFO dropped another glob, which burned him on the right side of the face.

It was about 2:00 a.m. on 30 June when Highway Patrolman Dennis Eisnach picked up Merchant Policeman James Ferguson's radio message. Ferguson asked Eisnach to meet him at the Montana-Dakota construction site in Rapid City, South Dakota.

When Patrolman Eisnach arrived at the construction site, Ferguson told him that he had been keeping 'something strange' under surveillance. Ferguson had just begun telling his fellow officer something of the nature of the unusual object when a craft with flashing lights lifted off the ground from behind a clump of trees and hovered just above the branches.

Eisnach watched the UFO through binoculars and was able to distinguish light coming through three windows. 'I couldn't distinguish the shape of the craft,' the patrolman said, 'just red, green, and white lights. It made several horizontal movements. I watched it move back and forth twice; then it sat back down on the ground again, out of sight.'

Eisnach drove his patrol car around on a back road, trying to get closer to the object. When he got behind it, about two blocks away, it once again rose off the ground and went over a hill.

'I had noticed', Eisnach said, 'that when the craft got closer to the ground the white light would get brighter – the closer to the ground the brighter the light.'

By this time a number of other law-enforcement officers had arrived on the scene and witnessed the strange, hovering craft. Soon an officer made the discovery that three similar craft were hovering a considerable distance away. Patrolman Eisnach focused his binoculars on them and said they looked the same as the object that had landed.

The officers watched the mysterious objects for over two and one half hours. 'We all couldn't be nuts,' said Ferguson. 'I never saw anything like that mass of lights before. It would be impossible that it was aircraft.'

An alien missile attack on a vehicle on 17 July may have produced a case similar to that of Betty and Barney Hill's famous 'interrupted journey'.

Village Patrolman Lewis Lindsay answered a report of a stalled automobile north of Millerton, New York, and found Mrs. Funk stunned and confused. Mrs. Funk said she had been traveling north on Route 22 at 11:25 p.m. when a shiny black object the size of a softball came from overhead, hit the windshield and then bounced away. At that precise moment, the headlights went out, the car stalled, a bright light seemed to flare inside her automobile, and Mrs. Funk lost consciousness. When she came to she was heading in the opposite direction on Route 22, about one mile south of where the alien missile had struck her car.

(On 19 September, William Donovan, president of Aerial Investigations and Research, Inc., said that Mrs. Funk's story had been 'verified' under hypnosis. While in hypnotic regression Mrs. Funk told of reaching over to turn off her car radio, which had suddenly become filled with static, when the black object came at her over the hood. She then told of 'them' turning her car around and striking her across the chest with a 'rod'. The hypnotic session was filmed by the BBC for a news special on UFOs scheduled to be broadcast early in 1968.)

APPENDIX 4

Major Flying Saucer Societies in America and Europe

Aerial Phenomena Research Organisation (APRO)
Main Aim or Activity: 'maintains a Field Investigators' Network to speedily and accurately investigate UFO cases'. Founded: 1952. Membership: 2700 (in 1979)

British UFO Research Association (BUFORA)
Main Aim or Activity: 'monthly meetings and production of detailed investigator's manual'. Founded: 1959

Center For UFO Studies (CUFOS)
Main Aim or Activity: 'to promote serious research into UFO phenomena'. Founded: 1973. Membership: 26 research scientists make up main core.

Centro Ufologico Nazionale (CUN)
Main Aim or Activity: 'maintains a serious scientific approach'. Founded: 1965.

Comitato Nazionale per lo Studio dei Fenomeni Aerei Anemali (CNIFAA)
Main Aim or Activity: 'a search for a real scientific approach to the UFO phenomenon'. Founded: 1973.

Contact International
Main Aim or Activity: 'a policy of promoting contacts between Ufologists everywhere'. Founded: 1967. Membership: 2000 (of whom 1000 in Britain).

Civilian Research into Interplanetary Flying Objects (CRIFO)
Founded: mid-1950s.

Ground Saucer Watch (GSW)
Main Aim or Activity: 'established for those persons who want to see positive scientific action taken to end the elements of cover-up and foul-up in UFO research'. Founded: 1957. Membership: 500.

Groupe d'Étude des Phénomènes Aérospatiaux non-identifiés (GEPLAN)
Main Aim or Activity: 'controlled by a council of seven scientists'. Founded: 1977.

Groupement d'Étude des Phénomènes Aériens (GEPA)
Main Aim or Activity: 'covers an extensive programme of research and publishes a periodical, *Phénomènes spatiaux*, and aims to attract attention of scientists worldwide to the UFO phenomenon'. Founded: 1962 (offshoot of a parent organization founded in 1952).

Mutual UFO Network (MUFON)
Main Aim or Activity: 'to resolve the UFO mystery and all of its ramifications in a scientific manner'. Founded: 1967. Membership: governed by a board of directors, there being a state or provincial director for every state in N.W. America.

National Investigations Committee on Aerial Phenomena (NICAP)
Main Aim or Activity: 'a research organisation willing to accept UFO reports in confidence from pilots, military personnel and others in sensitive positions. A national network of investigators and "sub committees" set-up, including operational units at major scientific and military establishments'. Founded: 1956. Membership: 10,000.

UFO Research, New South Wales (UFOR–NSW)
Main Aim or Activity: 'detailed investigations and documentation of UFO sightings and maintenance of the Australian computer file'. Founded: 1950.

The above list and details were taken from *The Encyclopedia of UFOs* (ed. R.D. Story, 1980). The titles of the above societies provide a revealing insight into the desires of their founders. The titles borrow from the language of the state science-bureaucracy hegemony, thereby hoping to appropriate an authority invested in 'official' activity. They also echo the titles of corporate organizations. These observations are reinforced by the entry under Main Aim or Activity, where research, communication and cataloguing are repeated themes: research becomes conflated with clerical activity, and both are 'serious' because they deal with 'reality'. Thus title and activity legitimate and bestow authority by association. Thus there is no society with a title such as 'Sky Watch', with an intent to 'observe the skies for UFO phenomena'.

APPENDIX 5

Prominent Ufologists and Contactees: Details taken from *The Encyclopedia of UFOS*

The Encyclopedia of UFOS gives extensive details of all the major 'ufologists' working in the field. The list below gives only a cross-section of the more prominent practitioners. Furthermore, it confines itself to those who are outside establishment science as promoters of UFO enquiry. Thus, for instance, Carl Sagan, a prominent science popularizer and advocate of the search for extra-terrestrial intelligence, is not included, since neither he nor the genre would consider him as being a 'ufologist'. What is itemized in the list of 'ufologists' is the educational attainment, which is almost invariably given. The evidence of this list shows that 'ufologists' are overwhelmingly male, and of, or aspiring to, what has been termed the professional-managerial class.

The second and much shorter list of prominent contactees has been limited to those contactees who went on to become saucer advocates and to found groups or movements dedicated to an organized attempt to extend the original contact with the saucers and/or their crew. Alternatively, or also, the contactees have written books about their experiences. Here there is a marked comparison in educational status. Whereas, therefore, the 'ufologists' appropriate the organizational forms of bureaucracy and science to validate their activity with authority, the contactees evoke mystic and religious significations and often proclaim a new millennium.

UFOLOGISTS

Andrews, Arlan Keith
BS degree in Mechanical
Engineering. MS and ScD degrees.
Consultant in mechanical
engineering for the AERIAL
PHENOMENA RESEARCH ORGANISATION,
the MUTUAL UFO NETWORK (MUFON)
and the New Atlanteans.

Andrus, Walter
Graduated from the Central
Technical Institute at Kansas City,
Missouri. International Director of
MUTUAL UFO NETWORK (MUFON).

Barker, Gray
Graduated from Glenville State
College with an AB degree.
Founded his own publication, *The
Saucerian*, edited and published
Saucer News.

Bowen, Charles
No educational details given. Editor
of *Flying Saucer Review*.

Cerny, Paul
No educational details given. Works
as miniaturization engineer in
electronics industry. Western States
Regional Director for MUFON.
Special investigator for the CENTER
FOR UFO STUDIES.

Chalker, William
Graduated in Chemistry and
Mathematics at University of New
England, New South Wales.
Australian representative for the
AERIAL PHENOMENA RESEARCH
ORGANISATION and scientific
consultant to the Australian
Coordination Section of the CENTER
FOR UFO STUDIES. Editor of the
Australian UFO Researcher.

Cohen, Daniel
Graduated in Journalism from the
University of Illinois. Edited *Science
Digest*. Has written over sixty books
within the genre.

Delair, J, Bernard
College education in Geography
and Geology. General Secretary of
CONTACT (UK), editor of (THE) UFO
REGISTER. He now coordinates
research conducted by the Data
Research Division of CONTACT (UK).

Druffel, Ann
BA degree in Sociology from
Immaculate Heart College,
Hollywood. Associate Editor for
the MUTUAL UFO NETWORK'S *UFO
Journal*.

Farabone, Roberto
Degree in Physics from the
University of Milan. A principal
founder of COMITATO NAZIONALE
INDIPENDENTE PER LO STUDIO DEI
FENOMENI AEREI ANOMALI, and
member of the scientific board of
CENTRO UFOLOGICO NAZIONALE.

Fouréré, René
No educational details given.
Telecommunications engineer.
Secretary of GROUPEMENT D'ÉTUDE DES
PHÉNOMÈNES AÉRIENS (GEPA).

Fowler, Raymond
Served a four-year term with USAF
Security Service. Graduated magna
cum laude from Gordon College,
Wenham, Massachusetts. Director
of Investigations for the MUTUAL UFO
NETWORK, a scientific associate for
the CENTER FOR UFO STUDIES, and a
consultant to the NATIONAL
INVESTIGATIONS COMMITTEE ON AERIAL
PHENOMENA (NICAP).

Hall, Richard
Philosophy graduate of Tulane
University, New Orleans. A
technical editor. Assistant Director
of NATIONAL INVESTIGATIONS COMMITTEE
ON AERIAL PHENOMENA (NICAP).
Editor of MUFON Journal and INFO
Journal.

Hendry, Allan
BA Degree in Astronomy from
the University of Michigan.
Chief Investigator for CENTER
FOR UFO STUDIES. Managing
Editor of International UFO
Reporter.

Hendry, Elaine
BS Degree in Astronomy from
the University of Michigan. MS
and PhD also in Astronomy from
North Western University. Editor
of The Journal of UFO
Studies.

Hewes, Hayden
Majored in Aeronautical and Space
Engineering, University of
Oklahoma. United States editor of
Psychic Australian and Contributing
Editor of the Canadian UFO Report
and the Hefley Psychic Report.

Hind, John
Electronic Engineering student.
Editor of Irish UFO News.

Hynek, Josef
Professor of Astronomy,
Northwestern University. Editor-in-
Chief of The International UFO
Reporter.

Jacobs, Daniel
PhD in History from the University
of Wisconsin. Consulting Editor to
The Zetetic Scholar & UFO Phenomena.
Consultant in History to the AERIAL
PHENOMENA RESEARCH ORGANISATION.

Jessup, Morris
BS, MS and PhD degrees at the
University of Michigan. Author of
four texts within the genre.

Keel, John
No educational details given.
Author and journalist. Six texts
within the genre.

Keyhoe, Donald
Graduate of US Naval Academy.
Director of NATIONAL INVESTIGATIONS
COMMITTEE ON AERIAL PHENOMENA.
Author of five texts within the
genre.

Le Poer Trench, Brinsley
Eighth Earl of Clancarty. Educated
at the Nautical College,
Pangbourne, Berkshire.
Advertisement Manager of RAF
Flying Review. Advertisement
Manager of Practical Gardening.
Editor of Flying Saucer Review.
Established INTERNATIONAL SKY
SCOUTS. Founder-President of
CONTACT INTERNATIONAL.

Leslie, Desmond
Educated at Ampleforth College, York and Trinity College Dublin. Co-author of 'classic' text, *Flying Saucers Have Landed*.

Lorenzen, Coral
Graduated from High School. Founder of AERIAL PHENOMENA RESEARCH ORGANISATION (APRO).

Lorenzen, Leslie
Graduated from High School. Trained as a radio-operator mechanic. International Director of the AERIAL PHENOMENA RESEARCH ORGANISATION (APRO).

Michel, Aimé
License in Philosophy and Letters, University of Marseilles. Overseas Consultant to British *Flying Saucer Review*.

Munday, John
AB in Physics at Cornell University, PhD in Biophysics at the University of Illinois. Consultant in Biophysics to AERIAL PHENOMENA RESEARCH ORGANISATION (APRO).

Olsen, Thomas
MS degree in Physics and Mathematics, University of Wisconsin. Founder of UFO INFORMATION RETRIEVAL CENTER (UFOIRC).

Randles, Jenny
No educational details given. Publications editor for NORTHERN UFO NETWORK (NUFON). Research Coordinator for BRITISH UFO RESEARCH ASSOCIATION (BUFORA). Helped create UFO INVESTIGATORS' NETWORK (UFOIN).

Steiger, Brad
No educational details given. Taught American literature and creative writing. Author of several major works on UFOs.

Stringfield, Leonard
No educational details given. Director of CIVILIAN RESEARCH, INTERPLANETARY FLYING OBJECTS (CRIFO) and publisher of its newsletter, *Orbit*.

Webb, David
BS degree in Physics and Astrophysics from Mount Union College. Member of AERIAL PHENOMENA RESEARCH ORGANISATION (APRO), a member of the NATIONAL INVESTIGATIONS COMMITTEE ON AERIAL PHENOMENA and co-chairman of MUFON's HUMANOID STUDY GROUP.

CONTACTEES

Adamski, George
Described by his disciples at the GEORGE ADAMSKI FOUNDATION, based in Vista, California, as 'author-lecturer on Unidentified Flying Objects, space travel, Cosmic Philosophy and Universal Laws of Life'. Claimed the title of Professor, as an honorary title bestowed upon him by his students.

Angelucci, Orfeo
Formal schooling ended early due to ill health. Shopfloor worker at Lockheed's Burbank Plant. He has founded no organization, claimed no grandiose titles or callings but has proclaimed a saucerian message based upon mystical experiences induced by direct contact with ufonauts. Wrote *Secrets Of The Saucers*.

Bethurum, Truman
An asphalt layer. Claimed to have met space people on numerous occasions. The 'Captain' of a flying saucer gave him information about the working of flying saucers. Once he was invited aboard a saucer by its female 'Captain', Aura Rhanes. Published details in *Aboard A Flying Saucer*.

Green, Gabriel
Professional photographer. Formed the LOS ANGELES INTERPLANETARY STUDY GROUPS, which evolved into the AMALGAMATED FLYING SAUCER CLUBS OF AMERICA (AFSCA). He claims over a hundred sightings of saucers as well as several direct contacts with persons from other planets. He was asked by the space people to run for political office, 'In an effort to plant the political seeds of reform'. He states that he is a 'vocal telepathic channel for the Space masters of the Great White Brotherhood – the Spiritual Hierarchy of Earth, and acts as a channel for energies from the Space People, which enables persons to read their own Akashic records and to re-experience their past lives without hypnosis'. He is an exponent of Universal Economics, the 'non-money system of economics' used on other advanced planets.

King, George
Taxi-driver. Claimed that he was contacted by a voice from space that informed him that he was to become the 'Voice of the Interplanetary

Parliament', and that he was also to become the 'Primary Terrestrial Mental Channel'. The voice from space was claimed to be that of a 3500-year-old Venusian Master called Aetherius. King subsequently founded the Aetherius Society. The messages from the Venusian Master include warnings against the use of nuclear energy in any form. The messages transmitted through King are all preserved on audio tape. King claims to have a PhD from London University.

Menger, Howard
Received an elementary and high school education. He worked for a year as a munitions handler and inspector in Picatinny Arsenal. War service in tank corps and military intelligence. After the war he established the Menger Advertising Company. He later formed Energy Systems Inc., to do basic research in electronics and to promote several of his inventions, including an emergency power pack. Took photographs of flying saucers. Was chosen to be one of a select group of 'earthlings' to be contacted by extra-terrestrials from Venus, Jupiter, Mars and Saturn. He was told that he and his second wife Connie were reincarnations of Venusians.

Van Tassel, George
Operator of Giant Rock Airport. Went into a trance by the large rock, for which Giant Rock is named. He was taken up to meet the 'Council of Seven Lights', a group of discarnate 'earthlings' inhabiting a spaceship circling the earth. He also was later contacted on earth by alien space travellers. He hosted the Giant Rock Space Conventions at which important contactees and their followers congregated annually. He was founder of the Ministry of Universal Wisdom, and the related College of Universal Wisdom. He built a large 'structure' for research known as the 'Integratron'.

BIBLIOGRAPHIES

BIBLIOGRAPHY 1: Techno-Occultism

ADAMSKI, GEORGE (WITH LESLIE), *Flying Saucers Have Landed,* 1977 Futura publications

ADAMSKI, GEORGE, *Behind the Flying Saucer Mystery.* This amazing book rips the curtain of secrecy from the flying saucer phenomena! 1967 Paperback Library, N.Y.

ASHPOLE, ADAMS, *The Search for Extra-Terrestrial Intelligence,* 1989, Blandford

BALL, BRIAN, *A Young Person's Guide to UFOs,* 1979 Granada

BERLITZ, CHARLES, *The Bermuda Triangle.* The bestselling saga of unexplained disappearances. 1975 Granada

—— *The Mystery of Atlantis,* 1977 Granada

—— *Without a Trace.* The latest investigation of the greatest unsolved enigma of all time. 1978 Granda

—— *The Philadelphia Experiment.* The true story behind Project Invisibility. 1980 Granada

—— *The Roswell Incident,* 1980 Granada

—— *Doomsday 1999.* Countdown to the new apocalypse. 1982 Granada

BLUMRICH, JOSEF, *The Spaceships of Ezekiel* Are the von Daniken theories really true? Was Earth once visited by beings from another planet? A major NASA engineer reveals some astonishing facts. 1974 Corgi

BOVA, BEN & BYRON PREISS (eds), *First Contact*; The Search for Extra-terrestrial Intelligence, 1990, Headline

BOYCE, CHRIS, *Extraterrestrial Encounter* A startling survey of alien intelligences and mankind. 1981 N.E.L

BRIAZACK, NORMAN (WITH SIMON MENNICK), *The UFO Guidebook,* 1978 N.E.L

BRENNAN, J., *Occult Reich,* 1974 Futura

BUTTLAR, JOHANNES, *The UFO Phenomenon* 'The existence of these machines is proved' – Air Chief Marshal Lord Dowding. 1980 Star

CATHIE, BRUCE, *Harmonic 33,* 1980 Sphere

—— *Harmonic 695,* 1980 Sphere

—— *The Pulse of the Universe: Harmonic 288,* 1981 Sphere

BIBLIOGRAPHY

CHAPMAN, ROBERT, *UFO* Flying saucers over Britain. 1968 Granada

CHARROUX, ROBERT, *Masters of the World* In the dawn of Time they came from space to become ... 1979 Sphere

—— *Legacy of the Gods*, 1980 Sphere

—— *100,000 Years of Man's History*, 1981 Sphere

CHATELAIN, M. *Our Ancestors Came from Outer Space*, 1980 Pan

COLLYNS, ROBIN, *Laser Beams from Star Cities?* A startling new theory of interstellar communication. 1977 Sphere

—— *Ancient Astronauts: A Time Reversal* New evidence of unearthly visitations. 1978 Sphere

—— *Prehistoric Germ Warfare* Is mankind an alien experiment? 1980 Star

DANIKEN, ERICH VON, *Chariots of the Gods* Was god an astronaut? 1971 Corgi

—— *Return to the Stars* Gods from outer space. 1972 Corgi

—— *The Gold of the Gods* From the author of Chariots Of The Gods and Return To The Stars comes explosive new evidence about the origin of man ... 1974 Corgi

—— *In Search of Ancient Gods* My pictorial evidence for the impossible. 1976 Corgi

—— *Miracles of the Gods*, 1977 Corgi

—— *According to the Evidence* My proof of man's extraterrestrial origins. 1978 Corgi

—— *Signs of the Gods?* 1981 Corgi

DELGADO, PAT & COLIN ANDREWS, *Circular Evidence*. A detailed investigation of the flattened swirled crops phenomenon. 1990, Headline

DEVEREUX, PAUL, *Earthlights*, 1982 Turnstone Press

DIONE, R. *God Drives a Flying Saucer* Astounding biblical revelations that prove the existence of UFOs and explain their spiritual significance to mankind! 1973 Corgi

DRAKE, W. RAYMOND, *Gods and Spacemen in the Ancient East* New evidence on the unexplained mysteries of civilisation in the ancient East. 1973 Sphere

—— *Gods and Spacemen in the Ancient West*, 1974 Sphere

—— *Gods and Spacemen in Greece and Rome*, 1975 Sphere

—— *Gods and Spacemen in Ancient Israel*, 1976 Sphere

FLINDT, MAX & OTTO BINDEN, *Mankind, Child of the Stars*, 1976 Coronet

FORT, CHARLES, *New Lands*, 1974 Sphere

GOOD, TIMOTHY, *Above Top Secret*. The worldwide UFO conspiracy. 1990 Grafton

GOODSAVAGE, JOSEPH, *Storm on the Sun* How the sun affects life on earth. 1980 Sphere

GRUMLEY, MICHAEL, *There are Giants in the Earth* Giant apemen – the true facts. 1976 Panther

HOBANA, ION & JULIEN WEVERBERGH, *UFOs from Behind the Iron Curtain*, 1975 Corgi

HOLROYD, STUART, *Alien Intelligence*, 1980 Abacus

HOYLE, FRED & N.C. WICKRAMASINGHE, *Diseases from Space*, 1981 Sphere

HOYLE, FRED, *Ice* A chilling scientific forecast of a new ice age. 1982 N.E.L

HUGHES, DAVID, *The Star of Bethlehem Mystery*, 1981 Corgi

HYNEK, J. ALLEN, *The Hynek UFO Report* The latest bestseller by the world's leading UFO expert. 1978 Sphere

KEEL, JOHN, *UFOs: Operation Trojan Horse*, 1973 Abacus

—— *Visitors from Space* The Astonishing, true story of the Mothman prophecies. 1976 Panther

—— *The Cosmic Question* Man and the supernatural – a stunning new perspective. 1978 Panther

KEYHOE, DONALD, *The Flying Saucers are Real* True story behind the strangest phenomena in history! 1950 Hutchinson

—— *Flying Saucers from Outer Space* One thing's absolutely certain. We're being watched by beings from outer space. 1970 Tandem

KOLOSIMO, PETER, *Not of this World* Not since *Chariots of the Gods* has so provocative an examination of the unexplained mysteries of the past appeared in paperback. 1971 Sphere

LANDSBERG, ALAN & SALLY, *In Search of Ancient Mysteries* Did man begin on Earth – or was he sent here from other worlds? 1974 Corgi

—— *The Outer Space Connection* Contains astonishing new proof that we are not alone in the universe. 1975 Corgi

LESLIE, DESMOND & GEORGE ADAMSKI, *Flying Saucers Have Landed*, 1977 Futura

LEONARD, GEORGE, *Someone Else Is On Our Moon* Revealed – the astounding facts about intelligent life on the moon 1978 Sphere

MENZEL, DONALD, *The World of Flying Saucers*, 1963 Doubleday & Co

MITCHELL, JOHN, *City of Revelation*, 1973 Abacus

—— *The View Over Atlantis*, 1973 Abacus

—— *The Flying Saucer Vision*, 1974 Abacus

MOONEY, RICHARD, *Colony Earth* What were the origins of man? 1977 Granada

—— *Gods of Air And Darkness* Man – an extra-terrestrial experiment? 1976 Granada

NOORBERGEN, RENÉ, *Secrets of the Lost Races* The most controversial view of the past since *Chariots of the Gods*. 1977 N.E.L

NOYES, RALPH (ed.), *The Crop Circle Enigma*, 1990, Gateway

PAGET, PETER, *The Welsh Triangle* The astonishing account of UFO sightings in the corner of Wales. 1979 Granada

—— *U.F.O. U.K.*, 1980 N.E.L

PAUWELS, LOUIS & JACQUES BERGIER, *The Morning of the Magicians* The most startlingly original bestseller of the decade. 1972 Mayflower

—— *Impossible Possibilities*, 1974 Mayflower

—— *Eternal Man* Are we older and wiser than we know? 1973 Mayflower

PUGH, R.J. & F.W. HOLIDAY, *The Dyfed Enigma* Close encounters of the Welsh kind. 1981 Coronet

RANDLES, JENNY, *UFO Study: A Handbook For Enthusiasts*, 1981 Robert Hale

RAVENSCROFT, TREVOR, *The Spear of Destiny* How the Occult Power of the Spear which pierced the side of Christ became Hitler's greatest weapon in his bid to conquer the world ... 1974 Corgi

ROBERTS, ANTHONY & GEOFF GILBERTSON, *The Dark Gods*, 1980 Rider Hutchinson

SASSOON, GEORGE & RODNEY DALE, *The Manna Machine* The Most exciting challenge in cosmology since *Chariots of the Gods*. 1980 Granada

SCRUTTON, ROBERT, *The Other Atlantis*, Astounding revelations of the secrets of Atland, long-lost imperial continent of the North. 1979 Sphere

SHUTTLEWOOD, ARTHUR, *The Flying Saucerers*, 1977 Sphere

—— *U.F.O. Magic In Motion*, 1979 Sphere

SIMPSON, GEORGE & NEAL BURGER, *Thin Air*, 1979 N.E.L

SMITH, WARREN, *U.F.O. Trek*, Has science fiction become an amazing fact? 1977 Sphere

STEIGER, BRAD, *Atlantis Rising* Astounding insights into the mystery of the Lost Continent. 1977 Sphere

—— *Gods of Aquarius* Man's secret destiny revealed. 1980 Granada

STEIGER, BRAD & JOAN WHRITENOUR, *The New U.F.O. Breakthrough.* 1973 Tandem

—— —— *Flying Saucers are Hostile.* 1967 Tandem

STONELEY, JACK, *CETI (Communication with Extra-Terrestrial Intelligence)* The future of mankind may depend on . . . 1976 Star

STREIBER, WHITLEY, *Communion*, 1988 Arrow

—— *Transformation: The Breakthrough*, 1989 Arrow

STRINGFIELD, LEONARD, *Situation Red: The UFO Siege*, 1978 Sphere

SULLIVAN, WALTER, *We Are Not Alone* Close Encounters? Have there been visitors from outer space? 1966 Signet

THOMAS, PAUL, *Flying Saucers Through The Ages*, 1973 Tandem

TILMS, RICHARD, *Judgement of Jupiter* A frightening scientific probe into what the planets really have in store for us. 1980 N.E.L

TOMAS, ANDREW, *Atlantis: From Legend To Discovery*, Folk lore or fact? The author of *We Are Not The First* examines the legacy of the lost continent. 1973 Sphere

TRENCH, BRINSLEY, *Operation Earth*, 1974 Tandem

—— *Mysterious Visitors*, 1975 Pan

—— *Secret Of The Ages*, UFOs from inside the Earth. 1976 Panther

VALENTINE, TOM, *The Great Pyramid* An astounding exploration into man's past and future. 1977 Panther

VELIKOVSKY, IMMANUEL, *Worlds in Collision*, 1972 Abacus

—— *Earth in Upheaval.* 1973 Abacus

—— *Mankind in Amnesia*, 1982 Sidgwick & Jackson

WARSHOFSKY, FRED, *Doomsday: The Science of Catastrophe*, 1979 Abacus

WATKINS, LESLIE, *Alternative Three* Life on Earth is doomed. The super-power governments have a plan to preserve a tiny nucleus of human survivors. 1978 Sphere

WILSON, CLIFFORD, *The Chariots Still Crash* The latest, fullest revelations about: the secrets of the pyramids; the legendary lost continents of the Mayas and the Incas; the golden artifacts of Ecuador; the clues in ancient writings; Stonehenge, Easter Island, and much, much more. 1976 Signet

WILSON, DON, *Our Mysterious Spaceship Moon* Is our nearest neighbour in space a huge alien spacecraft? 1976 Sphere

WINER, RICHARD, *The Devil's Triangle*. A saga of the mysterious sea where ships, planes and doomed human beings disappear forever. 1974 Bantam

—— *The Devil's Jaw* First time published! New startling evidence of mysterious disappearances around the world – phantom ships, bizarre sinkings, lost souls, unexplained disasters. 1977 Corgi

Compiled by the Editors of *Fate Magazine Strange Twist Of Fate* Startling, true accounts of how mysterious powers of UFOs, dreams, ESP, black magic and other amazing psychic phenomena influence our lives. 1967 Paperback Library, N.Y

BIBLIOGRAPHY 2: General

ARONOWITZ, STANLEY, 'The professional-managerial class or middle strata', in Walker, P., (ed.), *Between Capital and Labour: Marxist Theory And Contemporary Capitalism*, 1979 Harvester Press.

BADGER, ANTHONY J. *The New Deal and the Depression Years 1933–40*, 1989, Macmillan.

BALDERSTONE AND HUGHES, *Atomic Age: A Manual for Survival*, 1951, University of South California Press.

BALDICK, R., *The Life of J.K. Huysmans*, 1951, Oxford University Press.

BALL, BRIAN, *A Young Person's Guide to UFOs* 1979, Granada.

BALLARD, JACK, STOKES, *The Shock of Peace: Military and Economic Demobilisation after World War Two*, 1983, University Press of America.

BANKOFF, GEORGE, *The Boon of the Atom*, 1949, The Scientific Book Club.

BARTHES, ROLAND, *Mythologies*, 1980, Paladin.

BEDARIDA, FRANÇOISE, *A Social History of England, 1851–1975*, 1979, Methuen.

BEER, GILLIAN, *Darwin's Plots: Evolutionary Narrative in Darwin, George Eliot and Nineteenth-Century Fiction*, 1985, Ark Paperbacks, London.

BELL, DANIEL, *The Coming of the Post-Industrial Society*, 1973, Basic Books, New York.

BENNETT, TONY, 'Popular culture and the turn to gramsci', in Bennett, T. *et al.*, (eds), *Popular Culture and Social Relations*, 1986.

BERROW, LOGIE, *Independent Spirits: Spiritualism and English Plebeians (1850–1910)*, 1986, Routledge and Kegan Paul.

BESTERMAN, T., *Mrs. Annie Besant*, 1934, Kegan Paul.

BOOTH, WILLIAM, *In Darkest England and The Way Out*, 1890, London.

BOVERE, RICHARD, *Senator Joe McCarthy*, 1960, Methuen.

BOYLE, THOMAS, *Black Swine in the Sewers of Hampstead*, 1990, Hodder & Stoughton.

BRADBURY, MALCOLM, (WITH TEMPERLEY, HOWARD), *Introduction to American Studies*, 1981, Longmans.

BRANDON, RUTH, *The Spiritualists*, 1973, Weidenfeld and Nicolson.

BRAUNBECK, WERNER, *The Drama of the Atom*, 1958, Oliver and Boyd.

BRENDON, PIERS, *IKE: The Life and Times of Dwight D. Eisenhower*, 1987, Secker & Warburg.

BRIGGS, ASA, *Victorian Cities*, 1963, Odhams.

BROOKES, JOHN, *The Great Leap; 25 Years of Change: The U.S.A. and Ourselves, 1940–1965*, 1967, Gollancz.

BULWER-LYTTON, EDWARD, *Vril: The Power of the Coming Race* (1870), Rudolf Steiner Publications, 1972, New York.

CAMP, SPRAGUE DE, *Lost Continents: The Atlantis Theme in History, Science and Literature*, 1970, Dover.

CANNADINE, DAVID, *The Decline and Fall of the British Aristocracies*, 1990, Yale.

CARPENTER, EDWARD, *Towards Democracy*, 1913, George Allen & Co.

CARPENTER, GEORGE, *Civilisation: Its Cause and Cure*, 1889, London.

CAUTE, DAVID, *The Great Fear*, 1978, Secker & Warburg.

CHANCELLOR, JOHN, *Charles Darwin*, 1973, Weidenfeld & Nicolson.

CHILTON, PAUL, 'Nukespeak: nuclear language, culture and propaganda', in *Nukespeak: The Media and the Bomb*, 1982, Comedia.

CURTIS, RICHARD (WITH HOGAN, ELIZABETH), *The Perils of the Peaceful Atom*, 1970, Gollancz.

CUTCLYFFE-HYNE, C.J., *Beneath Your Very Boots*, 1889, London.

CUTCLYFFE-HYNE, C.J., *The Lost Continent*, 1899, London.

DAVIES, PAUL, *God and the New Physics*, 1986, Penguin.

DONNELLY, IGNATIUS, *Atlantis: The Antediluvian World* (1882), 1970, Sidgwick & Jackson.

DONNELLY, IGNATIUS, *Ragnarok: The Age of Fire and Gravel*, 1882, New York.

DYOS, H.J. (WITH WOLFF, MICHAEL), *The Victorian City*, Vol. 2, *Image and Reality*, 1973, Routledge and Kegan Paul.

EASLEA, BRIAN, *Science And Sexual Oppression*, 1976, Routledge and Kegan Paul.

EASLEA, BRIAN, *Fathering the Unthinkable: Masculinity, Scientists, and the Nuclear Arms Race*, 1983, Pluto Press.

EHRENREICH, BARBARA, *The Hearts of Men: American Dreams and the Flight from Commitment*, 1983, Pluto Press.

EHRENREICH, BARBARA AND JOHN, 'The professional-managerial class in Walker, P., (ed.), *Between Labour And Capital*, 1979, Harvester Press.

ENSOR, ROBERT, *England 1870–1914*, 1986, Oxford University Press.

FEARKISS, VICTOR, *Technological Man*, 1969, Heinemann.

FISHMAN, WILLIAM J. *EAST END 1988*, 1988, Duckworth.

GATLIN, ROCHELLE, *American Women Since 1945*, 1987, Macmillan.

GILBERTSON, GEOFF. (WITH ROBERTS, ANTHONY), *The Dark Gods*, 1980, Rider Hutchinson.

GILLESPIE, CHARLES COULSTON, *Genesis and Geology: The Impact of Scientific Discoveries upon Religious Belief in the Decades Before Darwin*, 1959, Harper Torch Books.

GISSING, GEORGE, *The Nether World* (1889), 1973, Everyman.

GOLDMAN, ERIC, *The Crucial Decade and After: America 1945–1960*, 1960, New York.

GOODRICK-CLARKE, NICHOLAS, *The Occult Roots of Nazism*, 1985, The Aquarian Press.

GOODSAVAGE, JOSEPH, *Storm on the Sun*, 1980, Sphere.

GRAZIA, ALFRED DE, *The Velikovsky Affair*, 1978, Abacus.

GRIFFITHS, ROBERT, *The Politics of Fear: Jospeh R. McCarthy and The Senate*, 1987, University of Massachusetts Press.

GRIFFITHS, ROBERT, 'American politics and the Rise of McCarthyism' in *A History of our Time: Readings on Post-War America*, (eds) Chafe & Sitkoff, 1987, Oxford.

HEUR, KENNETH, *The End of the World*, 1953, Gollancz.

HOWE, ELLIC, *Urania's Children*, 1967, William Kimber.

JACKSON, HOLBROOK, *The Eighteen Nineties* 1939, Penguin.

JACOBS, DAVID, *The UFO Controversy in America*, 1976, New York, Signet.

JALLARD, PAT, *Women, Marriage and Politics 1866–1914*, 1986, Oxford.

JONAS, HANS, *The Gnostic Religion*, 1963, Beacon Press.

JUERGENS, RALPH, 'Minds in Chaos', in DE GRAZIA *The Velikovsky Affair*, 1978, Abacus.

JUNG, C.G., 'Flying saucers; a modern myth of things seen in the sky', in *The Collected Works of C.G. Jung: Vol 10 – Civilisation In Transition*, 1953, R.K.P.

JUNG, C.G., *The Collected Works of C.G. Jung: Vol 12 – Psychology and Alchemy*, 1953, R.K.P.

JURG, MARTIN, GABRIEL, *The American Conception of Neutrality after 1941* 1988, Macmillan.

KEATING, P.J., 'Fact and fiction in the East End', in H.J. DYOS AND WOLFF, M. (eds.), *The Victorian City: Images and Reality: Vol 2*.

KNOEPFLMACHER, U.C., 'The novel between city and country', in DYOS & WOLFF op. cit.

KRASSA, PETER, *Erich von Daniken: Disciple of the Gods*, 1978, Star.

BIBLIOGRAPHY

LARSON, EGON, *Atomic Legacy: A Layman's Guide*, 1958, Henner Locke.

LIFTON, ROBERT J. (WITH FALK, RICHARD), *Indefensible Weapons: The Political and Psychological Case Against Nuclearism*, 1982, New York.

LONDON, JACK, *The People of the Abyss*, 1978, The Journeyman Press.

LUTYENS, ELIZABETH, *Candles in the Sun*, 1957, Rupert Hart-Davis.

LYND, HELEN MERRELL, *England in the Eighteen Eighties: Towards A Social Basis for Freedom*, 1945, Oxford University Press.

MACCABE, COLIN, *High Theory/Low Culture: Analysing Popular Television and Film*, 1986, Manchester University Press.

MACKENZIE, NORMAN AND JEANNE, *The First Fabians*, 1979, Quartet.

MAILER, NORMAN, *Fire on the Moon*, 1970, Pan.

MANUEL, FRANK AND FRITZIE, *Utopian Thought in the Western World*, 1979, Basil Blackwell.

MONTGOMERY HYDE, H., *The Atom Bomb Spies*, 1982, Sphere.

NEFF, MARY K., *Personal Memoirs of H.P. Blavatsky*, 1973, Rider.

NETHERCOTT, A., *The First Five Lives of Annie Besant*, 1961, London.

NEUBURG, VICTOR, *The Batsford Companion to Popular Literature*, 1982, Batsford.

PACKARD, VANCE, *The Status Seekers: An Exploration of Class Behavior in America*, 1963, Penguin.

PARRINDER, PATRICK, *Science Fiction: Its Criticism and Teaching*, 1980, Methuen.

PERKIN, JOAN, *Women and Marriage in Nineteenth Century England* 1989, Routledge.

PRINGLE, PETER (WITH SPIGELMAN JAMES), *The Nuclear Barons*, 1983, Sphere.

PUNTER, DAVID, *The Literature of Terror*, 1980, Longmans.

RAUSCHNING, HERMAN, *The Beast from the Abyss*, 1941, Heinemann.

RAVENSCROFT, TREVOR, *The Spear of Destiny*, 1974, Corgi.

RIDGE, MARTIN, *Ignatius Donnelly: Portrait of a Politican*, 1962, University of Chicago Press.

RIESMAN, DAVID, *The Lonely Crowd*, 1950, Yale.

ROLT, L.T.C., *Victorian Engineering*, 1970, Allen Lane.

ROOK, CLARENCE, *The Hooligan Nights* (1899), 1979, O.U.P.

ROY, ELIZABETH, *The Prince of Atlantis*, 1929, New York.

ROYLE, EDWARD, *Radicals, Secularists and Republicans: Popular Freethought in Britain, 1866–1915*, 1980, Manchester University Press.

SEAMAN, L.C.B., *Victorian England: Aspects of English and Imperial History 1837–1901*, 1973, London.

SHILS, EDWARD A., *The Torment of Secrecy*, 1956, New York.

SHILS, EDWARD A., 'Mass society and its culture' in JACOBS, NORMAN (ed.), *Culture for the Millions?*, 1961, Beacon.

SHERWIN, MARTIN J., 'The atomic bomb and the crisis of the Cold War', in CHAFE AND SITKOFF (eds) *A History of our Time: Readings in Post War America*, 1987, Oxford.

SNOWMAN. DANIEL, *America since 1920*, 1980, Heinemann.

SOLOVYOFF, VSEVOLOD, *A Modern Priestess of Isis*, 1895, Longmans Green.

SPILLANE, MICKEY, *One Lonely Night*, 1951, E.P. Dutton.

SPRAGUE, DE CAMP, *Lost Continents: The Atlantis Theme in History Science and Literature*, 1970, Dover.

STEDMAN-JONES, GARETH, *Outcast London: A Study in the Relationship Between Classes in Victorian Society*, 1984, Peregrine.

STONEMAN. C.F., *Space Biology*, Penguin Biology Topic Book, 1976.

STORY, R.D., *The Encyclopedia of UFOs*, 1980, N.E.L.

STORY, R.D., *The Space Gods Revealed*, 1978, N.E.L.

STORY, R.D., *Guardians of the Universe?* 1978, N.E.L.

SUTHERLAND, JOHN, *Fiction and the Fiction Industry*, 1978, R.K.P.

SUTHERLAND, JOHN, *Bestsellers*, 1981, R.K.P.

SWINGEWOOD, ALAN, *The Myth of Mass Culture*, 1977, Macmillan.

TAYLOR, GORDON RATTRAY, *The Doomsday Book: Can the World Survive?* 1970, Thames & Hudson

THEWELEIT, KLAUS, *Male Fantasies: Women, Bodies and History*, 1987, Polity Press

VERNE, JULES, *The Journey to the Centre of the Earth*, (1864), 1965, Airmont Classic

WEBB, BEATRICE, *My Apprenticeship* (1926), 1971, Penguin

WEBB, JAMES, *The Flight from Reason*, 1971, Macmillan

WEBB, JAMES, *The Occult Establishment*, 1976, La Salle, Illinois

WERNICK, ANDREW, 'The Shifting Image of the Modern Car', in *Cultural Politics In Contemporary America,* edited by IAN ANGUS & SUT JHALLY, 1989, Routledge

WHYTE, WILLIAM, *The Organisation Man*, 1967, Penguin

WIENER, MARTIN J., *English Culture and the Decline of the Industrial Spirit: 1850–1980*, 1981, Penguin

WILLIAMS, RAYMOND, *Culture and Society*, 1973, Penguin

WILLIAMS, RAYMOND, *The Long Revolution*, 1984, Penguin

WOLFE, TOM, *The Right Stuff*, 1981, Bantam

WRIGHT MILLS, C., *White Collar*, 1951, O.U.P.

WRIGHT MILLS, C., *The Sociological Imagination*, 1959, O.U.P.

WRIGHT MILLS, C., *The Power Elite*, 1981, O.U.P.

WYNN, NEIL, 'World War II and The Afro-Americans' in The Open University, *War & Society*, Unit 26

YATES, FRANCES A., *The Occult Philosophy in the Elizabethan Age*, 1983, Ark Paperbacks

YOUNG, G.M., *Portrait of an Age: Victorian England*, 1960, O.U.P.

YOUNG, ROBERT, M., 'The impact of Darwin on conventional thought', in *Darwin's Metaphor*, 1985, C.U.P.

MAGAZINES, NEWSPAPERS AND JOURNALS

(*Note:* **Articles are quoted in alphabetical order of author's name.**)

BARRUCH, BERNARD M., 'What of our futures?' *Saturday Evening Post*, 22 April 1949

CAREY, MICHAEL J., 'Psychological fall out', *Bulletin Of The Atomic Scientists*, January 1982

CONDON, EDWARD U., 'Velikovsky's catastrophe', *New Republic*, 24 April 1950

DUTTA, REX, 'Flying saucers: a deeper examination', *Adastra*, vol. I, October/ November 1978

FURTWANGLER, ROBERT, 'Growing up nuclear', *Bulletin Of The Atomic Scientists*, January 1981

HALDANE, J.B.S., 'St Quetzalcoatl & St Fenris' [A Review of *World In Collision*], *New Statesman & Nation*, November 1950

HELMUT, GERBER, 'The nineties: Edwardians and Late Victorians' *English Institute Essays*, 1959

BIBLIOGRAPHY

HILL, DAVID, L., RABINOVITCH, EUGENE AND SIMPSON, JOHN A. 'The atomic scientists speak up', *Life*, 29 October 1945

ICKES, HAROLD, 'National hysteria', *New Republic*, August 1950

KAEMPFFERT, HALDEMAR, 'The tale of Velikovsky's comet: a controversial view of how Joshua made the moon stand still', *The New York Times Book Review*, 2 April 1950

KAZIN, ALFRED, 'On the brink', *The New Yorker*, 29 April 1950

LARRABEE, ERIC, 'The day the sun stood still' [A review of *Worlds in Collision*], *Harper's*, January 1950

LAWRENCE, WILLIAM L., 'The truth about the hydrogen bomb', *Saturday Evening Post*, 24 June 1950

LEAR, JOHN, 'The heavens burst' [Excerpted accounts from *Worlds In Collision*], *Collier's*, February/March 1950

LEY, WILLY, 'Pseudo science in Naziland', *Astounding Science Fiction*, May 1947

LILJEGREN, S.B., 'Bulwer-Lytton's novels and Isis unveiled', *Essays and Studies on English Language and Literature*, no. xviii, Cambridge, Mass

MUSIL, ROBERT K., 'Growing up nuclear', *Bulletin of the Atomic Scientists*, January 1982

NAGL, MANFRED, 'S.F., occult sciences and Nazi myths', *Science Fiction Studies*, No. 1, 1974

OURSLER, FULTON, 'Why the sun stood still: a preview of Dr. Immanuel Velikovsky's sensational new book, *Worlds In Collision*, *Readers Digest*, February/April 1950

SMITH, SAMUEL, 'The industrial training of destitute children', *The Contemporary Review*, January 1885.

STEADMAN, JONES GARETH, 'Working class culture and working class politics in London, 1870–1900', *Journal of Social History*, Summer 1974

STRUVE, OTTO, Review of *Worlds in Collision*, *New York Herald Times Review of Books*, 2 April 1950

WAYS, MAX, 'The bright and dark perception', *Life* 28 December 1968

WOLFE, ALAN, 'The rise and fall of the Soviet threat: domestic sources of Cold War consensus', *Institute For Policy Studies*, Washington, 1978

WYLIE, P., 'Panic, psychology and the bomb', *Bulletin Of The Atomic Scientists*, February 1954

YEO, STEPHEN, 'A new life. The religion of socialism in Britain 1883–1896', *History Workshop*, no. 4, Autumn 1977

ARTICLES WITHOUT AUTHORIAL REFERENCE

(The) Bulletin Of The Atomic Scientists, August/September 1950 (Special double issue dealing with civil defence)

Encounter August 1973, 'Anatomy of a world best seller' (Review of Daniken's works to date)

Illustrated, 'Your friend the atom', 2 August 1958

New York Herald Tribune (Editorial on 'A' bomb), 7 August 1945

Reader's Digest, 'The facts that *MUST* prevent war', February 1949

Reader's Digest. 'New facts about the atom bomb', August 1949

(The) Saturday Evening Post, 'A life history of the 'A' bomb', 5 December 1953

(Der) Spiegel, 'Der Daniken-Schwindel. 9 Millionen Auflage', 19 March 1973.

BIBLIOGRAPHY

MAGAZINE FEATURES INSTANCED IN TEXT

(The) Aeroplane Spotter, 11 January, 9 February, 22 March, 5 April, 9 August, for year 1947

Life, 29 April, 10 June, 28 December for year 1968, and 20 January, 26 May, 6 July for year 1969

Man's Adventure

(The) Saturday Evening Post, April 1949 to April 1950

Time, March to December 1950, 27 September 1951, 15 October 1951

Wildcat Adventure.

THEOSOPHICAL AND PRIVATE PUBLICATIONS

BENTON, FLORIA, *Hollow Earth Mysteries and The Polar Shift*, Futura Press, Elkton, M.D. USA.

BESANT, ANNIE, *Karma*, 1895, Theosophical Publishing Society

BESANT, ANNIE, *Man and His Bodies*, 1896, Theosophical Publishing Society

BESANT, ANNIE, *The Path of Discipleship*, 1896, Theosophical Publishing Society

BESANT, ANNIE, *The Ancient Wisdom*, 1897, Theosophical Publishing Society

BESANT, ANNIE, *Evolution of Life and Form*, 1899, Theosophical Publishing Society

BESANT, ANNIE, *Esoteric Christianity*, 1901, Theosophical Publishing Society

BESANT, ANNIE, *The Immediate Future*, 1912, Theosophical Publishing Society

BLAVATSKY, H.P., *Isis Unveiled*, vols 1 and 2, 1877, Theosophical Publishing Society

BLAVATSKY, H.P., *The Secret Doctrine*, vol. 1 – *Cosmogenesis*, vol. 2 – *Anthropogenesis*, 1888, Theosophical Publishing Company

BLAVATSKY, H.P., *Lucifer*, July 1889

BLAVATSKY, H.P., *Studies in Occultism: The Exoteric Nature of the Gospels*, 1892, Theosophical Publishing Society

BLAVATSKY, H.P., *The Key to Theosophy*, Theosophical University Press, Pasadena, California

CONGER, ARTHUR, *Practical Occultism: From the Private Letters of William Quem Judge*, Theosophical University Press, Pasadena, California

HILLARD, KATHERINE, *An Abridgement of the Secret Doctrine*, 1907, The Quarterly Book Department, New York

HUBBARD, L. RON, *Dianetics: The Modern Science of Mental Health*, 1982, New Era Publications

JINARAJADASA, C., *First Principles of Theosophy*, 1938, Theosophical Publishing House

JONES, W. ANGUS, *Blavatsky and Hoerbiger: A Reconciliation*, Markham House Press

A Primer Of Theosophy: A Very Condensed Outline, 1914, Krotona, Los Angeles, California

SCOTT-ELLIOT, W., *The Story of Atlantis and the Lost Lemuria*, 1896, Theosophical Publishing House

SINNETT, ARNOLD PERCY, *Esoteric Buddhism*, 1898, Theosophical Publishing Society

STEINER, RUDOLF, *The Occult Movement in the Nineteenth Century*, 1973, Rudolf Steiner Press, London

INDEX